Tracing Your Caribbean Ancestors

THIRD EDITION

Tracing Your Caribbean Ancestors

A National Archives Guide

THIRD EDITION

Guy Grannum

The National Archives

BLOOMSBURY
LONDON · NEW DELHI · NEW YORK · SYDNEY

First published by the Public Record Office 1995
Second edition published by the Public Record Office 2002

This third edition published in 2012 by

Bloomsbury Publishing Plc
50 Bedford Square
London WC1B 3DP

A catalogue record for this book is available from the British Library

ISBN 978-1-40817-569-9

The National Archives logo device is a trade mark of The National Archives
and is used under licence.

This book is produced using paper that is made from wood grown in managed,
sustainable forests. It is natural, renewable and recyclable. The logging and
manufacturing processes conform to the environmental regulations of the
country of origin.

Design by Fiona Pike, Pike Design, Winchester
Typeset by Saxon Graphics Ltd, Derby, DE21 4SZ
Printed in the UK by MPG Books

CONTENTS

ILLUSTRATIONS

PREFACE

I joined the Public Record Office (now the National Archives (TNA)) in 1988 and for almost 20 years I have been advising researchers on how to make the best use of the National Archives' services and resources. I started tracing my Barbadian ancestors at about the same time and soon became aware that there were no general guides to help me like those familiar to family historians in the UK, America, Australia and Canada. Increasing numbers of people were visiting or writing to the National Archives for help in tracing their Caribbean ancestors and *Tracing Your Caribbean Ancestors* was written to help fill this neglected area. The aim of this guide is to describe the most important records in the National Archives for the study of Caribbean genealogy and heritage. These sources can also be used to study the social, economic and military history of the British Caribbean islands from the time of their settlement in the seventeenth century to the twentieth century.

The first edition was published in 1995 and the second in 2002. Since the last publication, the Public Record Office has become the National Archives following the merger of the Royal Commission on Historical Manuscripts (in 2003) and the Office of Public Sector Information (ex-HMSO in 2006), and the Family Records Centre has closed, the resources put online and services transferred to Kew. More significantly, since 2002 there has been phenomenal growth in the Internet and in particular for family and social historians there are online catalogues, finding aids and indexes, digitised images of documents and secondary sources, and new channels which allow researchers to store and share information instantaneously. This edition reflects these changes and in particular highlights online resources useful to Caribbean researchers.

Updates to this book and complementary resources will be published from time to time at www.caribbeanroots.co.uk.

Guy Grannum
March 2012

ACKNOWLEDGEMENTS

To Mrs Mary Pym, my grandmother, who sparked my interest in my ancestry and my late friend Ben Bousquet for his continual enthusiasm in promoting Caribbean heritage.

I would like to thank Karen Grannum, Mandy Banton, Nora Talty, Sheila Knight, Laura Simpson, Ellen Grace and numerous Caribbean researchers for their support and advice.

GLOSSARY

The records in the National Archives for the study of the West Indies and West Indians have many terms which are now obsolete or have changed their meaning and may now be considered offensive. Although I have tried to use modern words I have on occasion had to use historical terms. It may be useful, therefore, if I provide a short list of some of the more common words and terms which you will find in this guide and in the records:

Caribbean Used interchangeably with West Indies and West Indians. I have tended to preferentially use West Indies and West Indians in the book because this is how the region and people were described historically and was a convenient collective term to include related colonies which were outside of the Caribbean basin such as Bermuda and Guyana.

Coolie South Asian Indian labourer.

Creole Someone born in the West Indies or parts of North and South America. In the British West Indies the term is used for black and white inhabitants.

East Indian Someone from the Indian subcontinent. Large numbers of Asian Indians migrated to the West Indies between 1834 and 1920 (see section **3.7**).

Emancipate To free from slavery and interchangeable with manumission. In the British West Indies slaves were emancipated on 1 August 1834 under the Abolition of Slavery Act 1833.

Ethnicity and colour Colonial society and government officials were fairly consistent in their use of terms for colour and ethnicity since they had social and legal meaning (in the West Indies). It should usually be clear from the context of the record which ethnic groups are being referred to.

> **Asian** Someone from the Indian subcontinent. The nineteenth-century documents often use the word 'coolie'. Chinese West Indians were usually called Chinese.

Black Someone who was not white European. If black is found in context with other ethnic terms, for example Asian, Indian or coloured, then it means a person of African descent.

Coloured Someone who was not white European. If coloured is found in context with other ethnic terms, for example black, Indian or Asian, it means a person of mixed ethnic ancestry and more usually someone of mixed African and European ancestry. The term 'mulatto' is often used instead of 'coloured'.

Indian Until 1834 Indian meant indigenous Amerindian or of Amerindian descent, but after 1834, with the migration of Asian Indian labourers, Indian usually meant someone from the Indian subcontinent. Nineteenth-century documents often refer to Asian Indians as 'coolies'.

Negro African or a person of African descent. Frequently, used as an alternative word for enslaved Africans.

White Someone of 'pure' European descent, although in many colonies someone who was 1/16th black was legally white.

Many colonial authorities graded slaves and free people according to their ethnic origin. The terms varied slightly from country to country but the common usage in Jamaica was:

Mulatto The child of a white and a black (1/2 black, one black parent). The term 'mulatto' was more commonly used to describe someone of mixed European and African descent.

Quadroon The child of a white and a mulatto (1/4 black, one black grandparent).

Mustee The child of a white and a quadroon; sometimes also called mustifino or octoroon (1/8 black, one black great-grandparent). The child of a white and a mustee was white under Jamaican law (1/16 black, one black great-great-grandparent).

Sambo The child of a mulatto and a black (3/4 black, a single white grandparent). The child of a sambo and a black was black (7/8 black, one white great-grandparent).

Manumission Legally freed from slavery (see section **7.4**).

Maroon From 'cimarrones' (Spanish for wild or unruly), maroons were Spanish runaway slaves who settled in the mountains of Jamaica and fought the British. Their numbers were later increased by British runaway slaves.

Slave Someone who was enslaved. In the British Caribbean most slaves were Africans or of African descent. They were treated as chattel (personal property) and were enslaved for life, as were their children. Slavery was abolished in British Caribbean colonies on 1 August 1834; although most adults were 'apprenticed' to their former slave holders until 1 August 1838.

West Indian Originally a West Indian was someone who was born, or was settled in the West Indies, or someone based in the UK who had interest in the West Indies, such as an absentee proprietor or merchant. Later it was only used to describe people born or settled in the West Indies.

West Indies Chain of volcanic and coral islands from Florida in North America to Venezuela in South America. For administrative reasons the British government included Bermuda, British Honduras (Belize) and British Guiana (Guyana) as West Indian possessions.

INTRODUCTION

When I first came to London in 1982 I knew nothing about my ancestry and thought it would be interesting to try to research my family history. I have an unusual surname and thought it would be easy. I searched the birth, marriage and death indexes and the indexes to wills for England and Wales and found references to my father and his brothers and sister, my grandfather and his sister (no mention of two of his siblings) and his father's second marriage, and that was it. There were virtually no other Grannums listed until the 1950s. I later discovered that my great-grandfather was born in Barbados and using sources at the National Archives, the Church of Jesus Christ of Latter-day Saints, publications, newspapers and, for a brief time, employing a researcher in Barbados, I have now traced my Barbadian Grannum family back to the 1730s. However, I still have not managed to get back further to a place of origin (Barbados was uninhabited when colonised by the British in 1627).

There are a great many Grannums around the world. In common with many West Indians they have migrated to Britain, other West Indian Islands, Latin America, the United States, Canada and Australia. They are a mixture of Europeans and African-Caribbeans, having descended from European settlers, slaves, and the children of slave owners and their slaves. They served in the armed forces, colonial civil service, local colonial government, the merchant navy, and some were imprisoned.

Much has been written on family history for most of the former British Empire, especially South Africa, Canada, the United States, New Zealand and Australia. Very little has been written about the British West Indies or the other British colonies in Central and South America. The British West Indies are among a chain of islands spreading from Florida to Venezuela. They contain a diverse population of indigenous Amerindians and the descendants of Dutch, Spanish, African, British, Portuguese, Chinese, Danish, Swedish, Indian and French settlers. This small group of islands was important to the development of Britain's empire during the sixteenth to eighteenth centuries. The wealth created by the plantations encouraged the banking and insurance industries and, it is said, sparked Britain's industrial revolution.

This guide aims to aid research in the British Overseas Territories and former colonies of Antigua, Bahamas, Barbados, Bermuda, Cayman Islands, Dominica, Grenada, Jamaica, Montserrat, Nevis, St Christopher

(St Kitts), St Lucia, St Vincent, Tobago, Trinidad, Turks and Caicos Islands, and the British Virgin Islands, together with Guyana (formerly British Guiana) and Belize (formerly British Honduras). It is not intended to be a guide to general genealogical sources and techniques nor is it meant to stand on its own. I have included short references for further reading in each chapter and you will find fuller details about these books in the Bibliography at the back. Some of these books may be hard to find in the United Kingdom as many are published in the US and the Caribbean, although increasingly older publications are becoming available on the Internet. You may also find detailed histories and research guidance online.

I have referred to relevant chapters of Amanda Bevan's *Tracing Your Ancestors in the National Archives* throughout the guide. The National Archives also has research guidance on many of the subjects covered in this publication at www.nationalarchives.gov.uk/records.

Overview

West Indians are a diverse population reflecting the social and economic development of the region comprising British, Dutch, Spanish, French, Portuguese, African (from a wide variety of countries and ethnic groups), Danish, American, German, Lebanese, Chinese and East Indian migrants. They are a mixture of voluntary (planters, merchants, adventurers, economic migrants, indentured servants and discharged soldiers), involuntary (transported prisoners and slaves) and displaced migrants (refugees from American colonial wars, from religious persecution, liberated Africans and fugitive slaves). Although people often refer to West Indians as if they are a single group, they are not: each country has its own cultural identity based on history, language, religion and ethnic make-up.

The majority of people in the Caribbean are immigrants. When Europeans first discovered the West Indies at the end of the fifteenth century, most of the islands had indigenous populations. Caribs and other indigenous Amerindians still live on many of the islands and in Central and South America, but these are now minority populations, having been reduced by war, disease and forced migration by European settlers.

The Americas were 'beyond the line', that is they lay outside the territorial limits of European treaties, so disputes in the Americas did not invalidate peace treaties in Europe. While the Spanish attempted to keep other European powers out of America, the gold of the Spanish Main acted as a lure to adventurers and pirates. During the seventeenth and eighteenth centuries the Spanish gradually lost their hold on the

Figure 1 *Photograph of the West Indies Cricket Team who toured in England in 1906 (COPY 1/500, registered 21 August 1906).**

Caribbean and Latin and North America. The Portuguese settled in Brazil, the French and English colonised fragments of North America and many of the West Indian islands, and the Dutch settled in Suriname and Guyana and some islands, as well as enjoying a brief spell in Brazil. The Danes and Swedes also colonised some of the islands.

Regular territorial disputes and European wars meant that islands frequently changed hands from one power to another. On islands

---

* The team arrived in Southampton on 4 June 1906 on RMS Trent (passenger list in BT 26/277) and included H. B. G. Austin (Barbados), C. K. Bancroft (Barbados), W. T. Burton (Guyana), G. Challenor (Barbados), L. S. Constantine (Trinidad), A. B. Cumberbatch (Trinidad), P. A. Goodman (Barbados), A. E. A. Harrigan (Trinidad), O. Layne (Barbados), G. C. Learmond (Trinidad), C. S. Morrison (Jamaica), R. Olliverre (St Vincent), J. Parker (Guyana) and S. Smith (Trinidad). Most returned on the Trent on 30 August 1906 (passenger list in BT 27/1517). Constantine, Learmond, Goodman and Burton also played in the first West Indies cricket tour of England in 1900 (see two photographs of the team in COPY 1/446, registered 18 June 1900; passenger list in BT 26/168, RMS Trent arrived in Southampton 6 June 1900).

captured by Britain from the Spanish, French and Dutch, there was little or no attempt to expel all the non-British. During the French Revolution and the Spanish-American independence wars many refugees fled to 'friendly' British islands. These non-British populations would also have had their slaves and servants.

Labour was necessary for the settled islands to prosper and many thousands, free and unfree, were transported from Europe. From the 1650s the most significant change in the populations was the mass transportation of slave labour from the West Coast of Africa. The Spanish and Portuguese were already using African labour in Latin America, but the numbers enslaved escalated once the Dutch, French and British islands realised the necessity of a large unskilled workforce, used to tropical climate, food and diseases, to maintain their plantations.

It has been estimated that more than 11 million Africans were transported to the New World, with an estimated 1.6 million Africans sent to the British West Indies. By the mid-eighteenth century most of the British islands had black populations which far exceeded the white population. It is not easy to identify the origin of the black populations as very poor records were kept and, even where ethnic origins are noted, these are often the names of the areas of departure from Africa rather than the true ethnic group.

When slavery was abolished in the British Caribbean settlements in 1834 many colonies, notably Trinidad and British Guiana, suffered severe labour problems. Trinidad had established various schemes before 1834 to encourage labour, such as the immigration of Chinese labourers in 1806. Other people encouraged to settle were disbanded soldiers from the West India Regiments, black colonial marines who enlisted in America during the War of 1812, East Indians (from the Indian subcontinent), liberated Africans freed from illegal slavers, and Portuguese from Madeira and the Azores.

There has also been much migration between the islands and with Africa, Europe and North, Central and South America. It cannot be assumed that your ancestors came directly from the 'mother' country to the West Indies. For example, an English family in Jamaica may have reached there after first settling in Barbados, then migrating to South Carolina, and arriving in Jamaica as loyalists following the American Revolution. An African family in Trinidad may not be a product of Caribbean slavery but may be descended from a freed refugee from Georgia, US, who enlisted with the British forces during the War of 1812.

To use an extreme but possible example, an African family in Trinidad could have been descended from a slave who moved with his owner from Barbados to Jamaica and who later ran away and joined the maroons (see Glossary). A descendant was captured during the Maroon War against the British in 1796 and transported to Nova Scotia and was one of the black settlers to Sierra Leone in 1800. A son enlisted in the West India Regiment, was discharged and then settled in Trinidad.

The study of genealogy in the Caribbean relies on the same sources as used in Britain: parish records, legal records, military service, census returns, tax returns, wills, maps, private correspondence and newspapers. The National Archives (UK) does not hold the domestic records of colonial governments or the more important records for Caribbean genealogical research, such as church records and wills; these are held locally in the country's archives and register offices (see Chapter 10 for further information). The National Archives however, holds numerous references to people who lived in the West Indies, such as adventurers who planted sugar cane, slaves who toiled the land, soldiers and sailors who fought in the Napoleonic Wars, transported criminals, and Asian Indians who emigrated as indentured labourers.

Many Anglo-Caribbean countries were captured from or ceded by other European powers and records of their pre-British history may survive in provincial and national archives of other European countries (see Chapter 11 for addresses). For example, Guyana was Dutch, St Lucia, Grenada, Dominica and St Vincent were French, Trinidad was Spanish, and for eighty years St Christopher was jointly shared by both Britain and France. At various times the British also temporarily occupied islands held by other European powers, and the records in the National Archives may contain information about their inhabitants.

Further reading
Throughout the book you will find lists of suggested further reading. Full references for these can be found in the Bibliography, see page 199.

Dunn, *Sugar and Slaves: The Rise of the Planter Class in the English West Indies, 1624–1713*

Edwards, *The History of the British West Indies*

Higman, *A Concise History of the Caribbean*

Lucas, *Historical Geography of the British Colonies: Volume 2: The West Indies*

CHAPTER 1
FIRST STEPS

This book is not intended to be a guide to general genealogical sources or techniques and you may find it useful to have some general guidance to help start your research. There are many published guides to family history, which you may be able to obtain from your library and there is a lot of guidance on the Internet; I have included some at the end of this chapter (section **1.10**).

1.1 Be prepared

Family history can be very absorbing, almost addictive, and very rewarding, helping you find out more about yourself, your family and where you come from. It can be an emotional journey and you may discover exciting and interesting information, but you may also need to be prepared for disappointment and maybe even anger or distress at what you may find. You may discover family skeletons which your family wish to remain buried, and DNA analysis may throw up some surprises (see section **1.9**).

Points to consider:

- it may be worth asking your family if you need to know anything before you start (watch their reactions);
- records may be incomplete and you may not be able to go back many generations; you may find ancestral links to slaves, slave owners, slave traders and raiders – people of African Caribbean descent need to understand that it is likely that many, if not all, of their direct African ancestors were enslaved;
- if you have slave ancestors you will need to research your ancestor's owners to find out more. Without the name of an owner, or estate, it will be difficult to make progress beyond the 1840s;
- people of European Caribbean descent may have been slave owners;
- DNA tests may show you to be more ethnically diverse than you thought;
- DNA tests will only show your direct paternal and maternal ancestry;
- you may find out that your family aren't your family.

1.2 How do I start my research?

Tracing your family history relies on starting with what you know about yourself and immediate family and methodically working backwards one generation at a time, confirming links as you go back. Don't jump to conclusions and try not to skip generations – otherwise you could end up researching someone else's ancestors! Remember that spellings of surnames may change, dates and ages may be misremembered, and that people may be known by different names throughout their lives. You are aiming to use documentary sources to uncover facts, or make educated guesses in the absence of facts or where the 'facts' are wrong.

Firstly, write down what you know about yourself, your parents, brothers and sisters and aunts and uncles, spouses, partners and children. Note dates and places for events such as births, marriages and deaths, religion, schools and colleges, qualifications and employment etc. If you don't know dates, try to estimate – for example, put aunts and uncles into order by age. Start sketching a family tree. You might find it useful to use printed forms, family history software or websites to store your research and notes.

It is important to talk to your family, especially elderly relatives, who may be able to give you more information. Remember that memories fade or may not be reliable, that elderly people may not have the stamina for long sessions of question answering, and people may not want to talk about 'skeletons' such as illegitimacy, mixed-race relationships, divorce or bankruptcy – even if you do not consider these sensitive subjects. Be respectful; if they do not want to give you information do not press them, and treat anything given in confidence as confidential.

Look around your house for any photographs, heirlooms and other memorabilia that may give you clues (ask your relatives if they have any that you can copy), for example:

■ family bibles;
■ birth, baptism, marriage and death certificates (for names, dates and locations);
■ notices, cards and newspapers announcing births, baptisms, marriages, deaths or funerals of family members;
■ passports (for information on nationality, date and place of birth, visa and immigration stamps, and photographs);
■ wills (which may give names, relationships and locations of family members);

- medals and other awards (which may give clues on military services, or educational and sporting attainments);
- certificates of nationality or citizenship;
- photographs (which may give clues about dates and locations. Also, names and other information may be written on the reverse. Photographs are useful conversation pieces and someone may be able to describe the events and people depicted in the picture);
- postcards, letters and diaries.

The facts you are aiming to get are:

- official names as used by the church, school and state – you won't get very far without these;
- nicknames as used by friends and family – this is how people may be described in letters, photographs, and in conversation;
- places – you need at least the name of the country and ideally the name of a parish or village;
- dates – or at least estimated dates based on ages, clothing, medals, older/younger family;
- ethnicity – understanding your ethnicity will help decide what sort of records to look for and when.

1.3 Surnames

Until the twentieth century and the advent of universal education surnames were not standardised. The spellings of surnames could vary during a person's life and among family members, so it is important to look for variants when researching your ancestry. Listen to your surname and imagine how others may hear it, especially if it is said with a Caribbean accent. Do you have experience of correcting other people's spelling of your name or always having to spell it? For example, outside of Barbados my name is always written as 'Granham'.

Standard genealogical research in the UK relies on two assumptions: that people have surnames passed from a father to his children and that most parents get married usually before, or around, the time of the first child. For most Caribbean researchers this is not necessarily the case and you may find children of the same parents having two different surnames.

Common-law relationships were common in the West Indies and most children were born outside of marriage; they were therefore registered under their mother's name. To complicate matters they may have later adopted their father's name. So you may find examples of a birth but not find a marriage or death, or a death but no birth. This is a particularly challenging aspect of Caribbean genealogical research as the father of children born to common-law parents is not usually recorded on the birth certificate, the mother is not recorded on the children's marriage certificates, and neither are recorded on the death certificate. You need to use other records to trace such relationships.

Difficulties also arise when tracing ancestors from an era when a particular religion was not recognised by the state. In Trinidad, for example, Muslim marriages were not recognised until 1936 and Hindu marriages were not recognised until 1946 and so before these dates couples needed to undergo Christian or civil marriages for their children to be considered legitimate. Furthermore, couples often married late, for example, once they had saved enough to buy a plot of land with the result that children born before marriage have the mother's maiden name and those born after marriage have the father's name.

1.3.1 Slave surnames

Until freedom slaves did not have legal surnames. However, it is apparent, from runaway notices and manumission registers that many slaves used surnames before freedom even if they were not recognised by the owner or state. It is commonly believed that slaves took the surname of their owner and that this will help in identifying records for family history. Although this did occur, it was not always the case. British slave law denied slaves surnames because they had no legal father and they were the property of their owner. A good example of this can be found in the baptismal entries of slaves where usually only their first name is given. Contrast this with records after 1834, following the abolition of slavery, where most former slaves used surnames. There was no established way for slaves and free people to have a surname. It is possible that on freedom former slaves found that they needed a surname for personal or legal reasons, for example, when baptised or married, or to purchase or rent land or property, or for employment.

Little is known on the origins of slave surnames or the local practices on how they were adopted and used. Gutman, in *The Black Family in Slavery and Freedom*, shows that American slaves were often known by the name of their original owner, who was not necessarily their last owner. A brief examination of manumission returns and the 'Book of Negroes' compiled by the British military authorities in 1783 of black refugees from the American Revolution (PRO 30/55/100, no 10427) shows that few slaves possessed the same surnames as their owners; a digital copy of the 'Book of Negroes' is available online at the Nova Scotia Archives (www.gov.ns.ca/nsarm/).

The orders in council establishing the slave registries (see section **7.1**) in Trinidad (1812) and St Lucia (1814) say that the registers should record the surnames of slaves where they were already in use. Where the slaves did not have surnames they were to be chosen for them by the owner, or person making the return, as they thought fit. Families were to use the name of the 'superior relation' (usually the mother) unless there was already a family with that name. If that was the case, another name was to be chosen so that 'no two families on the same plantation, or belonging to the same owner' had the same surname. These orders further state that these surnames were to be passed onto descendants. If the parents were married, the father's name was to be used, otherwise the mother's name was to be used. The returns do not show which surnames were already in use when the registers were introduced, or which surnames were chosen for them.

Therefore, surname practices of slaves and freed men and women can have several origins:

- *the surname of the owner* – chosen or used by the slave, or given it by an official as a locative or paternal name. For example William, of Jordan's estate, may become William Jordan;
- *the surname of the original or former owner* – chosen by the slave or used by the new owner to differentiate between slaves with the same first name. For example, Eliza Redman on John Ellis's estate may have come from a Redman owner and Eliza may have retained Redman as a surname on freedom;
- *the surname of the father* – who could be the owner, a white employee, a slave on the plantation/household, or a slave from another plantation/household. The children of slaves by their owner or white employees often took their father's surname and this is shown in manumission registers and wills;
- *the mother's surname* – since slaves could rarely marry, children often took the mother's surname, for example, the slave registers for St Lucia and Trinidad show slaves listed in families with the children having the surname of their mother. Children might later adopt their father's name;

■ *the last name* – many slaves had more than one forename. Usually this was to differentiate between several slaves with the same name. For example, an owner might have on the estate a Tom, Tom William, Thomas and Thomas Edward. It is possible that Tom William later became known as Tom William(s) and Thomas Edward known as Thomas Edward(s). It is also possible that the last forename was the surname of a previous owner;

■ *chosen* – for official and legal reasons. Such surnames may have been chosen from influential, prominent or popular individuals or families;

■ *given* – by the church or by a government official for official and legal records. This is likely to be the case for liberated Africans freed from illegal slavers who only had their African name.

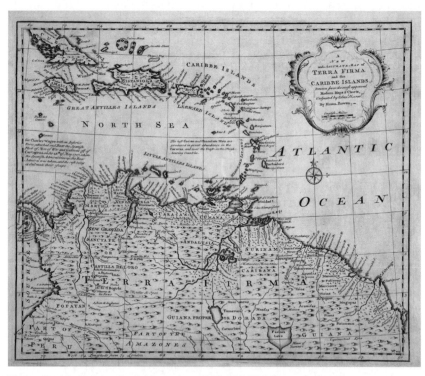

Figure 2   *Map of the Caribbean circa 1750 (CO 700/West Indies12)*

1.4 The Internet

Before visiting archives, use the Internet to help you find out more about your Caribbean home and to discover if anyone else is researching your family name. On discussion forums, social networking sites (e.g. Facebook and Flickr), Wikis (e.g. WeRelate) and family history websites you can share your experience and findings and maybe work together when visiting archives and libraries. Be careful when sharing your data, especially with strangers, respect people's right to privacy and confidentiality and try not to divulge too much about living people. Also bear in mind that some people are happy to take your information without offering anything in return.

Start searching for quick hits using your surname and such terms as 'family history' or 'genealogy' or 'ancestry'. If you get too many hits, add the country of origin. You should also try several search engines. While this approach should find family historians with an interest in your surname, most documentary sources are held in databases that cannot be found using standard search engines and you will need to search these databases directly from the compilers' sites. There are far too many sites to include here but I have included some in section **1.8**, in the relevant chapters of the guide, and on my website www.caribbeanroots.co.uk. Please note that website addresses may change and it is important to verify family history information with the original sources.

1.5 Archives and libraries

To find out more you are, at some point, going to have to visit archives and libraries in the UK and in the Caribbean.

When the British settled in the Caribbean they took with them British laws, government administration and local customs. This means that if you have undertaken family history research in Britain you will find that sources and techniques are very similar. For example, during the nineteenth century registration offices were established but for information before this you will need to use church records, wills, British army and navy records, and parish records. Britain does not hold the locally created records of her dependencies or former colonies; these should be found in the archives and other repositories of the relevant country, and therefore you need to know which country your family is from. There are, of course, some other factors to consider:

- some countries, e.g. St Lucia, Grenada and Guyana, had previously been administered by other European countries so records may be in France, Spain or the Netherlands. Early records will not be in English and even after Britain took over, documents may not always be in English;
- many records have been destroyed through the ravages of tropical insects, the environment (especially hurricanes), volcanic eruptions, earthquakes and intermittent warfare (until 1815) against the French, Spanish and Dutch;
- most employers and householders in the Caribbean used enslaved workers on their estates, businesses and households. They were legally the personal property of their owners with very few rights and were rarely recorded by the church or state. It can be extremely difficult tracing descendants of slaves during the period of slavery before 1834 but there are some sources which can help (see Chapter 7).

Most archives and libraries will not carry out general speculative research for you. You will have to visit or arrange for someone to visit on your behalf, which may mean employing a local researcher.

Before visiting an archive or arranging for research to be carried out, decide what you are looking for and identify the types of records that may hold that information. Most archival material is not indexed or catalogued beyond the title and asking for information on a specific individual will not usually be fruitful. The records may also be arranged according to who created them rather than by parish, subject or person.

Contact the archive to find out if they are likely to hold the material you want and if they have any other relevant material. Ask about opening hours, location, facilities and access conditions as well. For example, what kind of identification do you need? Do you need to book in advance? Is there a fee? Does the archive close at lunchtime? If you would like to use a tape recorder, computer or camera ask if these are allowed and if power points are available.

Many popular records, such as registers of baptisms, marriages, burials and wills, have been microfilmed to preserve them and you may find that the Church of Jesus Christ of Latter-day Saints has copies which can be ordered through one of their Family History Centres (see section **1.6**); increasingly archives are digitising their records (section **1.8**).

When using archives:

▮ write everything down and include the source such as family bible, certificate and spoken word. If it is from an archival record, note the archive and the full reference. You may need to recheck your information or pass the information on. Also record sources you have used even if the results proved negative because this information can be very important in itself and will help prevent you from repeating your research;

▮ when searching databases or looking at indexes bear in mind that a human has transcribed someone else's handwriting and in many cases this could be a copy of someone else's document. For example, the slave registers were completed by the slave holder and copied into two registers, one of which was sent to the Colonial Office and is now in the National Archives, and then transcribed for Ancestry;

▮ check original material whenever possible as errors may have crept into indexes or transcripts;

▮ most 'facts' were hearsay, being based on one person telling another person about an event. Such 'facts' are likely to be truthful but someone may lie in order to hide something such as adultery or illegitimacy, to prevent someone from being fined because of a late registration, or to enable someone to get married or enlist in the armed services.

1.6 Church of Jesus Christ of Latter-day Saints

The Church of Jesus Christ of Latter-day Saints (LDS), whose members are known as the Mormons, has microfilmed or purchased microfilms of many records and publications which can be used by family historians. These include parish registers, registers of wills, civil registration returns, censuses, military records and publications from around the world, including many relating to the Caribbean.

▮ Bahamas (births, marriages and deaths, 1850–1960)
▮ Barbados (census, 1679 and 1715, Anglican parish registers, 1637–1931)
▮ Bermuda (grant books, 1758–1937)
▮ Dominica (wills, 1750–1938)
▮ Grenada (civil registration returns, 1866–1940)
▮ Jamaica (wills, 1756–1930; parish register transcripts, 1664–1880; civil registration returns, 1878–1930)
▮ St Lucia (church registers, 1750s–1780s)

You can find lists of their microfilm from their online catalogue which you can order to be seen at a local Family History Library. They have also indexed millions of birth, baptismal and marriage events from parish registers and entries submitted by their members. The indexes, library catalogue and other resources are available at www.familysearch.org.

1.7 The National Archives (UK)

The National Archives holds the records of the UK central government and the law courts of England and Wales including the Treasury, the Cabinet Office, the Home Office, the Foreign Office, the War Office, the Admiralty and the Colonial Office. It does not hold locally created records of colonial administrations such as school records, court proceedings, or church registers etc; surviving records are to be found in appropriate Caribbean archives, libraries and departments (see Chapter 10 for details).

Therefore, the National Archives are not usually the first place to look for genealogical information on Caribbean families. The most useful and comprehensive records occur for those who worked for or came to the attention of the British government, for example, those who were:

- employed by the government as a colonial civil servant or in the military (not a local public servant or in the militia);
- regulated or registered by a UK government department – for example, merchant navy officers and men, ships' passengers, naturalisations in the colonies and registration as citizens of UK and Colonies;
- entered in the Slave Registers (c1817–1834) as a slave or slave holder (there are duplicates of registers which may survive locally);
- awarded, or who applied for, compensation under the terms of UK legislation following events such as the 1831 hurricane or the emancipation of slaves in 1834;
- in possession of estate in England and Wales but who had died overseas.

In general terms, the records in the National Archives are arranged first by the department which created, inherited or transferred the records to the National Archives and, second, by the series, which often represents the type of document, for example, musters, ships' logs, government gazettes or governors' correspondence. The records are then usually arranged chronologically or sequentially by former departmental file references.

Each document has a unique three-part reference. The first part is the department code, for example, CO for the Colonial Office, BT for the Board of Trade and PC for the Privy Council, according to the department that created it. The second part is the series number, which represents the series within the department code, for example, CO 141 for Jamaican government gazettes. The third and final part is the piece number, which represents the individual document. For example, the description book for those who enlisted in the 5th West India Regiment, 1811–1817, is WO 25/656 and the 1951 electoral register for Barbados is CO 32/124.

To identify documents you want to look at, consult the online catalogue at www.nationalarchives.gov.uk/discovery. There is no overall index to the records of the National Archives. The catalogue describes each record title, the detail of which varies greatly from a brief description such as 'minutes' to a detailed description of individual letters within a document. The catalogue has a very powerful search engine and you should read the help notes to make best use of it. You cannot usually search for names unless the record of the family or individual makes up a whole file or the description contains more than the document title, for example, when the catalogue describes individual letters or papers in a piece. Many popular genealogical records have been microfilmed by the LDS (section **1.6**) or digitised by the National Archives and commercial companies (see section **1.8**). Most administrative records and correspondence files have not been digitised or indexed and you will need to visit the National Archives to see them. You are strongly advised to check the website before visiting as it contains useful information such as up to date opening hours and identification requirements to obtain a reader's ticket.

You do not need an appointment and you do not need a reader's ticket to see surrogate records (digital and microfilmed records) but you will need to obtain a reader's ticket to see original (manuscript) records; most records referred to in this book are originals. To obtain a reader's ticket you must provide two forms of documentary evidence, one with your signature and the other with proof of address – again, check the website for details. Without a valid reader's ticket you will not be able to see original documents.

You may use only graphite pencils in the National Archives' reading rooms. Pens of any kind are not allowed. You may use personal computers and digital cameras in most of the reading rooms. The rules are on the website.

The National Archives does not undertake general speculative research. If you are unable to visit, the National Archives maintains a list of independent professional researchers on its website who, for a fee, may undertake research on your behalf. Researchers also advertise their services in family history magazines and directories, and on genealogical websites. Alternatively, if you know exactly what you are looking for, you can order copies if you know the reference and page numbers, or use the Freedom of Information paid research service; guidance and fees are on the website.

1.8 Digitised sources

Few archives from the Caribbean have been digitised but a large number of sources, especially for expatriate Caribbean people travelling to, residing in or settling in the UK, Canada and the US are available. Unless otherwise mentioned these are subscription or pay-per-view sites. There may be different subscription models allowing access to different datasets, or they may be time based, and there may be different rates for viewing transcriptions and digitised sources. Some services allow you to search their indexes without registering or subscribing, while others require you to register or subscribe before being able to use their indexes – you then need to pay to see the image of the document or dataset.

Many collections at the National Archives have been digitised and indexed by third party websites; most can be found by checking the record page at www.nationalarchives.gov.uk/records. In addition, the National Archives has its own digitised collections available through the online catalogue. I have listed many of the more useful resources for researching Caribbean ancestors below or in the relevant section in the book.

Please note that this list is a snapshot and more resources are frequently added. Also, while most of these digitised collections can be searched by name and other keywords, some can only be browsed and not searched.

The National Archives (TNA) – www.nationalarchives.gov.uk
■ Prerogative Court of Canterbury registered wills 1384–1858 (PROB 11)
■ WWI army medal index cards (WO 372)
■ Royal Navy seamen's services, 1854–1928 (ADM 139 and ADM 188)
■ Royal Navy medal rolls (ADM 171)
■ Royal Navy officers' records (ADM 196, ADM 340)

- Medals issued to merchant navy seamen (WWI BT 351 and WWII BT 395)
- Registers of passport applications 1851–61 and 1874–1903 (FO 611)

Ancestry

Ancestry has a number of regional websites and different subscription models. There are thousands of datasets from original records and secondary (published) sources. Those particularly useful for Caribbean researchers include:

www.ancestry.co.uk

- Censuses, for England and Wales, and Scotland 1841–1911
- General Register Office (GRO) indexes to births, marriages and deaths for England and Wales, from 1837
- Slave Registers of former British Colonial Dependencies 1812–34 (incomplete TNA T 71 – free to access but need to register)
- Index to the Prerogative Wills of Ireland 1536–1810
- British Army First World War papers (TNA WO 363 and WO 364)
- Soldiers who died in the Great War
- Index cards to WWI British army medal rolls (TNA WO 372)
- Copies of various publications of migration to the American colonies, including Dobson, Coldham and Hotten
- Incoming UK ships' passenger lists 1878–1960 (TNA BT 26)
- Certificates of arrivals into the UK 1810–69 (TNA CUST 102, FO 83, HO 2 & HO 3)
- Copies of various publications on wills and administrations including Coldham's *American Wills Proved in the Prerogative Court of Canterbury*
- Sanders' books on Barbados baptisms, marriages and wills as *English Settlers in Barbados 1627–1800*

www.ancestry.ca

- Censuses of Canada 1851–1916
- Canadian WWI army service records
- Passenger lists 1865–1935
- Border crossings from Canada to the US 1895–1956
- Loyalist claims
- Canadian birth, marriage and death indexes c1858–1934

www.ancestry.com

- Censuses of the Danish Virgin Islands 1835–1911
- Censuses of the USA 1790–1930 (including Panama Canal Zone and US Virgin Islands)
- Passenger lists into the USA c1800–1950s
- US passport applications 1795–1925
- US naturalisation records and indexes c1790–1974
- WWI US army draft registration cards
- WWII US draft registration cards and enlistment records
- Copies of published passenger lists to America, including the Caribbean

Family Relatives – www.familyrelatives.com

- GRO indexes to births, marriages and deaths for England and Wales, from 1837 (browse)
- GRO indexes to regimental births, marriages and deaths from 1761 (browse)
- GRO indexes to consular and High Commission returns to births, marriages and deaths from 1848 (browse)
- GRO indexes to marine births and deaths from 1837 (browse)
- Indexes to Irish Wills 1536–1857
- Index to Prerogative Wills of Ireland
- Canadian Civil Service List 1872–1918 (searchable by year)

FamilySearch – www.familysearch.org

- Indexes to US censuses 1910–1930 including Panama Canal Zone and US Virgin Islands
- Church registers for Danish/US Virgin Islands
- Church registers for Jamaica
- Indexes to US naturalisations
- Indexes to 1881 census for England and Wales
- Ad hoc worldwide indexes to baptisms, births and marriages and other records

Findmypast – www.findmypast.co.uk

- GRO indexes to births, marriages and deaths for England and Wales, from 1837
- GRO indexes to regimental births, marriages and deaths from 1761

- GRO indexes to consular and High Commission returns to births, marriages and deaths from 1848
- GRO indexes to marine births and deaths from 1837
- Censuses for England and Wales 1841–1911
- Outbound ships' passenger lists 1890–1960 (TNA BT 27)
- Registers of passport applications 1851–61 and 1874–1903 (TNA FO 611 browse)
- British army service papers 1760–1913 (TNA WO 97)
- Merchant seamen service records 1835-1857 and 1918-1941 (TNA BT 112-BT 120, and BT 348-BT 350)

Moving Here – www.movinghere.org.uk

- Selected passenger lists for ships leaving the Caribbean to the UK 1948–60 (BT 26, free)
- Selected photographs of people, industry and places in the Caribbean (INF 10, free)

Scotland's People – www.scotlandspeople.gov.uk

- GRO Scotland registers of births, marriages and death from 1855
- Old parish registers for Scotland 1538–1854
- Censuses of Scotland 1841–1911
- Scottish wills and testaments 1513–1901

The Genealogist – www.thegenealogist.co.uk

- GRO indexes to births, marriages and deaths for England and Wales from 1837
- GRO indexes to regimental births, marriages and deaths from 1761
- GRO indexes to consular and High Commission returns to births, marriages and deaths from 1848
- GRO indexes to marine births and deaths from 1837
- Rolls of honour for the First and Second World Wars
- Censuses for England and Wales 1841–1911
- Non-conformist registers for England and Wales 1567–1858 (TNA RG 4–RG 8)
- Non-statutory overseas returns 1627–1969 (TNA RG 32–RG 36)
- Registrar General of Shipping and Seamen registers of births, marriages and deaths of passengers and British nationals at sea 1854–91 (TNA BT 158–BT 160)

1.9 Ancestral origins

Most Caribbean people are immigrants to the region and the culmination of your research may be to find your ancestral home in Europe, Africa, America or Asia. During your research you may have been fortunate to find clues to the homeland for your Caribbean ancestors such as information in a passenger list, a letter, a service record, a will or obituary, and in which case you may be able to start researching archives in that country.

Unfortunately, there are very few records of passengers or immigrants to the Caribbean (see Chapter 3 for information). While discovering the ancestral home for people of European and Asian descent can be difficult, it is particularly challenging for African-Caribbean people because most had their names, culture and heritage taken from them on their capture in Africa and subsequent enslavement in America and the Caribbean. There are no lists of people who were captured in Africa, held in forts, or who were transported to the Caribbean. Few records give an African ethnic group which would help cross the Atlantic divide – auction notices rarely give the names of slaves or purchasers and shipping records do not give any names or origins of slaves. It is possible that receipts and accounts may say where people were bought, which may help identify the ship and then it may be possible to track back the ship's movements to Africa.

Private papers, slave registers and newspaper notices of runaway slaves sometimes give ethnicity or describe physical characteristics such as tattoos and country marks, which may indicate a possible ethnic group. There may be family stories about African-born ancestors. However, the slave trade from Africa to the British Caribbean ended in 1807, and slavery ended in 1834, and so the tales may be diluted or exaggerated. Linguistic evidence and naming practices may give clues. Many African naming traditions survived in slavery and children were given African names, although many were anglicised.

These techniques can be used by other ethnic groups and nationalities. Most free migrants retained their surnames and cultural practices which may help find their ancestral homeland. Most Europeans have surnames which may give clues to their ancestor's nationality although foreign settlers in British colonies may have anglicised their names to fit in. Most migrants who arrived after the abolition of slavery were recruited by agents whose records may survive in the country of departure. Furthermore, most Caribbean countries recorded these groups, especially those with 'protectors of immigrants' (successors to the 'protectors of slaves') and information may survive in immigration departments or in the archives.

In the absence of documentary evidence or other clues it has been suggested that DNA analysis may help people reconnect with their ancestral homes. There are two principal DNA tests: Y-chromosome which is passed from father to son and traces the paternal ancestry – this can only be used by men; and mitochondrial DNA which is passed from the mother to her children and which traces the maternal line – this can be used by men and women but only women can pass it on. Genetic companies check the DNA at selected points to identify your haplotype (genetic group). Comparing the results can reveal if two people have a common ancestor, but they cannot show how closely they are related or how many generations separate them. DNA testing should be used to complement traditional documentary research and in cases where males have the same surname and DNA haplotype there is a strong likelihood of them being related. Unfortunately, because of Caribbean family structures, with most children being born outside of lawful marriage and not having their father's surname, it can be difficult to demonstrate these relationships.

DNA analysis also reveals your deep ancestry over hundreds or even thousands of years and may not always help you identify a country of origin, let alone a village or cultural group. For example, both my paternal and maternal haplogroups are commonly found throughout southern and western Europe so their ancestors could have come from anywhere in France, Spain, Germany, Scotland, Ireland, England etc.

The BBC 2 *Motherland* documentary analysed the DNA of African-Caribbean participants who had four African-Caribbean grandparents. The documentary illustrated a major weakness of this type of testing by revealing that 27 per cent of the men and 2 per cent of the women tested had European roots. This is because the DNA analysis shows the direct paternal and maternal ancestry only; if there are European genes on either line your results will be European.

In addition, these tests do not show the DNA of your other ancestors, for example, there have been about seven generations since the slave trade was abolished and therefore you could have 128 ancestors (64 men and 64 women) but the analysis will only reveal information on two of them; and only the maternal line for women. Autosomal tests can look at your overall genetic make-up and identify your ethnicity but these are not always reliable. However, a couple of companies have introduced whole gene tests which look for clusters of DNA that are passed from parents to children for several generations and can be used to find cousins who have similar clusters.

DNA testing companies often have useful online tutorials and guidance to help interpret results and describe the history of human migration and migration of your haplotype. Some sites allow you to upload your DNA test results so that you can compare them with other users or be notified if other researchers match your DNA results. Genetic genealogy is becoming mainstream as an additional genealogical research tool and most genealogical websites, publications and magazines now have sections on DNA analysis.

1.10 Further reading and useful websites
1.10.1 General genealogical guides

The sources and research techniques for Caribbean genealogy are very similar to tracing families in the United Kingdom and you should read general family history books, magazines or websites to help you get started. These will be particularly useful for researching your family after they settled in the UK or if any of your ancestors are from the UK. There are far too many family history books to list here, however, the following books relating to DNA, Caribbean and African-American history and genealogy are less likely to be available in your local library or archive service and may be useful, especially for people with enslaved ancestors:

African American Lives (DVD)
Ball, *The Genetic Strand: Exploring a Family History Through DNA*
Barrow, *Family in the Caribbean: Themes and Perspectives*
Burroughs, *Black Roots: A Beginner's Guide to Tracing the African American Family Tree*
Crooks, *A Tree Without Roots: The Guide to Tracing British, African and Asian Caribbean Ancestry*
Gates, *In Search of our Roots: How 19 Extraordinary African Americans Reclaimed Their Past*
Hart, *How to Interpret Family History and Ancestry DNA Test Results for Beginners: The Geography and History of Your Relatives*
Kennett, *DNA and Social Networking: A Guide to Genealogy in the Twenty-First Century*
Lane, *Tracing Ancestors in Barbados: A Practical Guide*

Mitchell, *Jamaican Ancestry: How to Find Out More*

O'Sullivan-Sirjue and Robinson: *Researching your Jamaican family*

Pomery, *DNA and Family History: How Genetic Testing Can Advance Your Genealogical Research*

Porter, *Jamaican Records: A Research Manual: A Two Part Guide to Genealogical and Historical Research Using Repositories in Jamaica and England*

Rose, *Black Genesis: A Resource Book for African-American Genealogy*

Smolenyak and Turner, *Trace Your Roots with DNA*

Streets, *Slave genealogy: A Research Guide with Case Studies*

Wells, *Deep Ancestry: Inside the Genographic Project*

Woodtor, *Finding a Place Called Home: A Guide to African American Genealogy and Historical Identity*

1.10.2 Useful websites

www.afrigeneas.com – African-American genealogy; especially www.afrigeneas.com/guide, *African-American Genealogy: An Online Interactive Guide for Beginners* by Dee Parmer Woodtor

www.aahgs.org – Afro-American Historical and Genealogical Society

www.ahc.umn.edu/bioethics/afrgen/ – papers from a conference held at the Center of Bioethics, University of Minnesota, July 2002 on African-American genealogy

www.ancestry.com/learn/ – Ancestry.com's learning centre which contains useful articles on genealogical sources and techniques including DNA

www.bbc.co.uk/history/familyhistory/next_steps/genealogy_article_01.shtml – guidance on African-Caribbean genealogy

http://blackfamilytrees.com – a social networking site for Caribbean genealogists

www.candoo.com/genresources/ – a list of useful addresses and resources in the Caribbean including professional researchers and material which has been microfilmed by the LDS

www.ccharity.com/ – Christine's African-American Genealogy website

www.centrelink.org – Caribbean Amerindian Centrelink, a website for those interested in Indigenous Amerindians of the Caribbean area such as Caribs, Arawaks and Tainos

www.cyndislist.com – a popular genealogical gateway, comprising research tools and links to over 50,000 genealogical websites

www.cyndislist.com/hispanic.html – a gateway to resources for Hispanic, South American and Caribbean family history www.everygeneration.co.uk – empowering and influencing the black community through history, genealogy and heritage

http://genealogy.about.com/od/dna_genetics/ – links to articles on DNA

www.genuki.org.uk – the United Kingdom and Ireland Genealogical Information Service. A handbook on British genealogy and a gateway to British Internet resources

www.isogg.org – International Society of Genetic Genealogy

www.jamaicanfamilysearch.com – a subscription site which contains a miscellaneous collection of indexes and transcriptions of Jamaican records

www.movinghere.org.uk/galleries/roots/caribbean/caribbean.htm – guidance on Caribbean genealogy

www.rootsweb.com – a genealogical gateway to web-based groups, discussion lists and online resources

http://lists.rootsweb.ancestry.com/index/other/DNA/GENEALOGY-DNA.html – Rootsweb DNA message board

www.rootsweb.ancestry.com/~caribgw/ – Caribbean Genealogical Web Project contains country-based resources and links to useful websites. Guyana is under the South American GenWeb Project (www.worldgenweb.org/~southamericangenweb/) and Belize under the North American GenWeb Project (www.worldgenweb.org/index.php/northamgenweb)

http://boards.ancestry.com/localities.caribbean/mb.ashx – Caribbean message boards on Rootsweb

www.thegeneticgenealogist.com – blog on DNA by Blaine Bettinger

http://en.wikipedia.com – has useful articles on many aspects of genealogy, DNA and Caribbean history

CHAPTER 2
RECORDS OF THE COLONIAL OFFICE

The most important records for the study of the West Indies and West Indians are those of the Colonial Office and its predecessors. The term 'Colonial Office', as used in the National Archives and this guide, refers to the various departments which at different times had oversight of the colonies. These include the various secretaries of state, the Lords of Trade and Plantations, the Board of Trade, various committees of the Privy Council, and the Colonial Office. See Banton's *Administering the Empire* for a description of the history and the records of the Colonial Office.

The records of the Colonial Office relating to individual colonies are arranged according to the type of document: original correspondence, entry books, acts, sessional papers, government gazettes, miscellanea (*Blue Books of Statistics*, naval office returns, newspapers and reports of protectors of slaves), registers of correspondence and registers of out-letters. These are the records received or created by the Colonial Office rather than the records of colonial governments; where they survive, these are held in the appropriate country's archives. Chapter 10 lists Colonial Office series for each country.

Many of the records described below may survive in the relevant country's archives, for example, incoming letters from the Colonial Office, other Caribbean governments and other British government departments, drafts of outgoing letters, draft and printed copies of the *Blue Books*, sessional papers, acts and government gazettes. Many have been published, for example, newspapers, government gazettes, *Blue Books*, sessional papers and departmental reports and acts, and it is possible that copies may be available in national, academic and specialist libraries.

2.1 Original correspondence

These are despatches (letters) and reports received by the Colonial Office from the governor and correspondence with other bodies concerning a particular colony. Until 1951, each colony or administrative unit has separate original correspondence series. Until 1800, the correspondence is arranged by date of despatch. From 1801 until 1926, the volumes are arranged first by the governor's despatches, then by letters from UK government departments, and finally by letters from individuals. From 1926, the correspondence is in subject files. Until 1926, few documents are well described in the catalogue with a typical description along the lines of 'Despatches March–June 1900' and in most cases you will have to use published and unpublished finding aids to identify specific letters. 'Your Caribbean Heritage' was a project to catalogue Caribbean Colonial Office documents; they completed selected documents mostly for Jamaica, Barbados, Bermuda and Grenada for the 1830s and early 1900s, and this project is being continued by volunteers.

The papers are mostly of an official and administrative nature. The following types of records are found, and although they do not occur for every colony, they give an idea of the usefulness of these records: petitions (also known as memorials), tax lists, censuses (most are statistical but some give the name of the head of household with the numbers of women, children, servants and slaves), colonial civil servants' application forms, land grants, newspapers (which sometimes give announcements of births, marriages and deaths), lists of prisoners, returns of government slaves, lists of manumitted people, correspondence concerning the repatriation of merchant seamen and military personnel who had been discharged overseas including in the United Kingdom, and records of the local courts such as chancery, petty sessions and vice admiralty sessions.

From 1873 and increasingly from the 1890s the original correspondence series have been extensively weeded and are described in the registers (section **2.7**) as 'destroyed under statute'. Most surviving papers, especially from 1926, tend to be of a purely administrative nature demonstrating the type of work carried out by the Colonial Office or those which set precedent in colonial affairs and in the colonies. There are few papers concerning individuals, such as petitions and applications, unless they raise an important or interesting matter. Drafts of these letters, usually without the enclosures, may survive in the relevant country's archives.

As the Caribbean countries became independent, diplomatic relations with Britain and matters relating to British nationality and citizenship were dealt with by the Commonwealth Office (DO series) until 1967, and the Foreign and Commonwealth Office (FCO series) from 1967 (see section **9.2.1** for information). The records of the Colonial Office finish in 1967 following its merger with the Foreign Office and governors' correspondence is to be found in FCO series.

Published reference books for these records are the *Calendar of State Papers, Colonial, America and West Indies*, 1574–1739 and *Journals of the Board of Trade and Plantations*, 1704–1782; the calendars have also been published on CD-ROM (by Routledge (2000)) and online, with digital images of documents from CO 1 (by PROQuest, http://colonial. chadwyck.com). Selected correspondence is described in Ragatz's *Guide to the Official Correspondence of the Governors*. Unpublished reference is through the registers of correspondence which are described in section **2.7** and the chronological indexes, 1815–1870, in CO 714.

2.2 Entry books

These record drafts of letters sent from the Colonial Office to governors and government departments. They also contain instructions, petitions, letters, reports and commissions, and include details of patents for grants of land. Before 1700 they record letters received as well as letters despatched. Entry books were superseded in 1872 by the registers of out-letters (section **2.8**). Enclosures are rarely entered in full. The original letters, together with enclosures, may survive in the relevant country's archives.

2.3 Acts

These are copies of local acts and ordinances. For family historians they can include private acts of naturalisation in the colony, sales of land to recover debt, grants of manumission, appointments of office holders, names of people transported or deported from the colony, and confirm the rights and privileges to freed men and women. Acts are listed in CO 5/273–282 (1638–1781) and CO 383 (1781–1892).

2.4 Sessional papers

These are the proceedings of the houses of assembly, executive councils and legislative councils which formed the government of each colony. They touch upon all matters handled by the local government and may include departmental reports. Genealogical information can include petitions to the assembly, grants of manumission of slaves, naturalisation, and appointments of officials and members of the council.

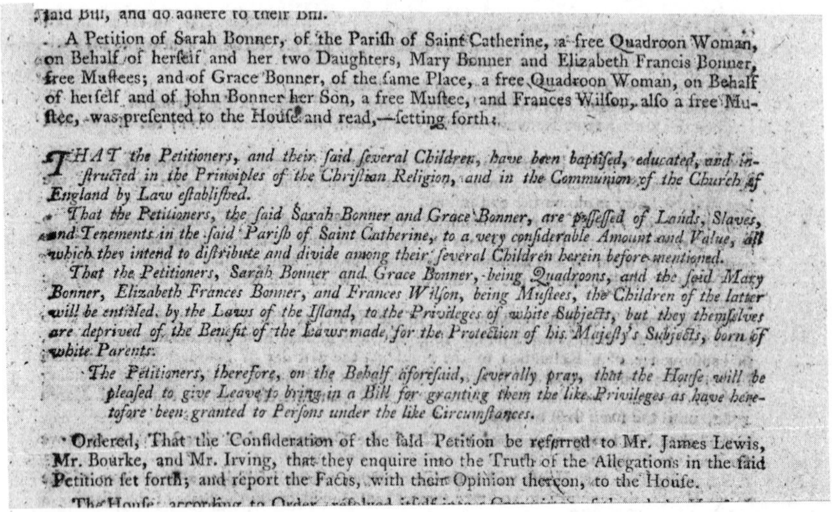

said Bill, and do adhere to their Bill.

A Petition of Sarah Bonner, of the Parish of Saint Catherine, a free Quadroon Woman, on Behalf of herself and her two Daughters, Mary Bonner and Elizabeth Francis Bonner, free Mustees; and of Grace Bonner, of the same Place, a free Quadroon Woman, on Behalf of herself and of John Bonner her Son, a free Mustee, and Frances Wilson, also a free Mustee, was presented to the House and read,—setting forth,

THAT the Petitioners, and their said several Children, have been baptised, educated, and instructed in the Principles of the Christian Religion, and in the Communion of the Church of England by Law established.

That the Petitioners, the said Sarah Bonner and Grace Bonner, are possessed of Lands, Slaves, and Tenements in the said Parish of Saint Catherine, to a very considerable Amount and Value, all which they intend to distribute and divide among their several Children herein before-mentioned.

That the Petitioners, Sarah Bonner and Grace Bonner, being Quadroons, and the said Mary Bonner, Elizabeth Frances Bonner, and Frances Wilson, being Mustees, the Children of the latter will be entitled, by the Laws of the Island, to the Privileges of white Subjects, but they themselves are deprived of the Benefit of the Laws made for the Protection of his Majesty's Subjects, born of white Parents.

The Petitioners, therefore, on the Behalf aforesaid, severally pray, that the House will be pleased to give Leave to bring in a Bill for granting them the like Privileges as have heretofore been granted to Persons under the like Circumstances.

Ordered, That the Consideration of the said Petition be referred to Mr. James Lewis, Mr. Bourke, and Mr. Irving, that they enquire into the Truth of the Allegations in the said Petition set forth; and report the Facts, with their Opinion thereon, to the House.

The House, according to Order, resolved itself into a Committee of the whole House upon

Figure 3 *Jamaica: Petition of Sarah Bonner, free quadroon, for rights and privileges, November 1783 (CO 140/66, p.57)*

2.5 Government gazettes

These are official newspapers produced by most colonies and can be extremely useful for local, family and social history. The starting dates and content varies between each colony but for family and local historians the gazettes can provide a wealth of information. Examples include: birth, marriage and death notices, including occasional obituaries of notable people; notices of proceedings and sales of property in the courts of chancery and petty sessions; lists of people applying for liquor, dog and gun licences; lists of jurors, druggists (chemists or pharmacists), constables, voters, solicitors, nurses, medical practitioners and militia; notices of sales of land; public appointments, leave of absence and resumption of duty; notices relating to cases of intestacy, guardianship and wills; notices on applications for naturalisation; inquests into shipwrecks; ships entering and clearing port, sometimes with the names of first class passengers; lists of people paid parish relief; and tax lists.

(226)

TABLE E.

Patients who have left the Infirmary cured or relieved during 1865.

Name.	age	Native Country.	Residence.	Occupation.	Date of admission.	Left cured.	Left Relieved.	Diseases and Remarks.
Solitude Celestin	50	Dominica	Barouie	Labourer	1864. Aprl. 20	1865. June 24		Extensive ulceration of the leg amputation below the knee.
Gustave Bona parte	20	do	W. House	do	May 27	Feb. 12		Severe ulcerat'n of the leg
Charles	21	do	do	do	June 24	Mar. 2		Ulceration of the foot
John Pierre	35	do	Mel. Hall	do	July 29	Apr. 24		Stricture
Joseph George	22	do	Rosean	do	Augst 30		Mar. 15	Epeliptic Fits
Whitfield	19	do	Canef Est	do	Sept. 13	Mar. 6		Ulcer of the leg [with f'ver
Laurent	24	do	Roseau	Groom	Oct 26	Sept. 2		Inflammation of the eyes
Thomas Valle	40	do	do	Boatman	Novr. 11	Jau. 26		heum affect'n of the back
Pierre African	50	Africa	Cur. Rest	Labourer	Novr. 26	" 7		Abscess of the hand
John Baptiste	40	Dominica	St Joseph	do	Decr. 3	" 6		Ulcer of the foot
Prince Lewis	16	do	M. Wallis	do	Decr. 2		Feby. 8	Frac. of leg, admittnd for relief the fracture having been neglected
George Train	51	England		Sailor	Decr. 16	" 4		Intermittent Fever
Avriette	20	Dominica	Roseau	Labourer	" 18	" 16		Fever &c.
Elizabeth St. Rose	24	do	Roseau	do	" 30	June 24		Ulcer of the toe
Caroline Baptiste	50	do	Genova Estate	do	1865. Jany. 7		Jany 24	Rolapsus Uteri
George William	21	do	Barouie	do	" 12	Feb. 15		Dropsy [head
Henry	31	Madras	Bal Town	do	" 15	" 6		Fever, with severe pain of
Maria	6	Mart'que			" 15	" 6		Cough
Angelle	3				" 15	" 6		Worms
Louisa Sam	37	Dominica	Roseau	W'woman	" 18	April 2		Inflammation of the eyes
Andria	24	do	do	Labourer	" 25	Mar. 26		Abscess of the breast
Jule	14	do	Gomier	do	" 30	April 8		Dropsy
Alfred Bellot	21	do	Newtown	Carpenter	Feby. "	Mar. 19		Inflammation of the eyes
Louisa Louis	46	do	Couliabre	Labourer	" 9	May 29		Ulcer of the foot
William George	60	do	River Est	do	" 11	Mar. 2		Pain in the chest
Rose J. Philip	17	do	Roseau	do	" 12	May 11		Ulceration &c.
Sophia	12	do	Campbell	do	" 18	" 14		Ulcer of the foot
Amelia Paul	13	do	Pt Michel	do	" 23	Mar. 6		Head & face severe injured by accident Sugar Mill
Jane Johnson	25	do	Roseau	H. Servant	" 23	Sep. 18		Ulceration of the foot
Henry Cooper	25	England		Sailor	" 23	Feb. 24		Sprained Arm
Pierre Billy	25	Dominica	Bell Vue	Labourer	" 27	Mar. 6		Fractured wound of the back by a bayonet
Elie Aladdin	48	Mart'que	Layou	do	" 27	" 14		Ulcer of the foot
Leger Bernard Dégazon	50	do	Roseau		" 27	April 3		Tumour of the neck—operation performed
Jean	50	Dominica	do	Labourer	March 5	" 27		Apoplexy
Louison George	50	do	Belvidere	do	" 8	July 15		Ulcer of the Scrotum
Josephine	24	do	Gomier	do	" 22	May 18		Rheumatic pains, swelling of the leg
Jeremie	14	do	Roseau V.	do	" 28	" 6		Gor'd in the thigh by an ox
Sammie	30	Madras	Roseau	do	" 29	pril 6		Pains in the back & side from a fall
Tasie Moise	16	Dominica	do	do	April 2		Apr 21	Dropsical swelling—removed from the Infirmary to her friends
Mary Jno Lewis	50	do	do	do	" 2	April 18		Dysentery
Andrea African	50	Africa	M prosper	do	" 4	June 19		Affection of the eyes
William	12	Dominica	River Est	do	" 6	Oct. 23		Ulceration of the toe
Pascal	64	do	Roseau	Baker	" 19		May 4	General Debility
Stephen	12	do	Antrim V	Labourer	" 19	ay 21		Fingers crushed in a sugar mill
Nicholas Pascal	22	do	Grandbay	do	" 6	" 6		Ulcer of toe
Daniel	20	do	do	do	" 23	" 18		Ulcer of leg
Ellen	49	do	Roseau	do	" 25	Sep. 23		Rheumatism
Henry	13	do	Souffriere	do	" 26	Aug. 23		Idiopathic Tetanus
Mary Ann	30	do	Roseau	do	" 27		June 27	Affection of the womb
Sophia	60	Africa	Mahaut	do	May 3		May 21	Prolapsus uteri
John Pierre	24	Dominica	P Ruperts	do	" 4	June 15		Ulcer of the toe
Barnes	14	do	Ma'uchrie	do	" 13	July 1		Severe sp ain of knee joint
Nelson	20	do	Chk. Hall	do	" 15		May 20	Finger broken
Jean	25	Gu'loupe	Roseau	do	" 16	June 10		Rheumatic pains

Figure 4 *Dominica:* Government Gazette, *1865, list of patients in the infirmary* (CO 75/1, p.226)

OFFICIAL GAZETTE, MONDAY, FEBRUARY 16, 1920.   35

List of TRADE LICENCES issued by the Treasurer from 1st August 1919 to 31st January 1920.

To whom granted.	Description of Licence.	Locality.	Date of Expiry.
Adrien Lelia	Huckster	Pte. Michel	
Alfred Anastasie	,,	Portsmouth	
Ambrose Evanah		,,	
Do.	6th Class Trade	,,	30 June 1920.
Andrew Garfield	,,	,,	
Anthony Frarcillia	Huckster	Old Street	
Augustin James	6th Class Trade	La Roche	
Baron A. A.	,,	Belle Hall	
Bank, The Colonial	Banker's	Long Lane	31 Decr. 1920.
Bank of Canada, The	,,	Old Street	Do.
Bellony Mary [Royal	Huckster	Portsmouth	
Benjamin Erene		Capuchin	
Bertrand John A.	6th Class Trade	St. Joseph	
Bertrand Elmira	,,	Hillsbro' St.	
Blanchard G. W.	,,	Market St.	
Bruno Knight	Huckster	Salisbury	
Birmingham Brenda	,,	Tete Morne	
Birmingham Anestine	,,	Picodeau	
Carbon Edwill	,,	Boetica	
Casey Ethel	,,	Portsmouth	
Charles Virginia	,,	Upper Lane	
Coipel Angelina	6th Class Trade	Brantridge	
Dickson, D. D.	5th Class Trade	Londonderry	
Destouche Roderick	,,	Pte. Michel	
Doram Elizabeth	Huckster	Marigot	
Ducreay Elmira	,,	Granby Street	
Dumas E. F.	,,	Church St.	
Dupigny Margaret	6th Class Trade	New Street	
Duverney Felicia	,,	New Town	
Edwards Marion	Huckster	Market St.	
Emanuel Moses J.	6th Class Trade	Portsmouth	
Emanuel Rosaline	,,	Balahou Town	
Eusebe Peter A.	Huckster	La Roche	
Fontaine Joseph B.	,,	Bagatelle	
Firmin John	,,	Soufriere	
Florent Clementine	,,	Granby St.	
Fraser Virginia	6th Class Trade	Layou	
Germain Virginia	,,	Granby Street	
Griffith Alcina	Huckster	River Street	
Hall James	,,	New Town	
Joseph Luvenia	,,	Upper Lane	
Jacob Fanny	,,	Grand Bay	
James Elizabeth	6th Class Trade	New Street	
James Elize	,,	Marigot	
Johnson Antoine	,,	New Town	
Johnson Valentine	Huckster		30 June 1920.
John Baptist Etheline	,,	Lake Road	
Joseph Paul	6th Class Trade	Mahaut	
Lecointe Ernestine	,,	Pte. Michel	
Leonard William	,,	High Street	
Magloire Beatrice	,,	Fond Canie	
Michel Mrs. Aaron	Huckster	Market St.	
Morancie Matilda	,,	New Street	
Myler Jessie	,,	Ship Street	
Mondesire Augustine	6th Class Trade	St. Sauveur	
Noel Nixon	,,	Morne Jaune	
O'Brien Mary	Huckster	Old Street	
Phillip, C. G.	,,	,,	
Pierre Ismenie	6th Class Trade	Colihaut	
Roberts Ann R.	,,	Granby Street	
Rossi Laura	Huckster	King's Lane	
Royer Mary	,,	Clifton	
Ryan Matilda	,,	Gt. Marlbro' St.	
Samuel George	,,	New Town	
Scotland Elfreda	,,	Castle Bruce	
Serrant Mary	,,	New Town	
Shillingford, E. P. &	6th Class Trade	Loubiere	
Shillingford Bros. [Co	,,	Balahou Town	
Shillingford St. Geo.,	,,	Salisbury	
Stedman Felicienne	Huckster	Carse O'Gowrie	

Figure 5   *Dominica:* Government Gazette, *1920, list of trade licences issued (CO 75/14, p.35)*

2.6 Miscellanea

Miscellanea series contain primarily *Blue Books of Statistics*. For some colonies they also contain naval officers' returns and newspapers.

2.6.1 Blue Books of Statistics

These annual volumes begin about 1820 and continue until the mid-1940s. They contain statistical information about each colony, such as population, education, religion and economy. They also include the names of public employees arranged by department, with their salary and date of appointment; the names of government pensioners; and the names of teachers, their salary and who paid them – for example, most early schools were set up by religious authorities.

2.6.2 Naval office returns

These are customs returns taken at colonial ports. They are organised by port and then by date of arrival or departure and record the names of vessels, the master, the owner, port of registry, tonnage, number of crew, type of taxable goods imported or exported, and the previous and next port. Slaving voyages have been identified and indexed on the Transatlantic Slave Trade database at www.slavevoyages.org.

2.6.3 Newspapers

These are an incomplete series of newspapers that were received by the Colonial Office during the 1830s to 1850s. Caribbean newspapers are extremely useful for local and family historians and in addition to local and international news they contain notices for runaway slaves and apprentices, court cases, shipping reports, and birth, marriage, death and funeral notices and obituaries; these can give information on extended families locally and living overseas. The style and content tends to be more like British local newspapers than the national newspapers.

The British Library Newspaper Library (see Useful addresses, page 196) contains collections of colonial newspapers. The newspaper catalogue can be searched online at www.bl.uk. Most modern Caribbean newspapers have online editions and historical copies of the *Jamaica Gleaner* from 1834 have been digitised and are available by subscription from www.newspaperarchive.com.

O 1   PENSIONS.

Name.	Amount of the Pension in Sterling.			Authority under which the Pension is granted.
	£	s.	d.	
PENSION.				
Alexander Ferguson	70	0	0	Ordinance 11, 1868
SUPERANNUATION ALLOWANCES. (a.)				
J. McSwiney	96	0	0	Ditto
George Fox	210	0	0	Ditto and No. 4 of 1861
D. Shier	480	0	0	Ordinance 22, 1860
N. J. Darrell	105	0	0	Ordinance 12, 1875
N. T. Vessey	130	0	0	Ditto
James Elliott	45	0	0	Ditto
J. Goring	33	6	8	Ditto
Mary Munro	17	10	0	Ditto
N. L. Brathwaite	204	3	4	Ditto
E. B. Bhose	170	0	0	Ditto
J. G. Austin (b)	253	17	8	Ditto
J. S. Hackett	660	0	0	Ditto
Horace E. Wickham	310	0	0	Ditto
H. W. Austin...	300	0	0	Ditto
A. Hitchins	72	0	0	Ditto
Samuel Johnstone	150	0	0	Ditto
F. A. Van Holst	88	0	0	Ditto
A. T. Hubbard	204	3	4	Ditto
J. J. Large	84	0	0	Ditto
H. P. Plummer	560	0	0	Ditto
F. J. Wyatt	576	0	0	Ditto
J. C. Lang	105	0	0	Ditto
Samuel Manning	198	0	0	Ditto
T. R. Milner	250	0	0	Ditto
D. M. Gallagher	384	0	0	Ditto

REMARKS.

(a) Superannuation Allowance is calculated at the rate of one-fiftieth of the average Salary for the three years preceding the date of retirement, in the case of Officers joining the Service after the passing of Ordinance 12 of 1875, and at a like rate on the Salary at the date of retirement in the case of those Officers who were in the Service before the passing of that Ordinance, and is available to every public servant drawing a salary of £30 and upwards after ten years' of service and 55 years of age.
(b) At the date of Mr. J. G. Austin's retirement, he held the office of Colonial Secretary of Hong Kong.

Figure 6 *Guyana:* Blue Book of Statistics, *1890, list of government pensioners (CO 116/259, pp.O1–2)*

PENSIONS.

O 2

Date from which the Pension has been paid.	Service for which Pension is granted.	Amount of Emolument when last employed in the Public Service.			Age of Pensioner on 31st Dec., 1890.	Cause of Retirement. (a)
		£	s.	d.		
Mar. 1, 1868	Minister of St. Luke's Parish	500	0	0	60	Ill-health.
April 1, 1868	Sheriff of Berbice & Stipendiary Magistrate	(b) 750	0	0	83	16 years of service.
May 16, 1872	Principal of Queen's College	500	0	0	77	21 do.
Aug. 25, 1873	Medical Inspector of Estates' Hospitals..	1,000	0	0	75	24 do.
Oct. 1, 1875	Commissary of Taxation...	375	0	0	76	14 do.
Sep. 29, 1875	Harbour Master, Georgetown	500	0	0	75	13 do.
April 11, 1876	Keeper, New-Amsterdam Prison ...	187	10	0	72	Ill-health.
April 7, 1877	Post Office Letter Carrier	83	6	8	62	Do.
Jan. 1, 1878	Matron of Georgetown Prison	62	10	0	79	14 years of service.
Jan. 11, 1879	Aid-Waiter, Customs	291	13	0	81	35 do.
April 1, 1879	Consulting Interpreter and Curate of St. Patrick's.	500	0	0	62	Abolition of office of Consul. Interpr.
Nov. 4, 1878	Immigration Agent General	(c)1,500	0	0	78	11 years of service.
May 1, 1879	Surgeon to Berbice Hospital, and District Medical Officer.	1,000	0	0	66	33 do.
May 26, 1880	Rector of St. Peter's Parish	500	0	0	67	31 do.
July 1, 1881	Comptroller of Customs	1,000	0	0	71	15 do.
Jan. 26, 1881	Curate of St. Paul's Parish	300	0	0	75	12 do.
April 1, 1883	Clerk, Immigration Department ...	250	0	0	64	30 do.
July 1, 1883	Aidwaiter, Customs, Berbice	200	0	0	73	22 do.
July 1, 1884	Weigher and Gauger, Colonial Bonded Warehouse.	291	13	4	81	34 do.
Jan. 1, 1884	Curate of St. Luke's	300	0	0	54	Ill-health.
Feb. 1, 1884	Stipendiary Magistrate	800	0	0	65	35 years of service.
Jan. 1, 1884	Rector of St. George's	900	0	0	63	32 do.
Nov. 2, 1884	Commissary of Taxation...	375	0	0	52	Ill-health.
Jan. 1, 1885	Curate, Trinity Parish	300	0	0	68	33 years of service.
Mar. 16, 1885	Rector, St. Michael's	500	0	0	61	25 do.
Aug. 1, 1885	Assistant Receiver General, Berbice ...	600	0	0	57	29 do.

REMARKS.

(a) Under this head—where years of service are given as the cause of retirement—the Officer at the date of his retirement had attained the age of 55.
(b) £450 of this from Imperial Funds.
(c) Superannuation allowed on average between salaries of £1,000 and £1,500 for the last three years of service.

2.6.4 Reports of protectors of slaves

The protectors of slaves looked after the welfare of slaves and there are returns for Trinidad, St Lucia and British Guiana. The reports include information on punishments, criminal cases, births, deaths, marriages, free baptisms and manumissions.

2.7 Registers of correspondence

Registers of correspondence are bound volumes which record correspondence received by the Colonial Office and its predecessors. Between 1703 and 1759 manuscript calendars of the correspondence of the Board of Trade are found in the General Registers (CO 326/1–51). From 1759 to 1782 a single, annual calendar was produced (CO 326/52–74). Between 1822 and 1849 all incoming correspondence was entered in a series of registers arranged by groups of colonies (CO 326/85–358).

In 1849 the Colonial Office introduced a system of registration whereby every incoming letter was allocated a number in the Daily Register (CO 382) which started with '1' each year. Details of the letter were then entered in a register for the colony. There is a series of these registers of correspondence, which run until 1951, for each colony.

Until 1926 the following details were noted in columns: date of registration, registered number (taken from the daily register), name of the correspondent, date of letter, letter number, subject of letter and a brief précis, related correspondence, action taken and remarks. The cross-references contained in the registers are abbreviated and usually refer to other correspondence recorded in the same register. For example, 'Gov' refers to governors' despatches, 'MO' to Miscellaneous Offices and 'C' to individuals with surnames beginning with letter 'C'; this also acts as an index to individuals referred to elsewhere in the register. A table of abbreviations is given in Banton pp.110–11.

Other information may be stamped into the register such as 'destroyed under statute' if the letter has been destroyed; 'printed for Parliament' with the date (these are in the House of Commons Sessional Papers); 'printed for the Colonial Office' with a colony and number noted (to be found in Colonial Office Confidential Print series); and 'secret' (these papers are often filed in CO 537). The letter was then given a minute sheet on which were written similar details as in the register; this was used by Colonial Office officials to make comments. Draft replies may be attached to the letter. If a letter from another government department has been destroyed, it may be possible to find a copy in the records of that department.

Until 1926 the registers are arranged first by the governor's despatches, then by letters from British government departments, and then by letters from individuals. Increasingly from 1868 the 'individuals' section may be used as an index to individuals and subjects mentioned in the correspondence. At the end of each register there is often a list of printed material received from the colony such as acts, *Blue Books* and sessional papers.

It is important to note that the registers are arranged by the date the Colonial Office received the letter but the original correspondence is filed by the date of the letter.

In 1926 a series of annual subject files was introduced and each colony was allocated a block of file numbers. The registers continue in the same series as before but they are arranged in file number order. There is usually a key to the files in the front of each volume. The registers give a brief description of each letter filed under the subject, the date and name of sender, and the action taken. If the letter was destroyed or printed, this will also be recorded.

2.8 Registers of out-letters

There is a series of registers of out-letters for each colony. They continue from the entry books (section **2.2**), starting in 1872 and finishing in 1926. These are compiled in the date order of the outgoing correspondence from the Colonial Office. The registers are arranged first by governor, then government department, and finally by the individual with whom the Colonial Office was corresponding. They record the name of recipient, date of despatch, number of despatch, a brief description, and the registered number of the letter to which it was the reply. Unlike the entry books, these give only a précis of each outgoing letter. If a draft copy survives it will be in the appropriate original correspondence series.

2.9 Other records

Most of these records are text but other types of records such as maps and photographs are found in the records of the Colonial Office and they can be used to illustrate the historical and social context in which your family lived. For example, maps show details such as topography, roads, towns, villages and railways and can help you visualise where your family lived and worked and how they travelled.

Photographs tend to be official in nature showing events, buildings, industry, landscapes and people, although with the exception of senior officials people are usually not named. Even so, they can be used to show leisure activities, occupations, living conditions, housing and clothing.

Maps and plans are described in Chapter 5. There are few photographic collections in the National Archives and most photographs are found as enclosures or as images in official letters and reports. Photographs extracted from Colonial Office files for preservation reasons are in CN 3. The Colonial Office library photographic collection is in CO 1069 and is being uploaded onto the National Archives' Flickr photostream (www.flickr.com/photos/nationalarchives). INF 10 contains photographs commissioned by the Ministry of Information illustrating the geography and life in the British Empire (1945–1965) and many of these are on Flickr and Moving Here (www.movinghere.org.uk).

2.10 Further reading

Acts of the Privy Council, Colonial Series

Andrews, *Guide to Materials for American History to 1783 in the Public Record Office of Great Britain*

Banton, *Administering the Empire, 1801–1968: A Guide to the Records of the Colonial Office in the National Archives of the UK*

Bell and Parker, *Guide to British West Indian Archive Materials in London and in the Islands for the History of the United States*

Calendar of State Papers, Colonial, America and West Indies 1574–1739

Journals of the Board of Trade and Plantations, 1704–1782

Ragatz, *A Guide to the Official Correspondence of the Governors of the British West India Colonies with the Secretary of State, 1763–1833*

Walne, *A Guide to Manuscript Sources for the History of Latin America and the Caribbean in the British Isles*

CHAPTER 3
MIGRATION TO THE CARIBBEAN

Most people from the Caribbean are migrants to the region. Although most of the islands once had indigenous populations, they were decimated by European settlers through disease, enslavement, forced migration and resettlement. Indigenous Amerindians still live on the Caribbean islands, but they are now a minority.

This chapter describes the main groups of migrants to the Anglo-Caribbean and sources for discovering more about why and when they migrated.

3.1 Emigration: general records
3.1.1 Passenger lists

Very few passenger lists survive in the National Archives before 1890. The British government did not register people emigrating from these shores or arriving in the West Indies, and until the First World War it was not necessary for emigrants to have passports.

Licences to pass beyond the seas (E 157) include registers of passengers going to America and the West Indies between 1634 and 1639, and in 1677. Port Books 1565–1798 (E 190) are customs accounts and often include names of passengers. The Privy Council registers (PC 2) contain many petitions and letters of people emigrating to, or already settled in, the colonies. These and other Privy Council papers relating to the colonies 1613–1783 are described in Acts of the Privy Council, Colonial Series.

Between 1773 and 1776 a register (T 47/9–12) was made of emigrants going from England, Wales and Scotland to the Americas. Information provided includes: name, age, occupation, reason for leaving the country, last place of residence, date of departure and destination; these lists include apprentices or indentured servants. People from T 47/9–11 are listed in Tepper's *Passengers to America* and Coldham's *Emigrants from England* and those from T 47/12 are listed in Dobson's *Directory of Scottish Settlers*, Volume I. Many early passenger lists are also found in Colonial Office original correspondence series (section **2.1**). Passenger lists in the

National Archives before 1890 do not usually contain much information relating to the emigrant apart from their name, where they sailed from and the intended destination of the ship. Many of these sources have been published and are included in the bibliography. Colonial newspapers and government gazettes (section **2.5**) occasionally give the names of first class passengers in the shipping intelligence sections.

Between 1890 and 1960 the Board of Trade kept passenger lists of people leaving from British ports to places outside Europe and the Mediterranean. These passenger lists (BT 27 – online at Findmypast) are arranged by date, port of departure and ship. Information given in the passenger lists includes the name, age and occupation of each passenger and, from the 1920s, often the place of residence in Britain. There are no passenger lists after 1960. It is possible that inwards passenger lists may also survive in the relevant country's archives. The National Archives does not hold any passenger lists of people who travelled by aeroplane.

3.1.2 Passports

Until the First World War it was not necessary to have a passport in order to emigrate. Early passports were issued to merchants, and to government and court officials to ensure safe conduct in foreign countries. SP 44/411 is an entry book of passes issued between 1697 and 1784. Later registers (FO 610) run from 1795 to 1948: they are arranged chronologically by date of issue and give the passport number, name of the applicant and destination. There are indexes (FO 611, online at TNA and Findmypast) for the period 1851–61 and 1874–1916 which give the name, passport number and date of issue.

The colonial secretary also issued passports to people wishing to go to the colonies. Correspondence relating to passes issued between 1796 and 1818 is in CO 323/97–116; later correspondence is in the relevant country series. Most of the earlier passes seem to have been issued to Dutch planters and businessmen wishing to return to the recently captured colonies of Surinam (Suriname) and Demerara; Demerara was later ceded to Britain as a state of British Guiana (Guyana).

Under the Colonial Regulations of 1868 governors were authorised to issue passports for foreign travel to people naturalised in the colonies. Interestingly, it was not until 23 September 1891 that governors were told they could issue passports to British-born subjects, although many colonies had already been doing this. These registers if they survive are in the relevant country.

3.1.3 Naturalisation

Until 1962 subjects in British colonies were also British citizens and did not need to naturalise. Citizenship conferred specific rights, subject to certain restrictions, which varied over time. These rights included the right to vote, inherit or bequeath property, serve in a public office, protection by the British Crown and government in foreign countries and, on occasion, exemption from some taxes.

Foreign subjects in the British colonies did not need to naturalise to reside or work there but if they wanted rights such as the vote, they did. Until 1914 naturalisation could be granted by local act or by the legislature, details of such grants may be found in the relevant country's acts or sessional papers. Correspondence and memorials relating to naturalisations may be found in original correspondence and sessional papers. Notices of naturalisations are often published in government gazettes (section **2.5**). Enrolled grants of naturalisations may be found in deeds or patent registers in the country's archive or register office.

Under the British Nationality and Status of Aliens Act 1914, naturalisations in the colonies needed to be first approved by the Colonial Secretary and then by the Home Secretary. A Colonial Office circular of 28 April 1915 (CO 854/51) describes the regulations for the granting of naturalisations by the non-self-governing colonies. The governor was to first send the completed, but unsigned, certificate of naturalisation to the Colonial Secretary, together with testimonials. If the application was approved it was signed by the Home Secretary and returned to the governor, who then signed and dated it and ensured that the applicant took the oath of allegiance. A copy of the certificate, with the oath endorsed, was then sent to the Colonial Secretary who forwarded it to the Home Secretary for registration.

These colonial certificates from 1914 to October 1986 are in HO 334, arranged by certificate number. The certificates contain the following information: full name, address, trade or occupation, place and date of birth, nationality, marital status, name of spouse and children if applicable, and the names and nationality of parents. These naturalisations are organised by certificate number and therefore to obtain a certificate you need to know the number. The Home Office indexes to these overseas naturalisations to 1980 have been added to the online catalogue and are searchable by name and date of naturalisation. To obtain the certificate number for colonial naturalisations between 1981 and October 1986 you need to write to the National Archives giving the full name of the person naturalised at time of application, country and date of birth, and the country and date of naturalisation. Naturalisation certificates after 1 October 1986 are held by the UK Border Agency (see Useful addresses).

The Home Office papers for colonial naturalisations have not survived but correspondence and memorials, especially in cases of doubt, may be found in the relevant original correspondence series (section **2.1**). Copies of the correspondence and duplicate certificates may also survive among the records of the governor's secretary's office, immigration office or register office in the relevant country. Announcements for naturalisations may be published in government gazettes (section **2.5**).

It is important to note that these certificates relate to the naturalisation of foreign subjects in the colonies and are not registrations of citizenship ('R' certificates) introduced in 1948 for Commonwealth British subjects who applied for British citizenship; see Chapter 9 for further information on these certificates.

3.1.4 Further reading

Acts of the Privy Council, Colonial Series, 1613–1783
Bevan, *Tracing Your Ancestors in the National Archives: The Website and Beyond*, Chapters 17–19
Coldham, *The Complete Book of Emigrants, 1607–1776*
Coldham, *Emigrants from England to the American Colonies*
Dobson, *Directory of Scots Banished to the American Plantations: 1650–1775*
Dobson, *Directory of Scottish Settlers in North America, 1625–1825*
Dobson, *The Original Scots Colonists of Early America, 1612–1783*
Filby and Meyer, *Passenger and Immigration Lists Index*
Games, *Migration and the Origins of the English Atlantic World*
Hotten, *The Original Lists of People of Quality...and Others Who Went from Great Britain to the American Plantations 1600–1700*
Kershaw, *Migration Records: A Guide for Family Historians*
Tepper, *Passengers to America*
http://www.findmypast.com
www.ancestry.com and www.ancestry.co.uk – contain a growing number of indexed and digitised images of published passenger lists to the American colonies including the Caribbean

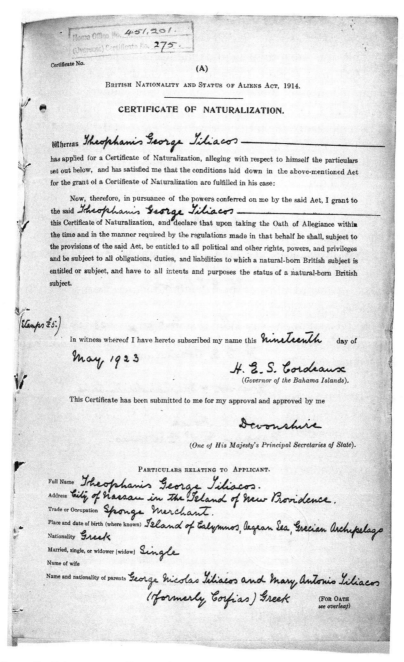

Figure 7   *Bahamas: certificate of naturalisation for Theophanis George Tiliacos, Greek, certificate number O275, 19 May 1923 (HO 334/249/275). Correspondence and testimonials relating to his naturalisation is in CO 23/293/11*

3.2 Indentured servants

Once the West Indies were settled there was a high demand for cheap labour. This was met initially by indentured servants and convicts (section **3.3**) from Britain. Indentured servitude was supposed to be freely entered into but many were children and paupers who had been kidnapped, and many thousands of Irish were transported to the Americas as servants; the term 'Barbadosed' entered the language at this time to describe people who were kidnapped and 'spirited' to the American colonies. The 'servants' were shipped to the colonies by agents (who arranged a transport fee through colonial merchants) and served a period of seven to ten years. After their period of servitude they were supposed to be allotted ten acres of land, but in the more densely populated islands, such as Barbados, this did not always occur. The National Archives does not hold comprehensive lists of indentured servants but some can be found among the passenger lists (section **3.1**) and in county record offices, especially for London, Liverpool and Bristol where the agents resided.

Indentured servitude was later restored following the abolition of slavery in 1834, with new groups of apprenticed migrants, mainly from India (section see **3.7**).

3.2.1 Further reading

Clark and Souden, *Migration and Society in Early Modern England*

Coldham, *The Bristol Registers of Servants Sent to Foreign Plantations, 1654–1686*

Galenson, *White Servitude and Colonial America*

Jordan and Walsh, *White Cargo: The Forgotten History of Britain's White Slaves in America*

Kaminkow and Kaminkow, *List of Emigrants from England to America, 1718–1759*

O'Callaghan, *To Hell or Barbados: The Ethnic Cleansing of Ireland*

Virtual Jamestown (www.virtualjamestown.org) – a database of indentured servants transported from Bristol to the American colonies in the seventeenth century

Wareing, 'Preventive and punitive regulation in seventeenth-century social policy: conflicts of interest and the failure to make "stealing and transporting Children and Other Persons" a felony, 1645–73'

3.3 Transportation

From 1615 until the loss of the mainland American colonies in 1783 many thousands of prisoners were sentenced to transportation, or had death sentences commuted to transportation (particularly under the 1718 Transportation Act, 4 Geo 1 cap 11), and were shipped to the American colonies including the Caribbean. Unfortunately, most records do not state the final destination. Transportation was for ten years as most of the colonies forbade longer sentences. Merchants arranged for the shipment of transportees and if, on arrival in the colonies, they were not already allocated an estate to work on, they were put up for auction.

State Papers, Domestic (SP series) contain correspondence and petitions concerning transportation and lists of reprieved people. Up to 1704 these are calendared in the *Calendar of State Papers, Domestic*. Lists of people to be transported occur in the Patent Rolls (C 66), the Treasury Papers (T 1, 1747–1772) and the Treasury Money Books (T 53, 1716–1744). Until 1745 the Treasury papers are described in the *Calendar of Treasury Books and Papers*.

Trials and verdicts of cases tried by the assize circuits are among various ASSI series. Governors' despatches and colonial entry books also describe cases and policy concerning transportation. Other records, such as quarter sessions papers, transportation bonds and landing certificates may be found in UK county record offices (see Coldham, *Bonded Passengers to America*, for a history of transportation to American colonies). Details of trials that took place in the Old Bailey, 1674–1913, are available at www.oldbaileyonline.org.

From 1783 other destinations were sought and Australia became Britain's next penal settlement. However, between 1824 and 1853 convicts were sent to Bermuda to build the naval base on Ireland Island; the convicts were able to return once their sentence had been served. Lists of convicts on the Bermuda hulks are in HO 8 and records of baptisms and burials, 1826–1946, for the naval base, Ireland Island, are in ADM 6/434–436.

3.3.1 Further reading

Baker, *An Introduction to Legal History*

Bevan, *Tracing Your Ancestors in the National Archives: The Website and Beyond*, Chapter 47

Calendar of State Papers, Colonial, America and West Indies, 1574-1739

Calendar of State Papers, Domestic, 1547-1704

Calendar of Treasury Books, 1660–1718
Calendar of Treasury Books and Papers, 1729–1745
Calendar of Treasury Papers, 1557–1728
Coldham, *Bonded Passengers to America*
Coldham, *The Complete Book of Emigrants, 1607–1776*
Coldham, *Emigrants in Chains*
Coldham, *More Emigrants in Bondage, 1614–1775*
Hallett, *Forty Years of Convict Labour: Bermuda, 1823–1869*
Hawkings, *Criminal Ancestors: A Guide to Historical Criminal Records in England and Wales*
Oldham, *Britain's Convicts to the Colonies*
Willis, 'Transportation versus imprisonment in the eighteenth- and nineteenth-century: penal power, liberty and the state'

3.4 Slave trade

Slavery became established in the British colonies from the 1640s when Dutch merchants from Brazil introduced sugar cane. Sugar farming created a monoculture which was physically demanding and required large numbers of labourers. Africans, used to tropical climates, diseases and food, were considered more suitable than white indentured labourers. It has been estimated that some 1.6 million Africans were enslaved and transported to the British Caribbean between 1640 and 1808, when the slave trade to British colonies was abolished.

The slave trade was essentially a triangular trade in which merchants traded British goods for slaves from trading settlements and forts on the West Coast of Africa. These slaves were then traded for goods such as sugar, rum and molasses in the West Indies. Before 1698 the Company of Royal Adventurers of England trading with Africa and its successors, monopolised the British slave trade. The various African companies administered British possessions on the West Coast of Africa until 1821 when the government abolished the company and took control of its West African forts and settlements (1 and 2 Geo 4 cap 28). The records of the African companies are in T 70. These records include details of payment for shipments of slaves, names of employees of the African companies and of their agents in Africa and the West Indies, and general correspondence.

Most of the records relating to the slave trade in the National Archives consist of petitions from merchants, statistics of imported slaves and navy office returns (section **2.6.2**) in the records of the Colonial Office. Details of the crews of slaving vessels can be found in the ships' musters in BT 98, although very few survive before 1800. Most sources detailing slaving voyages in the National Archives have been identified and are indexed on the Transatlantic slave trade database at www.slavevoyages.org.

Until 1808 there are no lists of slaves transported from Africa in the National Archives, and any after that date exist because slave ships had been seized for illegally transporting slaves. The released slaves then became forfeited to the Crown (**3.6**).

3.4.1 Further reading
Black, *The Atlantic Slave Trade*
Donnan, *Documents Illustrative of the History of the Slave Trade*
Eltis, *The Rise of Atlantic Slavery in the Americas*
Klein, *The Atlantic Slave Trade*
Tattersfield and Fowles, *The Forgotten Trade*
Thomas, *The Slave Trade: The History of the Transatlantic Slave Trade*
Transatlantic Slave Trade database (www.slavevoyages.org)
Walvin, *A Short History of Slavery*
Walvin, *Making the Black Atlantic: Britain and the African Diaspora*

3.5 American loyalists
During and after the American War of Independence 1775–83, many people lost their land and possessions because of their loyalty to the British Crown. Many loyalists fled to Britain, Nova Scotia and the Caribbean, in particular to the Bahamas, Dominica and Jamaica. Correspondence regarding these refugees to the Caribbean can be found in Colonial Office original correspondence (section **2.1**) and sessional papers (section **2.4**) series, for example CO 23/25, fo 131 lists 52 loyalist households who arrived in the Bahamas in 1784.

Under the Treaty of Peace (1783) and the Treaty of Amity (1794) loyalists were able to claim compensation for their losses. The records of Treasury Commissioners investigating claims, with pension and compensation lists, are in T 50, 1780–1835; T 79, 1777–1841; AO 12, 1776–1831; and AO 13, 1780–1835. Correspondence and petitions regarding relief and compensation can be found in T 1. In 1783 East Florida was ceded to Spain and loyalists made similar claims; many left for the Bahamas and Jamaica. The records of the East Florida Claims Commission are in T 77; T 77/19 relates to claims made by the settlers in the Bahamas.

Former slaves of Americans who fought for the British cause were allowed to remain free; many of these black loyalists who escaped to

Nova Scotia and England became the initial settlers of Sierra Leone. The 'Book of Negroes' (PRO 30/55/100, no 10427) compiled by British military authorities in 1783 lists black refugees in New York before they left for Nova Scotia. Sierra Leone was established in 1787 by a group of philanthropists as a settlement for freed slaves from Britain and the West Indies. The proceedings and other papers of the Committee for the Relief of Poor Blacks, 1786–1787, are among the papers in T 1/631–638 and 641–647. Four hundred poor blacks, together with some English women, were transported as the first settlers to Sierra Leone and a list of those at Plymouth, 16 February 1787, is in T 1/643, no 487.

The settlement did not survive and in 1791 a group of black loyalists from Nova Scotia was encouraged to settle. A list of the blacks of Birch Town, Nova Scotia, who gave their names for Sierra Leone, November 1791, is in CO 217/63, fos 361–366. Their numbers increased with the arrival in 1800 of Jamaican maroons, who had been expelled from Jamaica for Nova Scotia in 1796.

3.5.1 Further reading

Black loyalist information and some transcriptions on Library and
   Archives Canada Canadian digital collections (http://blackloyalist.com/
   canadiandigitalcollection/index.htm)
Braidwood, *Black Poor and White Philanthropists: London's Blacks and
   the Foundation of the Sierra Leone Settlement 1786-1791*
Brown, 'The American Loyalists in Jamaica'
Coldham, *American Loyalist Claims*
Walker, *The Black Loyalists: The Search for a Promised Land in Nova Scotia*

3.6 Liberated Africans

The slave trade was abolished on 1 May 1807 (Abolition of the Slave Trade Act 1807, 47 Geo 3 session 1 cap 36), although vessels which sailed before that date could under certain circumstances trade until 1 March 1808. Any vessels seized under the 1807 and subsequent acts for illegally carrying slaves were taken as prize, the master was fined and the slaves became forfeited to the Crown. This meant that they became government slaves and many were apprenticed or enlisted into the Royal Navy or the army, especially the West India Regiments and the Royal African Corps.

From 1808 Sierra Leone became the centre for British suppression of the slave trade on the West Coast of Africa and many liberated Africans settled there. Two Sierra Leone censuses include details of liberated

Africans living there in 1831 (CO 267/111) and 1833 (CO 267/127). In the 1840s many liberated Africans emigrated to Jamaica and other West Indian islands. Correspondence concerning this emigration, petitions and some passenger lists are in CO 267, for example, a nominal list of liberated Africans with their ages who left for Port Antonio, Jamaica on the *Morayshire* and the *Amity Hall* in 1848 is in CO 267/203. Nominal lists of liberated Africans who left for St Lucia and Jamaica on the *Una* in January 1849, for Jamaica on the *Etheldred* on 29 May 1849 and for Trinidad on the *Agnes* on 28 May 1849 are in CO 267/207.

The trials of illegal slavers were held at vice-admiralty courts in Africa, the West Indies, Havana and Rio de Janeiro. Under various treaties with slave trading powers, such as the Netherlands, Portugal, Spain and Brazil, ships of these and other nations could be sentenced at Mixed Commission Courts. Proceedings, and other papers relating to illegal slave trading are found mainly among the records of the Foreign Office, especially those of the Slave Trade Department (FO 84) and the Mixed Commission Courts.

The primary court was held at Sierra Leone (HCA 49/97, 1808–1817 and FO 315, 1819–1868). The other courts were at Cape Town (FO 312, 1843–1870), Havana (FO 313, 1819–1869), Jamaica (FO 314, 1843–1851) and Rio de Janeiro (FO 129/3–13, 15, 1819–1861, and FO 131/1–11, 1820–1885). These records include registers of slaves liberated, crew lists and log books of captured ships, and correspondence with the Admiralty and Foreign Office. Other records can be found in the papers of the Admiralty (ADM 1), the Slave Trade Adviser of the High Court of Admiralty (HCA 37), colonial customs returns (CUST 34), Colonial Office original correspondence series (especially for Sierra Leone, CO 267), and the Treasury (T 1).

Information on liberated Africans captured by colonial authorities or settled in the Caribbean can also be found in the appropriate colonial original correspondence series and C0 318. A 'Commission of Enquiry into the state of captured Negroes in the West Indies, 1821–1830' (CO 318/81– 98) was set up to look at the treatment and conditions of liberated Africans in the West Indies and includes some lists of liberated Africans, for example, CO 318/82 includes lists of liberated Africans in Tortola in 1823.

An Order in Council dated 11 July 1817 (revoking an Order in Council of 16 March 1808), relating to bounty payments for the capture of illegal slavers, required collectors of customs to send annual reports on liberated Africans they received to the Colonial Secretary to forward to the Privy Council. These returns were to include the names, ages and genders of the liberated Africans indicating if they were enlisted or apprenticed and to give the names of the people to whom they were apprenticed. No annual returns have been found among Privy Council or Colonial Office records although some returns which pre-date this Order in Council were printed for Parliament in 1821 (61) XXIII.119; others may be found among the Commission of Enquiry schedules in CO 318/81–98.

Some densely populated colonies could not cope with large numbers of liberated Africans and there were schemes to move them to colonies which needed labourers such as British Guiana and Trinidad. In addition, British colonies also received liberated Africans from Cuba under the Spanish cedula (law) of 1828, and correspondence relating to this movement for the period 1835–42 is in CO 318.

3.6.1 Further reading

Adderley, *New Negroes from Africa: Free African Immigrants in the Nineteenth-century Caribbean*

Howell, *The Royal Navy and the Slave Trade*

Lloyd, *The Navy and the Slave Trade: Suppression of the African Slave Trade in the Nineteenth Century*

Nwokeji and Eltis, 'The Roots of the African Disapora: Methodological Considerations in the Analysis of Names in the Liberated African Registers of Sierra Leone and Havana'

Ward, *The Royal Navy and the Slavers: The Suppression of the Atlantic Slave Trade*

3.7 Indentured labourers

When slavery was abolished in 1834 most newly freed slaves had to serve a period of four years for their former masters, which was known as apprenticeship. When apprenticeship ended in 1838, in colonies with available land such as Trinidad, St Vincent and British Guiana, many left their masters to establish their own smallholdings. As a result, many colonies suffered severe labour shortages and petitioned the Crown to help relieve this problem. Plans to transport Chinese settlers to Trinidad were first discussed in 1802 and to Jamaica in 1806, and the first group of 192 Chinese settlers arrived in Trinidad onboard the *Indianna Fortitude* on 12 October 1806 (BT 6/2). This was not successful and the Colonial Office and colonial authorities considered schemes to employ workers from other Caribbean islands, liberated Africans (section **3.6**), Portuguese from Madeira and the Azores and, to a lesser extent, labourers from

Britain, France and Germany. Jamaica published a pamphlet to encourage free blacks from the United States to migrate (CO 137/249, ff 288–295).

The largest group of migrants were Asian Indians from the Indian subcontinent, who are often referred to in the records as East Indians or 'coolies'. Policy papers concerning their recruitment, with reports and correspondence relating to welfare and employment in the colonies, are found among appropriate colonial correspondence series, CO 323 and CO 318. CO 318 contains documents devoted to Indian labour for the period 1843–73. These are continued in CO 323 and later in the Immigration Department records CO 571, 1913–1920. From the 1870s the records of the Land Board and Emigration Department, CO 384–CO 386 (registers in CO 428), include information on Chinese and Indian emigration. CO 384 and CO 385 include surgeons' reports for emigrant ships which sometimes list births and deaths. Other papers record ships commissioned to sail from Madras and Calcutta with the numbers of Indians on board. Some lists of these emigrants may be found in the colonial correspondence and government gazettes.

Several enquiries into the state of Indian labour were published in the British Parliamentary Papers. Reports of the various local bodies who administered and reported on apprenticed labour may be found in the appropriate country's archives.

The Indian subcontinent was administered by the East India Company and from 1858 by the India Office. The records of these organisations are held by the British Library Oriental and India Office collections (see Useful addresses). The records of the agents who arranged for the transportation of Indians to the West Indies may survive in the National Archives of India (see Useful addresses).

3.7.1 Further reading

British Library, *Indians Overseas: A guide to source materials in the India Office Records for the study of Indian emigration 1830–1950*, www.bl.uk/reshelp/pdfs/indiansoverseas.pdf

Cumpston, *Indians Overseas in British Territories 1834–1854*

Dabydeen and Samaroo, *Across the Dark Waters: Ethnicity and Indian Identity in the Caribbean*

Ferreira, 'Madeiran Portuguese Migration to Guyana, St Vincent, Antigua and Trinidad: A Comparative Overview'

Hansib publications www.hansib-books.com/root/icn.htm – selection of articles on Indian migration to the Caribbean

Lai, *The Chinese in the West Indies 1806–1995: A Documentary History*

63

SAINT VINCENT,
Immigration Office,
28th March, 1868.

THE following list of the arrival and distribution of Immigrants during the year 1867 is published in accordance with the provisions of the 24th Clause of the Immigration Act October 1857.

By Command,

JAMES H. BROWN,
Immigration Agent.

INDIAN Immigrants ex " Newcastle."
Indented to serve from 10th June 1867.

Ships No.	Col. No.	NAME	Male	Female
		MONTROSE ESTATE.		
242	766	Mansing	1	
437	777	Madutally	1	
206	778	Ramnuth	1	
308	779	Ramprotanb	1	
240	780	Gobind Sing	1	
278	781	Balgobind	1	
23	782	Sooktatee	1	
387	783	Biganah	1	
266	784	Ramchulown	1	
275	785	Sewtohul	1	
64	786	Edoo	1	
22	787	Eliebux	1	
65	788	Mohamad Ally	1	
450	789	Kurmoo	1	
246	790	Heeramon	1	
279	791	Korieu Box	1	
274	792	Sobat	1	
209	793	Jiblanl	1	
48	794	Mothie	1	
		MALES	19	
488	795	Ozzeerun		1
43	796	Scorjee		1
244	797	Tutury		1
251	798	Jelabia		1
254	799	Lookea		1
241	800	Matabia		1
252	801	Sawborkhee		1
44	802	Pooroah		1
190	803	Dewkolea		1
461	804	Kobotaree		1
397	806	Jenseah		1
691	805	Aukhajee		1
		FEMALES		12

Ships No.	Col. No.	NAME	Male	Female
		PEMBROKE ESTATE:		1
479	806	Soboseah		
481	807	Bhuttoo	1	
477	808	Jodhee	1	
478	809	Dusruth	1	
475	810	Sewborun	1	
473	811	Ghattoo	1	
113	812	Urjoon	1	
114	813	Lutchmon	1	
141	814	Phuleera	1	
471	815	Kunhie	1	
870	816	Badul	1	
62	817	Dwarka	1	
295	818	Buckus	1	
109	819	Ramsondur	1	
265	820	Ghoburdun	1	
220	821	Sheam	1	
			15	
467	822	Khadiah		1
483	823	Bhutanee		1
69	824	Gowdree		1
110	825	Phodeah		1
429	826	Dhunnia		1
414	827	Attesh		1
449	828	Bama		1
				8
227	829	Dorbejah	1	
			16	
122	830	Porgu	1	1
482	831	Ronoah	1	
72	832	Vodobothu		1
123		Sotura (Infant) MALES	17	1
480	833	Jogasuree		1
		FEMALES		12
		BELLEAIR ESTATE:		
201	834	Boyjoonath		1
174	835	Kerith		1
177	836	Gungabieson		1
160	837	Seetaram		1
350	838	Lalljee		1
26	839	Pokhon		1
178	840	Gowree		1
386	841	Gungah		1
181	842	Suukur		1
415	843	Guttee		1
36	844	Ramdhon		1
229	845	Persaud		1
183	846	Ramlogun		1
	847	Ramdoss		1
79	848	Sookhoo		1
				15

Figure 8   *St Vincent: list of Indians disembarked from the* Newcastle, *1867, and the estates they were indentured to (CO 264/9, p.63)*

Lai, *Indentured labour, Caribbean sugar: Chinese and Indian migrants to the British West Indies*

Pariag, *East Indians in the Caribbean: An Illustrated History*

Ramdin, *Arising from Bondage: A History of the Indo-Caribbean People*

Saha, *Emigration of Indian Labour, 1834–1900*

Saunders, *Indentured Labour in the British Empire, 1834–1920*

Thomas, *Indians Overseas: A Guide to Source Materials in the India Office Records for the Study of Indian Emigration, 1830–1950*

Tinker, *A New System of Slavery: The Export of Indian Labour Overseas, 1830–1920*

CHAPTER 4
LIFE CYCLE RECORDS

These are the most important sources for a family historian as they record the major events in the lives of individuals: birth, marriage and death, including censuses and wills.

4.1 Records of births, marriages and deaths

Birth, marriage and death records are usually the first sources for family historians and are the building blocks for most family trees. People often keep their own certificates safe and may hold originals or copies of certificates of other family members. They can provide you with such vital details as date and location of the birth, marriage or death, ages, occupations, addresses and parents, thus helping you go back generation by generation.

Please remember that most of the information was given by the people taking part in the event, for example, while the date of a baptism may be accurately recorded by the vicar, the date of birth of the child was given by the mother; the fathers' names recorded on a marriage certificate were given by the people getting married; and the personal information on a death certificate was given by an informant who may not be a family member – so they could contain errors and false statements!

4.1.1 Civil registers

Civil registration, the recording of births, marriages and deaths by the state, started in England and Wales in 1837 and was extended to other British territories, including West Indian colonies at different times from the mid-nineteenth century. Occasionally, different events were registered at different times, for example, in Barbados registration of births started in 1890 and registration of deaths in 1925. The National Archives does not hold any civil registration returns, which should be found in the relevant registry office and many are available through the LDS (see section 1.6).

The certificates are similar to those we are familiar with today and tend to be detailed; for example, birth certificates give name, sex, name of mother and her maiden name, and the name and occupation of father.

Note that in most countries, if the parents were not married the father's name was not recorded. Some countries such as Barbados and Guyana allowed baptismal names to be added later, and the Bahamas asked for 'colour'. Marriage certificates usually provide name, marital status, occupation, age, address and the father's name and occupation; the entry usually shows whether the father is deceased. Death certificates will give address, name, sex, age, occupation and cause.

4.1.2 Church registers

Before civil registration births, marriages and deaths were recorded by religious authorities. The Church of England was the primary church in the older British colonies until the early 1800s when other Christian churches were established such as Methodist, Moravian and Baptist. In the colonies ceded from France and Spain, the Catholic Church was more important. Church registers recorded baptisms, rather than births and burials rather than deaths. Other religions and Christian denominations are represented in the West Indies and may record other life events as part of their ceremonies.

Before the establishment of the Diocese of Jamaica and Barbados in 1824 the Bishop of London had jurisdiction over the West Indian Anglican churches but this responsibility was limited to the appointment and management of the clergy. No registers or Bishops' Transcripts were sent to London although copies of a few registers for the Bahamas (1721–28) and St George's, Nevis (1716–23) are in the Lambeth Palace Library (see Useful addresses).

The governor had responsibility for much of what would be considered in England as being the rights of the church such as the creation and disposal of parishes, issuing marriage licences, probate of wills and overseeing public morals. There were no church courts which, in England and Wales, dealt with moral offences. In the West Indies moral offences were regulated by the justices of the peace.

Some colonies passed local legislation to regulate such offences, for example, in 1722 Barbados passed an act to 'regulate the punishment of such crimes and vices as are cognisable in the ecclesiastical courts and for suppressing vice and profanities'. This act permitted the Bishop's commissary authority to act against offending clergy but reinforced the justices' jurisdiction over lay people.

Registers of baptisms (births), marriages and burials (deaths) may be deposited in the country's archive or registry office but many are still held by the individual church, which you will need to contact for access to its registers. Many registers have been microfilmed by the Church of Jesus Christ of Latter-day Saints (LDS) and can be accessed via their family history centres (see section **1.6**); many indexes to Caribbean baptisms, births and marriages can be found at www.familysearch.org. A few early eighteenth-century returns were copied and sent to the Colonial Secretary or Board of Trade and are found among the governors' despatches in the National Archives; these are listed under the relevant country in Chapter 10.

Early registers usually only describe the date of the event and the names. For example, baptisms may only give the names of child and parents. If the mother was unmarried the register usually only gives her name and the child was registered with her surname. The status of slaves and free black people is usually given such as 'free coloured' or 'adult negro'. Slaves were often baptised as adults but the baptismal entries usually only show the owners and not the parents. Marriage entries give marital status.

Until the late-eighteenth century, slaves are rarely recorded in the church registers. In the Protestant colonies owners were discouraged from baptising their slaves, although many were baptised. Slaves tended to be baptised as adults and the registers do not give ages or parentage, although the owner is recorded as his or her permission was needed. Many slaves chose to be baptised with a Christian name different from their slave name and this new name was used by the slave, especially if he or she became free; owners may also have used the new name in their lists of slaves.

Later registers from the mid-nineteenth century usually contain more information, for example, the address and father's occupation. Baptismal entries may also give date of birth and mother's maiden name; Catholic registers usually give the name of godparents and possibly any relationship to the child. Marriage entries usually give the name and occupation of the parties' fathers and record whether they are dead. Burials may give age at death and cause of death.

Marriage between slaves was extremely rare and the few examples I have seen occurred during the 1820s. Many plantation slaves were buried without Christian rites on the plantation. Slaves in more urban areas and household slaves were more likely to be buried in churchyards or separate slave cemeteries, or possibly in the grounds of the house. Slaves may be recorded in the usual baptism and burial registers, which were normally arranged chronologically by event, but they may be recorded at the end of the registers or even in separate registers.

Slaves were chattel, which meant that they were the personal property of their owner. Most of the events that affected their lives were plantation affairs, and records of births and deaths were events that would be recorded by their owner, if at all. On plantations, slaves had a value according to their occupation, sex and age and were often listed with livestock. These records are private records and are described further in section **5.3**.

4.1.3 Slave registers

An important source for the period 1812–34, and the most important for slaves, is the slave registers in T 71, which were compiled to establish legally held slaves (see section **7.1**). They can provide information not only on slaves but also their owners and most free people of modest means would have owned at least one slave as a domestic servant or to hire out. Registration was carried out approximately every three years and lists changes from the previous register. Slave births and deaths are recorded, which will help give the approximate date of the event. Changes in ownership are shown in the registers, for example, on the death of an owner slaves were often bequeathed to family members, on marriage slaves were transferred as property from wife to husband, as a dowry, and slaves were often gifted to children when they left home. Many registers are indexed, while others are arranged alphabetically by plantation, or name of the registered holder. The registers in T 71 are duplicates which were forwarded to the Slave Registry in London from 1821, and the originals may survive in the relevant country archive. Most of the slave registers have been digitised and indexed by www.ancestry.co.uk (free to access after registering).

4.1.4 Newspapers and gazettes

Newspapers and colonial gazettes sometimes have birth, marriage, death and funeral notices and obituaries, especially of prominent citizens. These notices sometimes list the extended family including people living overseas. See section **2.6.3** for more information on newspapers and section **2.5** on government gazettes.

4.1.5 Further reading

General Register Office, *Abstract of Arrangements Respecting Registration of Births, Marriages and Deaths in the United Kingdom and Other Countries of the British Commonwealth of Nations and in the Republic of Ireland*

Kemp, *International Vital Records Handbook*

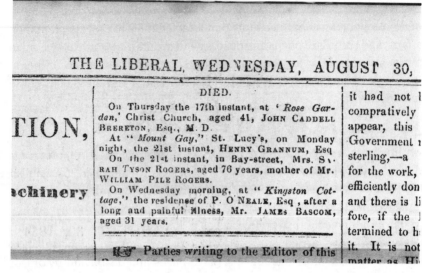

Figure 9 *Barbados: death notices announced in* The Liberal, *Wednesday 30 August 1854 (CO 33/12, fo 117). Henry Grannum is the author's great-great-great-grandfather*

4.2 Censuses and other listings

The English government started compiling information on colonial populations soon after settlements were established. Before 1670 few returns were made but with the creation of the Council for Foreign Plantations in 1670, regular reports from the colonies were sought. The information required was the numbers of men, women, children, servants, free people and slaves, the annual growth of the population and the number in the militia. This information was needed so that the government could record not only the population growth of the new colonies, but also its economic wealth and military strength. Some colonial governors sent regular returns, others waited for specific requests.

The majority of censuses returned to London were in the form of head counts of varying information. The simplest returns gave only the total population, the numbers of males and females and degrees of freedom. In more detailed censuses the population was broken down into sex, age group, marital status, degrees of freedom and colour or race. There are very few censuses giving names in the National Archives and most of these only give the name of the head of the household with numbers of women, children, servants and slaves. These are found among the original correspondence of the individual colonies, merely as a list or maybe with printed demographic analysis. Statistical counts of the population occur in the *Blue Books of Statistics* (section **2.6.1**) and government gazettes (section **2.5**) for the individual colonies, and are occasionally printed in the British Parliamentary Papers.

I have identified many West Indian censuses in the National Archives which give at least the name of the head of household (these are listed in Chapters 10 and 11). Details of pre-1776 American colonial censuses, with demographic analyses, are described in Wells' *Population of the British Colonies*. It is possible that other census returns containing names, especially any for the nineteenth and twentieth centuries, may be found in the islands' own archives or registration departments. If returns which list inhabitants have been kept it is possible that these will be closed or subject to certain restrictions.

The slave registers in T 71 provide a census of slave owners and slaves for the period 1812–34 (see section **7.1**). Although the information on owners is limited to their name and parish, and occasionally ethnicity, the information on the slaves is useful as the registers provide age, occupation and country of birth. The registers for the former Spanish and French colonies such as St Lucia, St Vincent, Trinidad and Grenada list the slaves in family groups, headed by the mother, and often record siblings if they are on the same estate. Unfortunately, the registers for the older British colonies such as Jamaica and Barbados list the slaves only by sex and age, although sometimes they may give the name of the mother.

The records of the National Archives include many other types of population returns, for example, petitions from prominent landowners, tax returns and electoral registers. The returns are in original correspondence (section **2.1**) and government gazettes (section **2.5**) series for the individual colonies; some are described in Chapter 10.

4.2.1 Further reading

Kuczynski, *Demographic Survey of the British Colonial Empire (Volume 3: West Indian and American Territories)*

Wells, *The Population of the British Colonies in America Before 1776*

	White Families	Free People of Color	Numb.ʳ in each Family.	Numbʳ of Slaves
George Town - formerly called the Hog-sties			.	**270**
	John Drayton		6	23
	Sarah Nixon		3	4
	Abraham Bodden		6	5
	Sterling Rivers		5	5
	Rachel Rivers		8	17
	William Jennett		3	
	Geo. Bodden		7	4
	Benjᵃⁿ Bodden		6	
	Willᵐ S. Prescott		5	2
	Eliz: Conior		1	5
	Mary Savery		6	5
	John Bodden		8	8
	John Edwᵈ Rivers		4	3
	James Thompson		7	5
	Cornelia Scott		5	1
	Mary Wilson		4	
	John S. Jackson		6	
		Chloe Parsons	1	2
		James Parsons	1	5
		Wᵐ Parsons	3	6
		Lind Rivers	1	1
		George Barrow	1	3
At West-Bay				
	John Bodden		6	2
	Thomas Hyde		8	6
	Jane Walker		1	9
	William Rivers		5	2
	Isabella Foye		1	2

Figure 10 *Cayman Islands: census of heads of households, 1802 (CO 137/108, fo 272)*

4.3 Wills and grants of administration

The governor was responsible for the probate of wills and grants of administration through the local courts. The types of information recorded include original wills and grants of administration, which were frequently copied into wills or probate registers or in the register of deeds and inventories of goods. Wills usually give details of the testator's immediate family and their bequests, together with some information about the property, including slaves. Administrations were grants made by the court and issued in the form of a letter to the next of kin, or creditors, in cases where a will was not made. Letters of administration, however, give very little information except the name of the administrator or administratrix. Inventories are lists of the testator's personal estate detailing its value. Since they list the testator's property they may include lists of slaves.

Most West Indian wills were proved locally and should survive in the relevant archive, register office or even with the courts. Following a French invasion of St Christopher and Nevis in 1711, powers of attorney were granted for payment of compensation. Copies of these powers, 1712–20, together with a number of wills are in CO 243/4–5. Lists of wills proved and letters of administration sometimes occur in the government gazettes (section **2.5**).

British subjects (including members of the British navy and army) dying abroad or at sea with personal estate and property in the United Kingdom had their wills proved or administrations granted in the senior church and probate courts in the UK.

The Prerogative Court of Canterbury (PCC) had jurisdiction for people with estate in England and Wales, and the records contain wills and administration of people who died in the West Indies with property in England and Wales. The PCC also includes wills of West Indians and others with estate or family in the West Indies who died in Britain. These wills can provide useful information on their property, including slaves, and family in the West Indies. Lists of West Indian wills proved in the PCC for the period 1628–1816 are in Oliver's *Caribbeana*.

The series of PCC records begin in 1383 for registered copy wills (PROB 11 – online at TNA) and 1559 for administrations (PROB 6); both these series are available through the LDS (see section **1.6**). Original wills 1484–1858 are in PROB 10 which also contains unregistered wills. Registered copy wills were made by PCC clerks after probate and include details of the probate. Original wills tended to be copied until about 1600. Unregistered wills may only be found in PROB 10 rather than PROB 11.

Until 1722 it was obligatory for every executor or administrator to return to the court's registry an inventory of the deceased's goods. After this date inventories were only called for as exhibits in the PCC court if the will was disputed. PROB 4, 1661–1720, is the largest collection of inventories, and there is a card index to the deceased as well as a topographical index. From 1722 some inventories are in PROB 31, exhibits, and PROB 37, causes. These records may also contain original and copy wills, and other papers, from courts outside the PCC.

Before 1858 there were many other church courts where wills could be probated. People who died in the West Indies and had property in only one diocese in Britain or West Indians who died in Britain could also have their wills proved in one of the other courts; see Gibson's *Probate jurisdictions* for descriptions and locations of these church courts. The ecclesiastical courts in England and Wales were abolished under the 1857 Probate Act, with effect from 12 January 1858, and responsibility for probate passed to the Court of Probate, now the Principal Registry of the Family Division. Wills and grants of administration later than this date are held at the Principal Registry of the Family Division (see Useful addresses). Indexes and summaries of wills proved between 1858 and 1945 are available as the National Probate Index on microfiche at many archives and most of the indexes are available online at www.ancestry.co.uk.

Indexes to and digitised images of Scottish wills and testaments 1500–1901 are available at www.scotlandspeople.gov.uk and later ones are at the National Archives of Scotland (see Useful Addresses).

4.3.3 Further reading

Bevan, *Tracing Your Ancestors in the National Archives: The Website and Beyond*, Chapter 9

Coldham, *American Wills and Administrations in the Prerogative Court of Canterbury 1610–1857*

Coldham, *American Wills Proved in London 1611–1775*

Grannum and Taylor, *Wills and Probate Records: A Guide for Family Historians*

Oliver (ed.), *Caribbeana*. Volumes 2 to 5 contain lists of Prerogative Court of Canterbury (PCC) wills, 1628–1816, and some abstracts of early PCC wills for Nevis and St Kitts. Volumes 1 and 2 contain lists of Jamaican wills and volumes 4 and 5 have lists of Barbadian wills

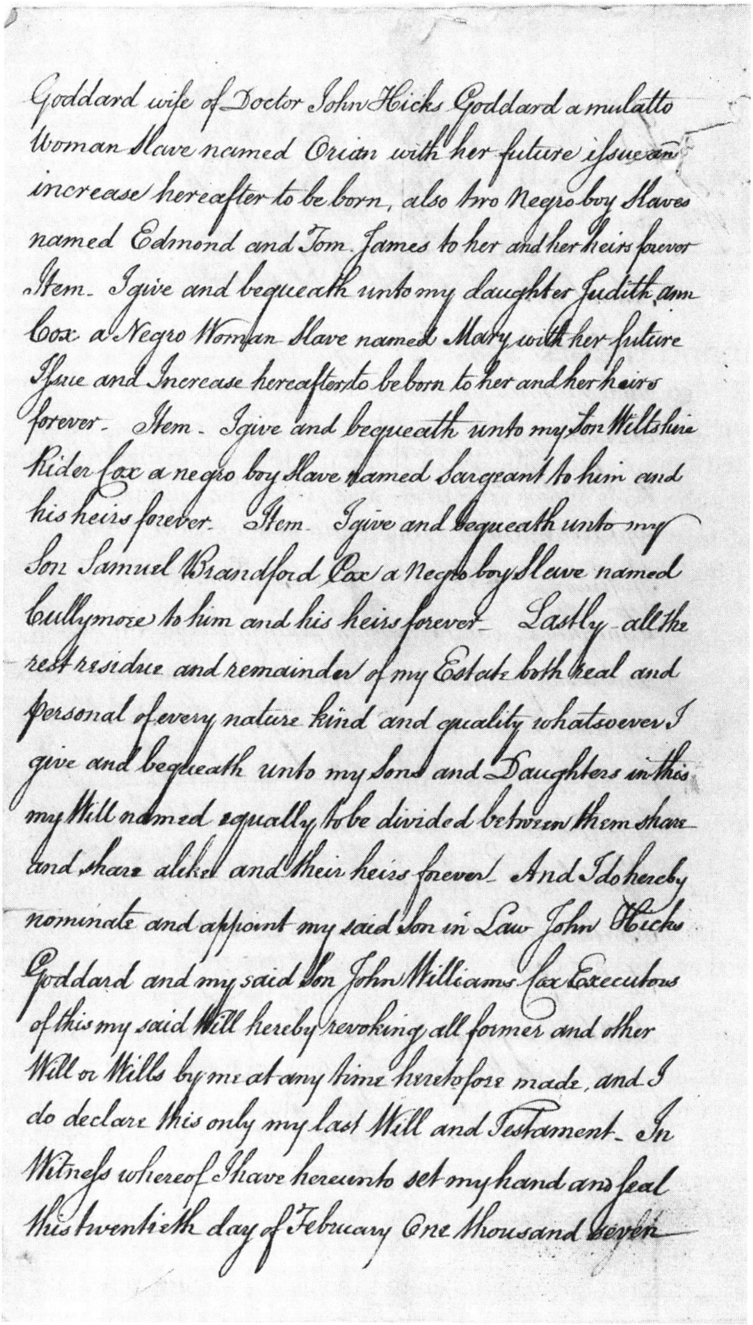

Goddard wife of Doctor John Hicks Goddard a mulatto
Woman Slave named Orian with her future issue and
increase hereafter to be born, also two Negro boy Slaves
named Edmond and Tom James to her and her heirs forever
Item. I give and bequeath unto my daughter Judith Ann
Cox a Negro Woman Slave named Mary with her future
Issue and Increase hereafter to be born to her and her heirs
forever. Item. I give and bequeath unto my Son Wiltshire
Rider Cox a negro boy Slave named Seargeant to him and
his heirs forever. Item. I give and bequeath unto my
Son Samuel Brandford Cox a Negro boy Slave named
Cullymore to him and his heirs forever. Lastly all the
rest residue and remainder of my Estate both real and
personal of every nature kind and quality whatsoever I
give and bequeath unto my Sons and Daughters in this
my Will named equally to be divided between them share
and share alike and their heirs forever. And I do hereby
nominate and appoint my said Son in Law John Hicks
Goddard and my said Son John Williams Cox Executors
of this my said Will hereby revoking all former and other
Will or Wills by me at any time heretofore made, and I
do declare this only my last Will and Testament. In
Witness whereof I have hereunto set my hand and seal
this twentieth day of February One thousand seven

Figure 11   *Barbados: will of Fearnot Cox dated 30 July 1784, showing slaves being bequeathed to family members (PROB 37/897)*

CHAPTER 5
LAND AND PROPERTY RECORDS

5.1 Land grants

In early colonial America the ownership of the land was vested in the Crown by right of discovery and settlement by its subjects. The Crown granted land to companies and to proprietors to organise settlement. During the Commonwealth, 1649–60, most of the colonies reverted to the state, which granted land through its appointed governors.

During the eighteenth century many colonies of other European powers were occupied by and then ceded to Britain, among them Dominica, Grenada, Trinidad, Tobago, British Guiana, St Vincent and the French portion of St Christopher. The British authorities sought to encourage British settlement and began to require returns to be made of lands granted, purchased or rented on many of these islands. Returns were also made of non-British proprietors. These returns can be found in Colonial Office original correspondence series and in T 1 (Treasury in-letters) especially relating to sales of land of the islands ceded to Britain after the Seven Years War (Dominica, Grenada, Tobago and St Vincent) and related French claims (many are listed in Chapter 10).

Land granted directly by the Crown or Parliament can be found among patent (C 66) and close rolls (C 54). However, most land grants were recorded locally rather than in London, and these survive in the former colonies in deeds or patent registers. Some copies and abstracts of land grants were forwarded by governors and can be found in Colonial Office records (Chapter 2). Information on lands granted by the governor can be found in the original correspondence series and the entry books for each colony. Lands granted through local government may be recorded in sessional papers or acts.

From the mid-nineteenth century the government gazettes are a rich source of information, and contain notices for sales of Crown land, auction notices for plantations, arrears of rent for government properties, land and house tax defaulters, land rolls, electoral lists, grants of land, grants of homesteads, transfer of land (sometimes known as transports), mortgages and applications for land claims.

5.2 Maps and plans

The National Archives holds numerous maps and plans relating to the Caribbean and the individual colonies. The most important collections are CO 700 (1595–1909), CO 1047 (1779–1947) and CO 1054 (1897–1984) for the Colonial Office, WO 78 (1627–1953) for the War Office, and FO 925 (1700–1944) for the Foreign Office. Most maps, however, are found in the Colonial Office records for each colony (Chapter 2), especially as enclosures to reports and despatches among original correspondence series; often these maps have been extracted to better preserve them and have different references. Many of these are described in Penfold, *Maps and Plans in the Public Record Office: Volume 2 America and West Indies*. There is also a card catalogue and printed supplementary catalogues to maps and plans held by the National Archives; most of these are in the online catalogue and can be found by using such key words as 'Barbados AND (map OR plan)'. Please note that most maps and plans are to be found as enclosures in military, naval and colonial despatches and reports and have not been catalogued.

Maps of the islands can provide a lot of information about landowners. Plantations, which were often named after the owner, are usually listed and many have since become villages bearing the same name. Many maps were produced under subscription, and these include lists of the subscribers with their addresses. Some include the names of landowners, for example, the plan of St George's, Grenada, surveyed by the Commissioners for the Sale and Disposal of His Majesty's Lands 1765 (CO 700 Grenada no 5) identifies each parcel of land and lists the proprietor. Many of the owners are included in the list of town lots granted by Governor Smith between 1762 and 1764 (CO 101/1, fos 245–246).

Collections of maps can also be found in local Caribbean archives and libraries, the British Library and the Royal Geographical Society (see Useful addresses).

The Directorate of Overseas Surveys and its successor, Ordnance Survey International, undertook aerial surveys of many of the islands from the 1930s and these photographs have been used to create topographic maps of the islands. Files on the surveys are in OD 6 in the National Archives. In 2005 maps, photographs and documentation formerly held by Ordnance Survey International were transferred to a number of repositories in the UK and overseas including to Caribbean lands and surveys departments; see www.ordnancesurvey.co.uk/ oswebsite/aboutus/international/collection/dispersal.html for details of which records have been transferred where.

Many historical maps can be found online using the image search function of most search engines using such phrases as 'historical map Barbados' or 'antique map Jamaica'. Modern maps can also be found using image search and online mapping and aerial or satellite services are useful showing you estates, topography, major and minor roads, footpaths, and maybe even street names, and many allow users to add descriptions and photographs.

5.3 Plantation records

The National Archives holds very few records of plantations because they are private papers. Surviving records can be found in a variety of places which reflect the movements of the owner. For example, if the owners were absentee landlords and lived in Britain, or eventually returned to Britain, these records may survive in a British local record office. The papers of families who remained in the colony may survive in that country's archive. It is also possible that the records may still remain with the family who owned, or managed, the estate.

The National Register of Archives database contains information on private papers and can be searched at www.nationalarchives.gov.uk/nra. Many English and Welsh local authority archive catalogues can be searched on the NRA and Access to Archives (A2A) www.nationalarchives.gov.uk/a2a and the Scottish Archives Network (SCAN) at www.scan.org.uk.

The few records of plantations held by the National Archives survive because the estate or its owner was involved in litigation or involved in a claim. The equity side of the courts of Chancery and Exchequer dealt with a large and varied range of disputes such as inheritance, lands, debts, bankruptcy and marriage settlement. Papers such as accounts, deeds, journals and correspondence were provided as evidence in the Court of Chancery. Those that were not returned to the owner have survived as Chancery Masters Exhibits (C 103–C 114 and J 90) and Exchequer Exhibits (E 140, E 192, E 214 and E 219). Many of these records include lists of slaves and plantation accounts. The proceedings contain much information on the individuals, families and property involved in the suits and the records are in numerous C and E series; I suggest that you read the two guides by Henry Horwitz and the online catalogue for

Figure 12 *Grenada: plan of Georgetown, 1765 (CO 700/Grenada5) map of Georgetown 1765*

further information. Counterclaims among the records of the Slave Compensation Commission (section **7.2**) often provide descriptions of disputed estates, details of mortgages and lists of slaves which may pre-date the slave registers (section **7.1**).

Other plantation records are found among the records of the West Indian Incumbered Estates Commission (CO 441, 1854–1893) and the West Indian Hurricane Relief Commission (PWLB 11, 1832–1881); many records pre-date the setting up of these commissions and some include schedules of slaves.

The West Indian Relief Commission was set up in 1832 following insurrections in Jamaica and hurricanes in Barbados, St Lucia, St Vincent, British Guiana and Trinidad, and was extended to Dominica following a hurricane in 1835. Money was made available to the colonial governments to relieve people affected and as loans to individual estate owners to rebuild their plantations. The loans were secured by the mortgage of the estates to the Crown. The records of the Commission (PWLB 11) contain records of about 120 estates in Jamaica, Barbados, St Lucia, St Vincent and Dominica and include mortgage indentures, schedules of slaves and evidence of ownership. No other records of the Commission such as correspondence and minute books appear to have survived. However, correspondence between the Treasury and the Commission, colonial governments and individuals concerning the effects of the hurricanes and relief in general, including correspondence from other affected islands is in T 1/4395–4397 and in original correspondence series for the affected countries.

The West Indian Incumbered Estates Commission was set up under the West India Incumbered Estates Act 1854 to investigate estates which had become overburdened by mortgages and, in some cases, to sell them. The Commission existed until 1892 and sold 382 estates. Some estates were sold by agents locally on the islands but the majority (350) were sold in London. CO 441 contains the records of the Commission and the papers of 205 estates, the majority in Jamaica and Antigua. The records are arranged by date of sale and contain transfer of mortgages, newspapers advertising sales and various accounts and deeds, including plans.

Some correspondence and reports relating to both these commissions are published in the British Parliamentary Papers.

Other West Indian estate records may survive in the National Archives but these will be difficult to find, for example, WO 9/48 includes accounts of John Moffat's Blenheim and Cranbrooke Plantations in Jamaica 1806–1807 and ADM 65/59 includes accounts and schedules of slaves of Golden Vale Plantation, Portland, Jamaica, c1793–1811.

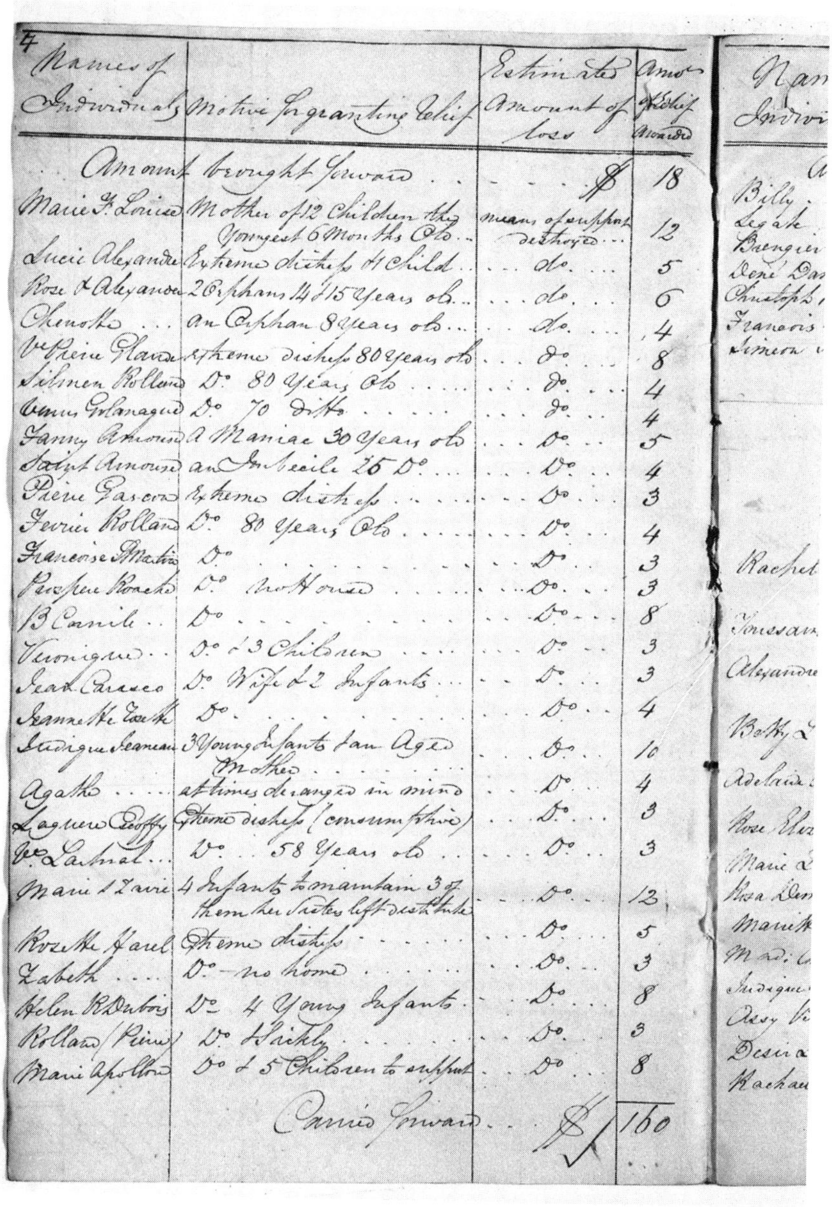

4

Names of Individuals	Motive for granting Relief	Estimated Amount of loss	Amo. of Relief awarded
Amount brought forward		$	18
Marie St. Louise	Mother of 12 Children the Youngest 6 Months Old	means of support destroyed	12
Lucie Alexandre	Extreme distress & 1 Child	do.	5
Rose & Alexandre	2 Orphans 14 & 15 Years old	do.	6
Chenotte	an Orphan 8 Years old	do.	4
Ve Pierre Plava	Extreme distress 80 Years old	Do	8
Silmen Rolland	Do 80 Years Old	do	4
Venus Grlanague	Do 70 ditto	do	4
Fanny Amoured	a Maniac 30 Years old	Do	5
Saint Amoured	an Imbecile 25 Do	Do	4
Pierre Gascon	Extreme distress	Do	3
Ferrier Rolland	Do 80 Years Old	Do	4
Francoise St Martin	Do	Do	3
Prosper Roache	Do no House	Do	3
B Camile	Do	Do	8
Veronique	Do & 3 Children	Do	3
Jean Carasco	Do Wife & 2 Infants	Do	3
Jeannette Zoeth	Do	Do	4
Sedigue Jeaneau	3 Young Infants & an Aged Mother	Do	10
Agathe	at times deranged in mind	Do	4
Laguerre Geoffy	Extreme distress (consumptive)	Do	3
Ve Lastnal	Do 58 Years old	Do	3
Marie & Xavier	4 Infants to maintain 3 of them her Sisters left destitute	Do	12
Rosette Harel	Extreme distress	Do	5
Zabeth	Do no home	Do	3
Helen R Dubois	Do 4 Young Infants	Do	8
Rolland (Pierre)	Do & Sickly	Do	3
Marie Apollon	Do & 5 Children to support	Do	8
Carried forward		$	160

Figure 13 *St Lucia: return of relief paid to persons in distress following the great hurricane of August 1831, Laborie Quartier, 16 January 1833 (T 1/4396, paper 6312/33)*

5.4 Further reading

Barck and Lefler, *Colonial America*

Bevan, *Tracing Your Ancestors in the National Archives: The Website and Beyond*, Chapters 58 and 59

Horwitz, *Chancery Equity Records and Proceedings, 1600–1800*

Horwitz, *Exchequer Equity Records and Proceedings, 1649–1841*

Penfold, *Maps and Plans in the Public Record Office, Volume 2: America and West Indies*

Many sources of family, plantation and estate papers are listed in the various guides to sources for West Indian history in Chapter 10.

CHAPTER 6
MILITARY AND RELATED RECORDS

From the first European settlements in the West Indies until the mid-nineteenth century there was almost constant military conflict between the European powers in the West Indies, even when they were at peace in Europe. To protect her colonies from attack and internal unrest, Britain had a permanent military presence. Every colony possessed local militia and troops of the regular British Army were stationed on most islands. The Royal Navy patrolled the seas, moved troops and protected convoys and the colonies from pirates and enemies. The merchant navy transported goods between Europe and the colonies, including slaves, and was a source of manpower for the Royal Navy. Many soldiers and sailors who served in the West Indies did not return to Britain: thousands died through tropical diseases and warfare, many deserted, and some remained in the colonies after discharge.

West Indians also served in all of the military services and in the merchant navy. However, with the exception of periods of war, black and coloured West Indians, as well as other non-Europeans, were discouraged from joining the army and Royal Navy. Only 'British-born men of British-born parents of pure European descent' could be commissioned officers. During the First and Second World Wars the armed services reluctantly recruited black and coloured servicemen and women and a few received temporary commissions, mainly in the Royal Air Force. Black and coloured West Indians also experienced prejudice in the merchant navy and were mostly restricted to ships which travelled to and from the West Indies.

There are many records among WO, CO, BT, MT (Ministry of Shipping and Transport) and LAB (Ministry of Labour) series discussing the issue of race and colour in the armed services and the merchant navy. Discrimination in the army is also described in several articles and books listed in Further reading (section **6.1.5**). The colour bar was officially lifted in 1948 but until 1968 the army had a quota of about 4,000 non-European recruits, although there were rarely more than 2,000 coloured recruits. I have not been able to determine if the other services also had quotas for coloured recruits. See the Ministry of Defence's 'We Were There' exhibition at www.defenceimagedatabase.mod.uk/fotoweb/wewerethere/indexhtml.html for information on colonial contribution to the armed services.

As the records of the services are well described elsewhere in genealogical publications and on the National Archives website, I will simply highlight records which are pertinent to the West Indies and West Indians.

6.1 Army

The British Army was permanently stationed in the West Indies as imperial regiments (administered by the War Office) did a tour of duty there, and most colonies had barracks. The forces were made up predominantly of recruits from Britain, with a small number of other Europeans and some local men. Many foreign regiments on British pay also served in the West Indies, especially during the American War of Independence and the French Revolutionary and Napoleonic Wars. For example, the York Light Infantry Volunteers was raised from Dutch garrison battalions after the loss of the Dutch colonies of Berbice, Demerara and Essequibo in 1803; this corps was disbanded in 1817. The army also raised African and West Indian regiments who saw service in West Africa, the Caribbean and America.

Most colonies also had a locally raised militia force administered by the colonial governments (see section **6.1.3**). These were composed initially of European settlers but increasingly from the 1790s of black and coloured slaves and freemen. Until the twentieth century West Indian regiments and militia regiments consisted of European officers and non-commissioned officers (NCOs) such as corporals and sergeants, and black and coloured soldiers, although many black and coloured soldiers were promoted to NCO ranks.

Records relating to military activities in the West Indies, recruitment, policy and West Indian local forces and imperial regiments are found in a wide variety of War Office (WO) and Colonial Office series. For the period before about 1900 it is best to start with PRO Lists and Indexes Volume LIII, *An Alphabetical Guide to Certain War Office and Other Military Records*. Thereafter, the main series are WO 32, Registered files, 1845–1985; WO 106, Directorate of Military Intelligence and Operations, 1837–1962; CO 323, Colonies general: original correspondence, 1689–1951; CO 318, West Indies original correspondence, 1624–1951, relevant country original correspondence series; CO 820, Military original correspondence, 1927–1951; and CO 968, Defence departments original correspondence, 1941–1967.

6.1.1 Records of service
Officers

The starting point for information about officers is the *Army List*, which details the officer's regiment and the dates of his commission. The manuscript army lists, 1702–1752, are in WO 64. From 1754 they are published and copies are available at the National Archives. Personal details of officers can be found among the Commander-in-Chief's memoranda in WO 31, 1793–1870, and in the widows' pension applications among the miscellaneous certificates in WO 42, 1755–1908. There is an incomplete run of officers' services in WO 25 for various periods between 1808 and 1872, and in WO 76 for various periods between 1829 and 1919; there is an incomplete card index of names for these returns.

Correspondence files of officers who served between 1914 and 1922 are held by the National Archives in WO 339 and WO 374. The main series of files was destroyed by bombing in 1940: these are supplementary files but in some cases the supplementary file had been destroyed before 1940. Both WO 339 and WO 374 can be searched using the National Archives' catalogue by surname and initial. These are indexed by WO 338 (online at TNA) which includes references to officers who continued serving after March 1922 and whose records are still held by Ministry of Defence (see Useful addresses and www.veterans-uk.info).

Other ranks (pre-1914)

The most detailed record of a soldier's service, for those who were discharged to pension between 1760 and 1913, is provided by the attestation and discharge papers in WO 97 (online at Findmypast). These record the place of birth, age on enlistment, place of enlistment, a physical description and the record of service. From 1883 details of next of kin, wife and children are given. WO 97 is arranged by date of discharge: 1756–1854 (soldiers have been listed in the National Archives' catalogue and can be searched by first and last names and by regiment); 1855–72, arranged alphabetically by surname under the regiment; 1873–82, alphabetically by name under the type of corps (infantry, cavalry, artillery); and 1883–1913, alphabetically by surname and including not only those discharged to pension but also those discharged after limited engagements or by purchase. There are also two supplementary series of papers in WO 97 which had been misfiled; these are for discharges between 1843 and 1899 and between 1900 and 1913.

If the attestation and discharge papers do not survive, then details of a soldier's service can be obtained by searching the regimental musters and pay lists; you will need to know the regiment or brigade for artillery regiments. The musters for infantry and cavalry 1740–1878 are in WO 12, artillery 1708–1878 are in WO 10, and engineers 1816–78 in WO 11. From 1878 until 1898 they are all in WO 16; there are no musters or pay lists after 1898.

These volumes can be used to trace the date of enlistment, movements and the date of discharge or death of soldiers. On enlistment the pay books often give the age and place of birth. From 1868 details of marriages, with the numbers and ages of children, are shown. The regimental description books in WO 25 and depot description books in WO 67 give the physical description of soldiers on enlistment, which can include tattoos, markings and ritual scarring which may help identify ethnic origin for African-born soldiers.

Until 1855 the artillery and engineers were the responsibility of the Board of Ordnance. Some additional musters and description books are in WO 54 and service records in WO 69.

If you do not know the regiment but have information such as a date and a place where the person served then you may identify possible regiments by using the regimental returns in WO 17, WO 73 and WO 379. A useful guide to the stations of regiments for the period 1640 to the First World War is in Kitzmiller's *In Search of the 'Forlorn Hope'*.

Soldiers who were discharged after completing an agreed term of service or as invalids were entitled to a pension. The Royal Hospital Chelsea administered pensions for the army and their records include those who were discharged and received pensions in the West Indies. The out-pension admission books are arranged chronologically by the date of the examination board for assessing the pension claim and are in three series: pensions awarded for disability, WO 116, 1715–1913; pensions awarded for length of service, WO 117, 1823–1920; and WO 23, 1817–1903, for pensions awarded in the colonies and to black pensioners. These admission books are arranged by date of pension board and by Chelsea pension number (which is usually recorded on the discharge papers in WO 97), and give a brief description, age, place of birth, particulars of service and reason for discharge.

In addition there are pension pay registers (WO 22, 1845–1880), arranged by colony, which give details of payment and the date of death if it occurred within the period of the register. Sometimes the regiment is noted, which will aid research in the pay lists, and in the soldiers' documents. PIN 71 comprises selected war pensions award files for service before 1913; you can search this series by surname on the catalogue.

Other ranks (post-1913)

Records of service for soldiers who served in the First World War and were discharged before 1922 are held by the National Archives in two series. WO 363 is the main series of service records but unfortunately the majority (about 60 per cent) were destroyed by bombing in 1940. Unfortunately, the records of the British West Indies Regiment (BWIR) are listed among the army records destroyed by bombing in September 1940 (WO 32/21769 – online at TNA). Indeed, I have not yet found any records for the BWIR in this series although it is possible to find ex-BWIR soldiers who served in other units.

The second series, WO 364 comprises discharge papers of soldiers discharged to pension during the war or who received medical discharges. For example, it is possible to find medical discharge papers for the Jamaican soldiers who suffered frostbite and other effects of the cold in Halifax, Nova Scotia, in 1916. This series is in two main alphabetical sequences and was compiled from records formerly held by the Ministry of Pensions and the Ministry of Health. Both series are available online at www.ancestry.co.uk where you can search by surname, country of birth or residence and by regiment.

There is also a 2 per cent sample of pension papers, created by the Ministry of Pensions in PIN 26, which can be searched on the catalogue by surname.

The service records for soldiers who served in the British Army after 1922 are still held by the Ministry of Defence (see Useful addresses and www.veterans-uk.info).

Most West Indians who joined the army during the First World War enlisted in the British West Indies Regiment (see section **6.1.3**). West Indians also enlisted in imperial regiments but the War Office tried to prevent coloured West Indians enlisting in any corps except the BWIR; until the BWIR was established the War Office threatened to repatriate any who made their own way to the United Kingdom to enlist. In June 1918 the War Office informed the Colonial Office that it would allow coloured recruitment into the British Army (CO 323/781/59).

No. in Lincoln Regt.	No. in B.V.R. Corps.	Rank and Name.		Name and address of next of kin.	Relationship.
3	918	Pte.	Boorman F.J.	Mrs. Florence E. Dunston, Laffan St., Hamilton, Bermuda.	Mother.
4	862	Pte.	Bridges A.P.	Alfred Joseph Bridges, Somerset Bridge, Bermuda.	Father.
5	954	Pte.	Bruce Ed.	Dollie Louise Bruce, St. Georges, West Bermuda.	Wife.
6	810	Pte.	Burgess E.R.	Mrs. Ida Talem, Spanish Point, Bermuda.	Mother.
7	860	Pte.	Cannon C.R.	Elizb. Cannon, Hamilton, Bermuda.	Mother.
8	927	Pte.	Cannon J.R.	Elizb. Cannon, Hamilton, Bermuda.	Mother.
9	973	Pte.	Crone Jas.	John Crone, 136 Grosvenor Road, Belfast, Ireland.	Father.
17110	887	Pte.	Cooper J.C.	Joseph S. Cooper, Pembroke, Bermuda.	Father.
1	926	Pte.	Cooper A.L.	Orville Cooper, Somerset, Bermuda.	Father.
2	929	Pte.	Cuttenden C.H.	Edith Cuttenden, 109 Richmond Rd., Kingston-on-Thames.	Wife.
3	779	Pte.	Davies H.B.	Ernest Harrington Davies, Southampton W. Bermuda.	Father.
4	808	Pte.	Dickens A.E.G.	Edward Frank Dickens, Laffan St., Hamilton, Bermuda.	Father.
5	930	Pte.	Davison E.G.H.	Col. George Markham Davison, 11th Service Battn. Durham L.I.	Father.
6	711	Pte.	Doe A.E.	Henry Anstice Doe, Paget E. Bermuda.	Father.
7	82	Pte.	Farrell J.W.A.	Patrick Jos. Farrell, Spanish Point, Bermuda.	Brother.
8	888	Pte.	Farrell M.J.	Patrick Jos. Farrell, Spanish Point, Pembroke, Bermuda.	Brother.
9	968	Pte.	Foreman J.A.	Jas. Fredk. Foreman, Mangrove Bay, Somerset.	Father.
17120	984	Pte.	Hall B.E.	Maud Dellmer Davidson, Dellmer Cottage, Southampton E. Bermuda.	Mother.
1	863	Pte.	Herriott N.B.	Benjn. Jas. Herriott Paget E. Bermuda.	Father.
2	751	Pte.	Harris S.A.	Chas. Harris, New Road, Somerset, Bermuda.	Father.
3	886	Pte.	Heath F.E.	Wm. John Heath, Devonshire Bermuda.	Father.

Figure 14   *Roll of the Bermuda Volunteer Rifle Corps who were attached to the Lincolnshire Regiment (CO 318/336, War Office, 24 November 1915)*

In addition to the BWIR, Bermuda raised two corps: the Bermuda Volunteer Rifles, a white unit, which was attached to the 1st battalion Royal Lincolnshire Regiment, and the Bermuda Garrison Artillery, which was a coloured unit. There were two other organised contingents, the Trinidad Merchants' and Planters' Contingent Committee, and the Barbados Citizens' Contingent Committee, which paid for white officers and soldiers to enlist in the UK. They included clerks in the colonial service, planters, merchants and public school men.

However, from discussions in Colonial Office papers it is clear that many, especially Trinidadians, were not of 'pure European descent'. These contingents joined many different imperial regiments; returns of men waiting to be repatriated in 1919 show that many had served in the 1/15 and 2/16 London Regiment, the Artists' Rifles and the 2/6 Devonshire Regiment. Many, especially officers from Trinidad, were waiting to be repatriated from the Royal Air Force (see section **6.4**). Lists of the Trinidad Merchants' and Barbados Citizens' contingents, with information such as name, rank, regiment, contingent, date of enlistment and remarks (such as gallantry awards, deaths or pensioned etc) are found in CO 318/351/6, West India Contingent Committee, 2 April 1919 and CO 28/294, fos 457–460.

Many West Indians also joined the Canadian Overseas Expeditionary Force during the First World War and the records of service are held by the Library and Archives Canada (see Useful addresses). Service records are available online at www.collectionscanada.gc.ca and at www.ancestry.ca.

6.1.2 Other records

In addition to records describing soldiers' services there are many other records which are useful for those with British army ancestors.

Regimental and army chaplains' registers of births (baptisms), marriages and deaths (burials), 1761 to date, are held by the General Register Office (see Useful addresses); the indexes are available online from a number of genealogical websites. These returns include some original West Indian garrison and station registers: baptisms, marriages and burials for the St Lucia garrison, 1898–1905; deaths and burials for the Barbados Station (Windward and Leeward Islands Command) 1804–1906; and baptisms, births and marriages for the Trinidad and Martinique garrisons, 1812–16.

Campaign medal rolls, WO 100, 1793–1913, are arranged by campaign and then by regiment. First World War medal rolls (British War Medal,

1914 Star, 1914–15 Star, Victory Medal and Silver War Badge) are in WO 329 (indexed by WO 372, online at TNA and www.ancestry.co.uk). Later medal rolls are with the Ministry of Defence Medal Office (see Useful addresses and www.veterans-uk.info).

Casualty returns, 1809–75 (but covering the period 1797–1910) in WO 25, refer to absences, desertions, discharges, the wounded and the dead. The information includes name, rank, place of birth, trade on enlistment, date, place and nature of casualty, debts or credits and next of kin or legatee. Occasionally these records contain wills, inventories, correspondence and accounts.

WO 334, Army Medical Department: Returns and Reports, 1817–1892, includes annual death returns by country and by regiment, providing regiment, rank, name, disease, date of death and place of death; deaths of soldier's children are also recorded.

Information on soldiers who died in the First and Second World Wars can be obtained from the Commonwealth War Graves Commission (see Useful addresses). Their Debt of Honour register can be searched by surname from their website (www.cwgc.org) which provides brief details on the soldier such as date of death and place of burial or memorial; occasionally the names of parents or widows may be given. The Caribbean Roll of Honour http://caribbeanrollofhonour-ww1-ww2. yolasite.com aims to identify and provide additional information on Caribbean solders who died during the First and Second World Wars.

Soldiers Died in the Great War, first published in 1921, is available on CD-ROM and online on a number of websites. It gives place of birth, place of enlistment, cause of death, theatre of war where the soldier died and date of death. Unfortunately, this compilation only includes deaths in UK army regiments; the British West Indies Regiment and West India Regiment are excluded. Medical records of the field medical centres (MH 106) contain admissions and discharges with brief details of the medical condition.

The Second World War army roll of honour WO 304, published on CD-ROM, contains the following: name, service number and date of death, together with coded information on rank, unit first served in, unit at time of death, place of birth, residence and place of death.

War diaries for the First World War (WO 95, some are online at TNA) are arranged by theatre of war and then hierarchically by division, brigade etc. They describe, often very briefly, day-to-day activities of the unit. The amount of information varies significantly and they rarely name individuals apart from officers, although it is sometimes possible to find lists of soldiers, lists of wounded and killed, and citations for gallantry awards.

Second World War war diaries (WO 166 to WO 177) are also arranged by theatre of war and then hierarchically. The document descriptions are often abbreviated and to search the online catalogue you will need to try short forms and abbreviated forms of the regiment, for example 'Durham' or 'D.L.I.' or 'DLI' for the Durham Light Infantry. Activities in the Caribbean can be found in the relevant colonial original correspondence series for each colony and in CO 318, CO 323, CO 820 and CO 968.

6.1.3 West Indian regiments

West Indians served in all British regiments. However, except during periods of war the War Office resisted recruiting black and coloured soldiers into the regular European regiments, although for much of the eighteenth and nineteenth centuries most regiments had black musicians. Black West Indians were restricted primarily to joining the West India Regiments and the Corps of Military Labourers and, during the First World War, to the British West Indies Regiment.

West India Regiments

The West India regiments were raised in 1795 as a black corps to complement the European regiments. The troops were predominantly black with white officers and non-commissioned officers (NCOs), although some blacks did rise to become NCOs. The origin of these regiments was the Carolina Black Corps which was formed from several loyalist corps of Black Dragoons, Pioneers and Artificers raised during the American Revolution. After the revolution the Carolina Black Corps formed various black pioneer, garrison and infantry corps serving in the West Indies. Supplementing these corps were locally raised black pioneer and ranger corps. The West India regiments also bought slaves, first from existing slave owners but later directly from slave ships. It is estimated that from 1795 to 1807 the British army bought seven per cent of all slaves sold in the British West Indies.

In 1807 the slave trade was abolished, and under the Mutiny Act 1807 (7 Geo 3, session 1, c32, s102) all former military slaves were emancipated (freed) but remained in the army. The recruiters turned next to liberated Africans (see section **3.6**) seized from illegal traders by customs officials and the Royal Navy and established recruiting depots in ports such as

Freetown in Sierra Leone and Havana in Cuba. Other groups which enlisted included: soldiers from the Bourbon Regiment from Mauritius, which was merged with 1st West Indies Regiment in 1816; blacks from St Domingo, Martinique and Guadeloupe; Europeans, from Belgium and Germany; and American slaves who enlisted during the Anglo-American War of 1812.

Between 1795 and 1888 there were between one and 12 West India Regiments which served in the West Indies, West Africa and, during the Anglo-American War of 1812, in the United States. By 1888 there was one regiment of two battalions; a third battalion was raised in 1897 and disbanded in 1904; and the second battalion was disbanded in 1920. The West India Regiment was disbanded in 1927 and the soldiers transferred to local defence forces. It was re-formed for a short time between 1958 and 1961 during the short-lived Federation of the West Indies and on disbandment in 1961 the discharged soldiers formed the nucleus of the Jamaica Defence Force.

Corps of Military Labourers

Other locally raised corps were garrison companies and the military labourers, many of whom were also slaves and liberated Africans. The Corps of Military Labourers was formed on 25 August 1817 from supernumeraries from the 1st, 3rd and 6th West India Regiments administered by local staff officers of the Quartermaster General's Department for mainly garrison and general labouring duties. It was disbanded on 1 October 1888.

British West Indies Regiment

On the outbreak of hostilities in 1914 many West Indians left the colonies to enlist in the UK and were recruited into British regiments. However, the War Office became concerned with the numbers of black and coloured West Indians in the army and tried to prevent more from enlisting, threatening to repatriate any who arrived. After much discussion between the Colonial Office and the War Office, and following intervention by King George V, agreement to raise a West Indian contingent was approved on 19 May 1915 and on 26 October 1915 the British West Indies Regiment was established.

Twelve battalions were raised and saw service in East Africa, Egypt, Palestine, Jordan, France and Italy, mainly as labourers in the ammunition dumps and gun emplacements, often under heavy fire. Towards the end of the war two battalions saw combat in Palestine and Jordan against the

Turks. A total of 397 officers and 15,204 other ranks, representing all the Caribbean colonies, served in the BWIR and of these 15,601 men, 10,280 (66 per cent) were from Jamaica.

I have been advised by the Ministry of Defence that no records of service have survived for soldiers of the BWIR. The records of the BWIR are listed as having been destroyed following the bombing of the army records store at Arnside Street, September 1940 (WO 32/21769). I have not yet managed to find any among the 'burnt' documents in WO 363, although records for those discharged to pension should be found in WO 364. Some records relating to pensions were transferred to the colonial governments in the 1920s and 1930s.

Colonial governments accepted liability for paying separation allowances during the war and for pensions after the war. There is much correspondence in Ministry of Pensions (PIN series), Colonial Office and Treasury (T series) files concerning the paying of pensions in the colonies, including a cryptic message in CO 137/804/15 (Jamaica) dated 14 October 1935 which states that the 'work [payment of pensions] will be undertaken by the [Jamaican] Treasurer and the handing over of all of the records will be completed in the course of the next few days'; this correspondence is also found in Treasury and Ministry of Pensions files. Unfortunately, there is no mention of what these records were and it may be that only files of soldiers who were receiving pensions were passed to the Jamaican treasurer. It is also possible that the records were transferred to the local defence forces, especially when the West India Regiment was disbanded in 1927.

However, among the Colonial Office papers, especially CO 318 and the appropriate colonial original correspondence series, there are numerous lists of West Indian soldiers. Most of these are for the various contingents of the BWIR but also include the Bermuda Volunteer Rifle Corps, the Trinidad Merchants' and Planters' Contingent, and the Barbados Citizens' Contingent. These records include: separation allowances, nominal rolls, embarkation returns, casualty lists, pensioners, and lists of those found unfit and returned.

For example, a list of 199 Jamaicans who were discharged in 1916, including 184 who were pensioned following the effects of the cold in Halifax on the *Verdula* in March 1916, is in CO 137/717/76, gov 30 Dec 1916. The information includes regimental number, date embarked, date returned to Jamaica, date discharged and date pension awarded.

These records are incomplete and unfortunately there are very few after 1916. The Colonial Office registers show that they were regularly received by the Colonial Office but were 'destroyed under statute' and no longer survive in Colonial Office files. Those for 1915 and 1916 may have been kept as examples of the types of records created and since the War Office would keep such documents as nominal rolls, casualty returns and personal records, the Colonial Office decided not to keep them. Most rolls and casualty lists were routinely copied to the governors and it is possible that they may survive in the relevant archives.

The first contingent of the BWIR arrived at Seaford Camp, Sussex on 5 September 1915 for training. Further contingents arrived at Seaford in 1915 and 1916 and in April 1916 left for Egypt. Later contingents sailed directly for Egypt. Some passenger lists for the contingents who arrived in Britain, which give name and age, are in BT 26 (online at www.ancestry.co.uk); most however, only give the numbers of soldiers. The few lists with names include: SS *Danube* with 120 of the 1st British Guiana contingent who disembarked at Plymouth on 5 September 1915 (BT 26/616/72); SS *Danube* with British Guiana (with 30 other ranks) and Barbados (29 other ranks) contingents and Trinidad Merchant Contingent (109 other ranks) who disembarked at Plymouth 1 November 1915 (BT 26/617/43); SS *Quillota* with 145 mainly Jamaican and Bahamian other ranks who disembarked at Plymouth 12 Jan 1916 (BT 26/629/39); and SS *Balantia* which arrived on 17 January 1916 with three of the 1st and 69 of the 2nd Trinidad contingents (BT 26/629/38). Among the medal rolls is WO 329/2373 which is a list of soldiers from the BWIR who were awarded the British War and Victory Medals arranged by colony (excluding Jamaica) and occasionally gives addresses and next of kin.

Caribbean Regiment

At the outbreak of the Second World War, West Indians again tried to enlist in the British Army and again met with resistance. The War Office did not want to raise a West Indian regiment: West Indians who wanted to enlist had to arrange their passage to the UK and almost 10,000 West Indians enlisted individually in the British Army. In 1940 Churchill suggested re-forming the West India Regiment but the War Office only considered pioneer (labour) corps. After much deliberation the Caribbean Regiment was formed in April 1944 with just over 1,200 men, most of whom were volunteers from the local defence forces including Bermuda. The regiment was trained in Virginia and on 8 June 1944 became the first British regiment to celebrate the King's birthday in the US since the American Revolution. Without seeing any combat the regiment returned to the West Indies in 1946 and was disbanded.

New Regtl. No. Alltd.	Prev. Col. No.	Rank.	Name.	Christian Name.	Name of next-of-kin.	Particulars of next-of-kin.	Address of next-of-kin.
5086	2641	Pte.	Davis	James	Alberta Aquart	Sister	Bloomfield, Port Antonia, Jamaica.
5087	2474	Pte.	Dias	Samuel	L. Diaz	Brother	Guala Guatemala, Central America.
5088	3230	Pte.	Diego	Lino	Juana Lodriquez	Mother	Stann Creek, Br. Honduras.
5089	2609	Pte.	Dixon	Alvern Ogilvie	A.H.McNab	Cousin	French Harbour, Puatton, Spanish Honduras.
5090	2601	Pte.	Domingo	Meshach Augustus	Emeline Domingo	Mother	1297 Freetown Rd., Belize, Br. Honduras.
5091	2359	Pte.	Domingo	Simeon	Emeline Domingo	Mother	1297 Freetown Rd., Belize, Br. Honduras.
5092	2449	Pte.	Duncan	Charles Daniel	James Duncan	Brother	Monkey River, Br. Honduras.
5093	2366	Pte.	Duran	Phillip	Jane Crawford	Mother	King St., Belize, Br. Honduras.
5094	2584	Pte.	Edwards	Faben George	Amelia, Henrietta Edwards.	Wife	Lataste St. Patricks, Grenada.
5095	2493	Pte.	Edwards	William	John Edwards	Nephew	Orange Walk, Belize, Br. Honduras.
5096	3220	Pte.	Ellis	Ernesto (Decease)	Mrs J.Ellis	Mother	Farmers Town, Stann Creek, Br. Honduras.
5097	2576	Pte.	Ellis	Richard	Amelia Greenfield	Grand-mother	Monkey River, Br. Honduras.
5098	2338	Pte.	Elmandarez	Emmanuel	Ann Walker	Mother	Rocky Rd., & Geo.St., Belize, Br. Honduras.
5099	578	Pte.	Elkington	Peter Louis	Jane Elkington	Mother	303 South St., Belize, Br. Honduras.

Figure 15   Roll of 5th battalion of the British West Indies Regiment comprising men mainly from British Honduras (Belize) (CO 318/340, War Office, 28 October 1916)

The National Archives does not hold service records for the Caribbean Regiment and it is unlikely that the Ministry of Defence holds them. As most members were recruited from local defence forces, I suggest that any personal records will be with the relevant defence force.

6.1.4 Militia

The militia were locally raised forces, formed to protect the colony itself. They were not expected to serve overseas. The National Archives does not hold the records of West Indian militia. However, the government gazettes among the Colonial Office records often contain lists of militia, and notices of promotion and retirement. Useful material, such as military policy and activities, war diaries, lists of officers and applications for commissions can be found in original correspondence series, CO 318, CO 820 and CO 968; CO 820/50/1 to CO 820/51/28 contain nominal rolls of European officers and men in colonial local forces, 1941–1942. Lists of officers and men of the various local defence and police forces awarded defence and war medals for the Second World War are in CO 820. Service records of West Indian militia may survive with the local defence forces or in the islands' archives.

6.1.5 Further reading

Andrade, *A Record of the Jews in Jamaica: From the English Conquest to the Present Time*

Atkinson, 'Foreign Regiments in the British Army 1793–1802'

Bevan, *Tracing Your Ancestors in the National Archives: The Website and Beyond*, Chapters 23–7

Bousquet and Douglas, *West Indian Women at War: British Racism in World War II*

Buckley, *Slaves in Red Coats: The British West India Regiments, 1795–1815*

Cundall, *Jamaica's Part in the Great War, 1914–1918*

Dyde, *The Empty Sleeve: The Story of the West India Regiments of the British Army*

Ellis, 'George Rose: An exemplary soldier'

The First Black Britons [DVD]

Healy, 'Colour, climate, and combat: The Caribbean Regiment in the Second World War'

Holmes, *The Bahamas during the Great War*

Howe, *Race, War and Nationalism. A Social History of West Indians in the First World War*

Ingham, *Defence not Defiance: A History of the Bermuda Volunteer Rifle Corps*

Joseph, 'The British West Indies Regiment 1914–1918'

Kieran, *Lawless Caymanas: A Story of Slavery, Freedom and the West India Regiment*

Kitzmiller, *In search of the 'Forlorn Hope': A Comprehensive Guide to Locating British Regiments and Their Records (1640–World War I)*

Metzgen and Graham, *Caribbean Wars Untold: A Salute to the British West Indies*

Murray, *Lest We Forget: The Experiences of World War II Westindian Ex-service Personnel*

Public Record Office Lists and Indexes, Volume LIII: *An Alphabetical Guide to Certain War Office and Other Military Records Preserved in the Public Record Office*

Sherwood, *Many Struggles: West Indian Workers and Service Personnel in Britain, 1939–1945*

Sherwood and Spafford, *Whose Freedom Were Africans, Caribbeans and Indians Defending in World War II?*

Smith, *Jamaican Volunteers in the First World War*

Spencer, *Army Records: A Guide for Family Historians*

Spencer, *Army Service Records of the First World War*

Watson, *The Carib Regiment of World War II*

Watts and Watts, *My Ancestor was in the British Army. Guide to British Army sources for family historians*

http://freepages.genealogy.rootsweb.com/~portwestind/research/archives/service_in_great_war.htm – a list of people of Portuguese descent who left Trinidad to serve in the First World War, translated from Charles Reis's, *Brief History of the Associação Portuguesa Primeiro de Dezembro* (Port-of-Spain, 1926)

www.bermuda-online.org/warveterans.htm – history of the regiments in Bermuda

www.jdfmil.org – official website of the Jamaica Defence Force

www.ttdf.mil.tt – official website of the Trinidad and Tobago Defence Force

6.2 Royal Navy

The Royal Navy patrolled the islands, protecting them against invasions, pirates and privateers. It also protected merchant shipping between the colonies, and escorted convoys between Africa and the West Indies, and between the islands and Britain.

6.2.1 Records of service

Officers

The starting point for tracing an officer's service is *Commissioned Sea Officers* by Syrett and DiNardo (see Bibliography) and the published *Navy List* from 1782. Service registers were started during the nineteenth century, but few begin before the 1840s. The most important registers are ADM 196 (online at TNA), which begin in 1840, although some returns are retrospective to the 1750s, and run to the 1930s, and ADM 340 (online at TNA) which contains selected service cards and files covering the period c1880–1950s for officers born before 1900. Other returns and surveys of officers' services between 1817 and 1846 are in ADM 6, ADM 9, ADM 10, and ADM 11. Lieutenants' and engineers' passing certificates, 1691–1902 (ADM 6, ADM 107 and ADM 13) summarise an officer's career and training; they sometimes contain supporting papers such as certificates of baptism or birth.

The National Archives does not hold comprehensive service records for executive officers (cadets, midshipmen, lieutenants, captains and admirals etc) whose service began after May 1917 or for warrant officers whose service began after 1931. These records are held by the Ministry of Defence (see Useful addresses and www.veterans-uk.info).

Other ranks

The National Archives holds two series of registers for ratings: ADM 139, 1853–1872, and ADM 188, 1872–1923, with service to 1928 (both series are online at TNA). In addition to ships served on, these records give the date and place of birth and physical description. Certificates of service of warrant officers and ratings who applied for superannuation or admission to Greenwich Hospital are in ADM 29, 1802–1894.

Before 1853 if there are no records in ADM 29, then you must refer to the ships' musters and pay lists, ADM 36–ADM 39, ADM 41, ADM 115 and ADM 117. A muster should provide a man's age and place of birth from 1764 and, from about 1800, description books (which give age, height, complexion, scars and tattoos) may be included. These records cover the period 1667 to 1878 and are arranged by ship. The ship must be known, although if the place where the sailor was serving is known it may be possible to identify the ships attached to the particular station; you can then search the musters of each ship on that station.

The records for ratings who joined after 1923 or whose service continued after 1928 are still held by the Ministry of Defence (see Useful addresses and www.veterans-uk.info).

6.2.2 Other records

The primary source for naval operational records and correspondence relating to individuals is ADM 1, which contains correspondence from naval officers, other government departments and individuals on naval activities and individuals. Case papers are in ADM 116, ADM 137 (for the First World War) and ADM 199 (for the Second World War). Ships' logs: ADM 51, ADM 52 and ADM 53, describe ships' movements and activities.

Casualty returns can be found in a variety of sources: ADM 104 contains registers of deaths, 1854–1956. Seamen's wills, 1786–1882, are in ADM 48; ADM 142 contains registers of seamen's wills, 1786–1909 (both series online at TNA). Seamen's effects, ADM 44, 1800–1860 (indexed by ADM 141), contains claims by executors or next of kin for the back pay of ratings who died in service and can include wills, birth and marriage certificates and other supporting evidence. Wills for officers and warrant officers are in ADM 45. ADM 242, War Graves Rolls, contains information on Royal Navy and Royal Marines officers and men who died during the First World War. The information is: full name, rank, service number, ship's name, date and place of birth, cause of death, where buried and next of kin. Brief information on Naval service personnel who died in the First and Second World Wars can be obtained from the Commonwealth War Graves Commission (www.cwgc.org).

Registers of Naval births, deaths and marriages from 1881 are held by the General Register Office (see Useful addresses; the indexes are available online from a number of genealogical websites); marriages held on board Royal Naval ships, 1842–89, are in RG 33/156; some naval registers of baptisms, marriages and burials are in ADM 6; and the Chaplain of the Fleet's registers of baptisms, confirmations, marriages and burials, 1845–1995, are in ADM 338.

Information on naval personnel who died in the First and Second World Wars can be obtained from the Commonwealth War Graves Commission (see Useful addresses). Their Debt of Honour register can be searched by surname on their website (www.cwgc.org) which provides brief details on the soldier such as date of death, place of burial or memorial and, occasionally, the names of parents or widows may be given. The Caribbean Roll of Honour (http://caribbeanrollofhonour-ww1-ww2.yolasite.com) aims to identify and provide additional information on Caribbean naval personnel who died during the First and Second World Wars.

Medal rolls, ADM 171, are arranged by campaign or service medal. Early rolls are arranged by ship and for the First World War are arranged by naval service (RNR, RNVR, RN) in alphabetical order and give the service number. Later rolls are held by the Ministry of Defence Medal Office (see Useful addresses and www.veterans-uk.info).

6.2.3 Royal Naval Reserve

The Royal Naval Reserve (RNR) was raised in 1860 from officers and men of the merchant navy (see section **6.5**) who could be called upon for service in the Royal Navy in times of emergency. Records of service of officers who served before the First World War and of honorary officers between 1862 and 1960 are in ADM 240 and selected cards and files for officers born before 1900 are in ADM 340 c1880–1950s (online at TNA). A selection of records of ratings who served between 1860 and 1913 are in BT 164 (online at TNA). Indexes to service numbers from 1860 to 1922 are in BT 377. BT 377 also holds service details of ratings who served during the First World War. Medal rolls are in ADM 171 (online at TNA).

6.2.4 Royal Naval Volunteer Reserve

The Royal Naval Volunteer Reserve (RNVR) was formed in 1903 and was composed of volunteers, except merchant seamen who went into the Royal Naval Reserve. Records of service for officers, 1914–22, and ratings, 1903–18, are in ADM 337 (online at TNA) and selected officers' cards and files of officers born before 1900 are in ADM 340 (online at TNA). Ratings' service records are arranged by division and then by service number, which can be found in the medal rolls in ADM 171 (online at TNA). Most RNVR divisional records have not survived although there is a selection in ADM 900/75–86. Later records of service are with the Ministry of Defence (see Useful addresses and www.veterans-uk.info).

In December 1939 the Trinidad Royal Naval Volunteer Reserve was formed to carry out patrols and to distribute supplies to the West Indies. The Trinidad RNVR comprised men from most of the British Caribbean countries and lists of those awarded the War Medal, 1939–45, are in CO 820/63/1 to CO 820/63/3.

6.2.5 Naval dockyards

Most of the islands possessed naval dockyards for the maintenance, refitting and victualling of Royal Naval ships. Musters and pay lists for the larger yards are in the Yard Pay Books, ADM 42. Those for the minor yards and establishments are in ADM 32, ADM 36 and ADM 37. The main series of yard musters and lists survive into the mid-nineteenth century. The only later surviving records are the pensions registers in ADM 23, 1830–1926, and the naval establishment: artificers' and labourers' civil pensions, PMG 25, 1836–1928. There are pay lists, musters and pension registers for many West Indian islands including: Antigua, for the period 1743–1835; Barbados, 1806–16; Bermuda, 1795–1857; Cape Nicholas, Haiti, 1798; Jamaica, 1735–1835; and Martinique, 1775–1815.

The Bermudas were important as a naval and military station and in 1810 work was begun on the naval station on Ireland Island, using convict labour. Between 1824 and 1863 some 9,000 convicts were sent from Britain but it never became a penal settlement and they were able to return to Britain on the completion of their sentence. Quarterly returns of prisoners on the Bermuda hulks in Ireland Island are in HO 8 and provide the following information: number, name, age, offence, where and when convicted, sentence, health, behaviour and remarks. The National Archives holds baptisms, 1826–1946, and burials, 1826–48, for the naval base at Ireland Island in ADM 6/434–436. Later baptisms for Ireland Island, 1947–57, are in ADM 338/11.

6.2.6 Further reading

Bevan, *Tracing Your Ancestors in the National Archives: The Website and Beyond*, Chapter 28

Cock and Rodger, *Guide to the Naval Records in the National Archives of the UK*

Crewe, *Yellow Jack and the Worm: British Naval Administration in the West Indies 1739-1748*

Pappalardo, *Tracing Your Naval Ancestors*

Rodger, *Naval Records for Genealogists*

Stranack, *The Andrew and the Onions: The Story of the Royal Navy in Bermuda 1795-1975*

Syrett and DiNardo, *The Commissioned Sea Officers of the Royal Navy 1660-1815*

6.3 Royal Marines

The Royal Marines were the Royal Navy's soldiers, and records for them survive among the records of the Admiralty (see section **6.2**).

6.3.1 Records of service

Officers

The sources for tracing Royal Marine officers are the same as those for tracing Royal Navy officers (section **6.2.1**). From 1782 the published *Navy List* gives all commissioned Royal Marine officers by substantive rank and seniority, and the ships they were attached to. The *Army List* from 1740 also contains details of Royal Marine officers. The main series of service records is ADM 196, 1770s to 1920s (online at TNA). An index to the service records of all Royal Marine officers commissioned between 1793 and 1970 is in ADM 313/110.

Other ranks

The basic arrangement of records of other ranks' service is according to Division (Portsmouth, Chatham, Woolwich, Plymouth, Royal Marine Artillery or Deal). There are three main series for records of service: description books, 1755–1940 (ADM 158); attestation forms, 1790–1925 (ADM 157); and records of service from 1842 (ADM 159, online at TNA). These registers are closed for 75 years. Indexes to these records are in ADM 313, and there is an incomplete card index of names to ADM 157 in the Research Enquiries Room. The effective and subsistence lists, 1688–1837 (ADM 96) list Royal Marines by company. If a marine is known to have served on board a particular ship then the ships' musters and pay lists in ADM 36–ADM 39, ADM 115 and ADM 117 (1667–1878) may contain some information; there are no musters after 1878.

For information on officers and men who enlisted less than 75 years ago, enquiries should be made to the Ministry of Defence (see Useful addresses and www.veterans-uk.info).

6.3.2 Other records

Operational records for the Royal Marines are included with the Royal Navy (see section **6.2.2**). Medal rolls are in ADM 171. Before the First World War they are arranged by campaign and then by ship. For the First World War they are arranged alphabetically and give the division and service number, which will help obtain service records. Later rolls are with the Ministry of Defence Medal Office (see Useful addresses and www.veterans-uk.info).

6.3.3 Colonial Marines

This corps was established during the Anglo-American War of 1812. The British forces offered to free any American slaves who joined them. Many enlisted in the West India regiments and the Royal Navy, but some 800 formed the 3rd, or Colonial, battalion of the Royal Marines. Black refugees who did not enlist were discharged in Bermuda and then moved to Nova Scotia; a few went to Trinidad.

The Colonial Marines were formed in May 1814 but most of the records do not begin until September 1814. There appear to be no attestation papers for these marines in ADM 157. The only lists of these marines are in the ships' musters (ADM 37) and in the effective and subsistence lists (ADM 96). For example, the musters for HMS *Albion* in ADM 37/5005 and 5006 and HMS *Severn*, ADM 37/5430, list Colonial Marines and black American refugees for April 1814 to March 1815. ADM 96/366 includes the lists for the Colonial Marines for 1816. The corps was disbanded in August 1816 in Bermuda and the marines were settled in the military townships in Trinidad.

6.3.4 Further reading

Bevan, *Tracing Your Ancestors in the National Archives: The Website and Beyond*, Chapter 29

Brooks and Little, *Tracing Your Royal Marine Ancestors*

Divall, *My Ancestor was a Royal Marine*

Rodger, *Naval Records for Genealogists*

Weiss, *The Merikens: Free Black American Settlers in Trinidad, 1815–1816*

Weiss, 'The Corps of Colonial Marines 1814–16: A summary'

6.4 Royal Air Force

The Royal Air Force (RAF) was formed on 1 April 1918 with the amalgamation of the Army's Royal Flying Corps (RFC) and Royal Naval Air Service (RNAS). Officers and men of these services were transferred to the RAF and joined by later recruits. Many West Indians served in the RAF and saw service in the First and Second World Wars. For example, many officers and soldiers of Trinidad Merchants' and Planters' Contingent and the Barbados Citizens' Contingent were repatriated from the RAF after the First World War. Lists of these contingents with information, such as name, rank, regiment, contingent, date of enlistment and remarks (e.g. gallantry awards, deaths, pensioned etc) are found in CO 318/351 (West India Contingent Committee, 2 April 1919) and CO 28/294, fos 457–460.

Many thousands of West Indians joined the RAF during the Second World War. Most were ground crew but about 1,000 served as air crew. Policy regarding recruitment in the West Indies is in CO 820. AIR 2/6876 contains two lists of West Indian RAF personnel:

1 A list of 298 British West Indians (including 50 officers) who attested in Canada for training as air crew in about 1944. Information includes: number, name, colony, date attested, disposal (rank and date embarked for UK), colour (white or coloured), officer's personal number, rank, decorations, date appointed to commission and details of casualties.

2 Nominal roll of 340 coloured candidates (including 47 officers) of October 1944. This roll includes candidates from other colonies. It contains: colony, name, trade, date of attestation, notes such as awards and casualties.

Information on RAF personnel from this document together with personal recollections, photographs and information from other sources is being added to www.caribbeanaircrew-ww2.com: A record of West Indian volunteers who served in the Royal Air Force during the Second World War.

6.4.1 Records of service
Officers
The career of RAF officers can be traced in the *Air Force List* and in the *Confidential Air Force List*, 1939–1954, in AIR 10. It is possible to identify to which squadrons officers were attached from the *Air Force List* between March 1920 and April 1939, and afterwards in the confidential lists. AIR 76 (online at TNA) contains records of service for officers in the RAF and RFC who were discharged before 1920. Service records of officers formerly in the RNAS for the period 1914 to March 1918 are in ADM 273.

Service records for those who joined after 1920 are still held by the Ministry of Defence (see Useful addresses and www.veterans-uk.info).

Other ranks
If an airman died or was discharged before the formation of the RAF on 1 April 1918 records of service will be under the army for RFC (see section **6.1.1**) or Royal Navy for RNAS (see section **6.2.1**) as appropriate.

Service records for RFC and RNAS airmen who joined the RAF are in AIR 79, indexed by AIR 78 (online at TNA).

Service records of men whose service number is greater than 329001 or who served in the Second World War are with the Ministry of Defence (see Useful addresses and www.veterans-uk.info).

6.4.2 Other records

The majority of records relating to operations during the First World War are in AIR 1. This series includes squadron war diaries, recommendations for gallantry awards and details of officers' careers. Later operational records are in the Operations Record Books (ORBs): AIR 24 commands, AIR 25 groups, AIR 26 wings, AIR 27 squadrons, AIR 28 stations and AIR 29 miscellaneous units. ORBs record daily events of the squadron and usually list flying personnel in each plane with the times they left and returned; casualties during operations are usually listed. ORBs sometimes include nominal rolls, lists of officers, and details of promotions, transfers and awards.

The National Archives does not hold campaign medals rolls for the RAF but medal rolls for the RFC are in WO 329 (indexed by WO 372, online at TNA and www.ancestry.co.uk) and RNAS in ADM 171 (online at TNA). Other rolls are with the Ministry of Defence Medal Office (see Useful addresses and www.veterans-uk.info).

Flying casualties are listed in the Operations Record Books. Deaths of RAF personnel, 1939–48, are held by the General Register Office (see Useful addresses), who also hold registers of births, marriages and deaths, from 1920, of RAF personnel serving overseas. The indexes are available online from a number of genealogical websites.

Information on flying personnel who died in the First and Second World Wars can be obtained from the Commonwealth War Graves Commission (see Useful addresses). Their Debt of Honour register can be searched by surname from their website (www.cwgc.org) which provides brief details on the soldier such as date of death, place of burial or memorial, and occasionally the names of parents or widows may be given. The Caribbean Roll of Honour (http://caribbeanrollofhonour-ww1-ww2.yolasite.com) aims to identify and provide additional information on Caribbean flying personnel who died during the First and Second World Wars.

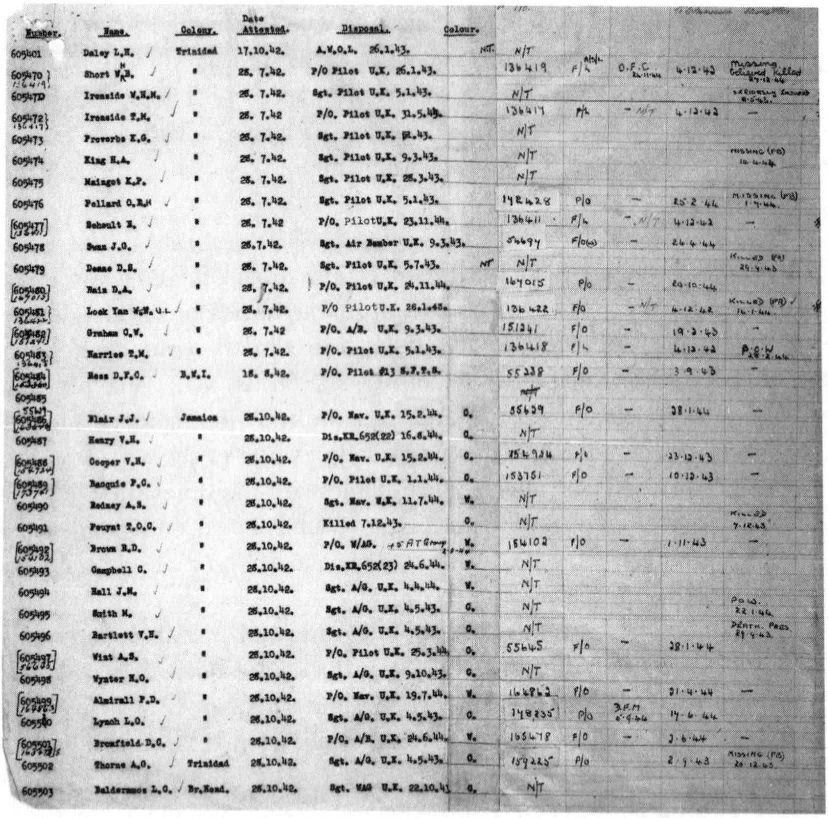

Number.	Name.	Colony.	Date Attested.	Disposal.	Colour.					
605401	Daley L.H.	Trinidad	17.10.42.	A.W.O.L. 26.1.43.	N.T.	N/T				
605470 (136419)	Short W.R.B.	"	28. 7.42.	P/O Pilot U.K. 26.1.43.		136419	F/L	O.F.C. 24.11.44	4.12.42	Missing believed killed 27.12.44
605470	Ironside W.H.M.	"	28. 7.42.	Sgt. Pilot U.K. 5.1.43.		N/T				Seriously injured 8.5.43.
605472 (136417)	Ironside T.M.	"	28. 7.42	P/O. Pilot U.K. 31.5.43.		136417	F/L	– N/T	4.12.42	–
605473	Proverbs E.G.	"	28. 7.42.	Sgt. Pilot U.K. 2.43.		N/T				
605474	King H.A.	"	28. 7.42.	Sgt. Pilot U.K. 9.3.43.		N/T				Missing (FB) 16.4.44
605475	Maingot K.P.	"	28. 7.42.	Sgt. Pilot U.K. 28.3.43.		N/T				
605476	Pollard O.R.H	"	28. 7.42.	Sgt. Pilot U.K. 5.1.43.		142428	P/O	–	25.2.44	Missing (FB) 1.7.44.
605477 (136411)	Schoult E.	"	28. 7.42	P/O. Pilot U.K. 23.11.44.		136411	F/L	– N/T	4.12.42	–
605478	Swan J.O.	"	28.7.42.	Sgt. Air Bomber U.K. 9.3.43.		54694	F/O(w)	–	26.4.44	
605479	Deane D.S.	"	28. 7.42.	Sgt. Pilot U.K. 5.7.43.	NT	N/T				Killed (FA) 29.4.43
605480 (164015)	Bain D.A.	"	28. 7.42.	P/O. Pilot U.K. 24.11.44.		164015	P/O	–	20.10.44	
605481 (136422)	Look Yan W.W. U.L.	"	28. 7.42.	P/O Pilot U.K. 26.1.43.		136422	F/O	– N/T	4.12.42	Killed (FA) 14.1.44.
605482 (151241)	Graham C.W.	"	28. 7.42	P/O. A/B. U.K. 9.3.43.		151241	F/O	–	19.3.43	–
605483 (136418)	Harries T.M.	"	28. 7.42.	P/O. Pilot U.K. 5.1.43.		136418	F/L	–	4.12.42	P.O.W. 28.2.44
605484	Ross D.F.C.	B.W.I.	18. 8.42.	P/O. Pilot #13 S.F.T.S.		55238	F/O	–	3.9.43	–
605485						N/T				
605486 (55629)	Blair J.J.	Jamaica	28.10.42.	P/O. Nav. U.K. 15.2.44.	C.	55629	F/O	–	28.1.44	–
605487	Henry V.H.	"	28.10.42.	Dis.KR.652(22) 16.8.44.	C.	N/T				
605488 (154924)	Cooper V.H.	"	28.10.42.	P/O. Nav. U.K. 15.2.44.	C.	154924	F/O	–	23.12.43	–
605489 (153751)	Basquie P.C.	"	28.10.42.	P/O. Pilot U.K. 1.1.44.	C.	153751	F/O	–	10.12.43	–
605490	Rodney A.S.	"	28.10.42.	Sgt. Nav. U.K. 11.7.44.	W.	N/T				
605491	Peuyat T.O.C.	"	28.10.42.	Killed 7.12.43.	C.	N/T				Killed 7.12.43
605492 (154102)	Brown R.D.	"	28.10.42.	P/O. W/AG. 45 AT Group 2.8.44	W.	154102	F/O	–	1.11.43	–
605493	Campbell C.	"	28.10.42.	Dis.KR.652(23) 24.6.44.	W.	N/T				
605494	Hall J.M.	"	28.10.42.	Sgt. A/G. U.K. 4.4.44.	W.	N/T				
605495	Smith M.	"	28.10.42.	Sgt. A/G. U.K. 4.5.43.	C.	N/T				P.O.W. 22.1.44.
605496	Bartlett V.H.	"	28.10.42.	Sgt. A/G. U.K. 4.5.43.	C.	N/T				Death Pres. 29.4.43.
605497 (55645)	Wint A.S.	"	28.10.42.	P/O. Pilot U.K. 25.3.44	C.	55645	F/O	–	28.1.44	
605498	Wynter H.O.	"	28.10.42.	Sgt. A/G. U.K. 9.10.43.	C.	N/T				
605499 (164862)	Almirall F.D.	"	28.10.42.	P/O. Nav. U.K. 19.7.44.	W.	164862	F/O	–	21.4.44	–
605500	Lynch L.O.	"	28.10.42.	Sgt. A/G. U.K. 4.5.43.	C.	148235	P/O	D.F.M. 6.9.44	14.6.44	
605501 (165478)	Bromfield D.C.	"	28.10.42.	P/O. A/B. U.K. 24.6.44.	W.	165478	F/O	–	2.6.44	–
605502	Thorne A.O.	Trinidad	28.10.42.	Sgt. A/G. U.K. 4.5.43.	C.	159225	P/O		2.9.43	Missing (FB) 20.12.43.
605503	Balderamos L.O.	Br.Hond.	28.10.42.	Sgt. WAG U.K. 22.10.43	C.	N/T				

Figure 16 *Roll of West Indian RAF recruits who trained in Canada (AIR 2/6876)*

6.4.3 Further reading

Bevan, *Tracing Your Ancestors in the National Archives: The Website and Beyond*, Chapter 30

Grant, *A Member of the RAF of Indeterminate Race*

Noble, *Jamaica Airman: A Black Man in Britain, 1943 and After*

Spencer, *Air Force Records: A guide for family historians*

Tomaselli, *Tracing Your Air Force Ancestors*

6.5 Merchant navy

Merchant ships transported goods between Europe, Africa and the Caribbean and between the islands and other parts of the British Empire. There are historical links between the merchant navy (civilian) and the Royal Navy (armed services) and many merchant seamen moved between the two services. During periods of war the Royal Navy looked for trained personnel and many merchant seamen found themselves pressed into the Navy or part of the reserve force; merchant ships were requisitioned to transport weapons and troops, and many became privateers supporting naval activities.

6.5.1 Records of service
Officers

In 1845 a system of voluntary examinations of competency for those intending to become masters or mates of foreign-going ships was introduced. Masters and mates passing the voluntary examination between 1845 and 1850 should be found in BT 143. In 1850 certificates of competency for foreign-going ships were made compulsory and gradually extended to other categories. These certificates were obtained either by long service (service) or by examination (competency). The certificates were entered into registers in numerical order. The details entered were name, place and date of birth, register ticket number, rank examined for or served in, and date and place of issue of ticket. Additional information can include names of ships sailed in, deaths, injuries and retirement. For the period 1845 to 1921 the indexes are in BT 127 and the registers to which they relate are BT 122 to BT 126, and BT 128. These registers are continued in BT 317, 1917–1968, and BT 352, 1910–1969.

Seamen

The registration of seamen was introduced in 1835 and continued until 1857. The registers and indexes are in BT 112 to BT 120 (online at Findmypast). The details given include name, date and place of birth, date and capacity (rank) of first going to sea, capacity since, Royal Navy ships served on and home address.

In 1913 registration was re-introduced, with the *Fourth Register, 1913–1941,* continuing from the *Third Register,* which ended in 1857. Unfortunately cards for 1913 to 1920 of the two main series (CR 1 and CR 2) were destroyed in 1969. Four series have been transferred on microfiche to the National Archives; the original cards are now in the Southampton Archive Service (see Useful addresses). The four series are: BT 350 (CR 10), 1918–1921, an alphabetical series which gives date and place of birth, rating, discharge number, description, photograph and list of ships served on by official number, and the date signed on; BT 348 (CR 1), 1921–1941, alphabetical, includes date and place of birth, discharge number, rating and description;

BT 349 (CR 2), arranged numerically by discharge number and contains a list of ships on which the seaman served, usually by the ship's official number, and dates of signing on; some cards have photographs; and BT 364, which comprises a mixed selection of CR 1, CR 2 and CR 10 cards extracted from the other series – it is arranged numerically by discharge number. BT 348, BT 349 and BT 350 are online at Findmypast.

In 1942 the *Fifth Register, the Central Register of Seamen*, was started and continued until 1972. CR 1 and CR 2 cards of seamen who were serving in 1941 were removed from the *Fourth Register* and added to the *Fifth Register*. There are two series, the first being BT 372 (CRS 3) Seamen's Pouches, c1913–1972. When seamen were discharged some or all of their documents were placed in the pouches. The pouches are arranged by discharge number and the catalogue lists all pouches, with discharge number, surname, initials and date and place of birth, and you can search for seamen on the catalogue by using their surname. The second series is BT 382 (CRS 10) Docket Books, 1941–1972, arranged alphabetically within a number of sub-series. The information includes date and place of birth, discharge number, rating, qualifications, list of ships with date and place of engagement and discharge. Please note that for data protection reasons there are some restrictions accessing these records if the person was born less than 100 years ago.

6.5.2 Other records

For officers and seamen who served before the start of registrations or whose record of service is incomplete or absent, you will need to use musters, and agreements and crew lists. These lists contain brief details of the voyage and the crew, including the previous ship they served on. The agreements and crew lists include the town or county or country of birth. The musters run from 1747 to 1835, but only those for Shields, Dartmouth, Liverpool and Plymouth survive before 1800. Agreement and crew lists were started in 1835. All surviving musters and agreements before 1861 are in BT 98. Before 1854 these are arranged by the port of registration of the ship but later ones are arranged by the ship's official number, which can be found in Lloyds' *Register of Shipping* and the *Mercantile Navy List*.

Most crew lists later than 1860 are in BT 99 but the National Archives holds only a ten per cent sample for the periods 1861–1938 and 1951–89. Most of the remainder between 1863 and 1972 are in the Maritime History Archive (see Useful addresses). They will do a search for a fee if the name of the ship and the years of service are known. The National

C.R.S. 178   MINISTRY OF PENSIONS AND NATIONAL INSURANCE

APPLICATION FOR THE INITIAL ISSUE OF
A BRITISH SEAMAN'S CARD
A DISCHARGE BOOK

FOR OFFICIAL USE

Dis. A No. *R 755406*

B.S.C. No. *299034*

[Before completing this form you should read carefully the Notes on the back. Completed forms should be submitted to the Superintendent of a Mercantile Marine Office in the United Kingdom.]

PART I. PERSONAL PARTICULARS OF APPLICANT [BLOCK CAPITALS, PLEASE]

1. Surname *BROWNE*   2. Christian or first names *Edward Valentine*
3. Date of birth *23 April 1931*   4. Place of birth *Plymouth, Montserrat, W.I.*
5. Colour of (a) eyes *Brown*   (b) hair *Black*   6. Complexion *Brown*   7. Height *5* ft. *10* ins.
8. Distinguishing Marks (Tattoos, etc.)
9. Home address *34 Hawke Road   Ipswich*

10. **Married Women only**—Maiden name .... Date of marriage
11. Next-of-kin.   Name *D. Browne*   Relationship *Brother*
    Address *4 Slewyn Road, London N.W. 10*

12. National Insurance No. *Z S 94 44 92 C*   13. Union or Society No. *Sec 5 A*
14. Rating *II Engr.*
15. Particulars of seaman's documents held (If none, write None) *None*
16. Certificates held.   Grade .... No. ....

PART II. APPLICATION AND DECLARATION

I hereby apply for the issue of a ~~British Seaman's Card*~~ ~~Discharge Book*~~   (*Delete as necessary.*)
I declare :

(i) that the information given in this form is correct to the best of my knowledge and belief and that I am, or propose now to become, a merchant seaman.

*(ii) that I do not possess a Discharge Book issued in the United Kingdom, the Irish Republic or any Commonwealth country or Colonial territory.

†(iii) that I have not previously held or applied for a British Seaman's Card.

†(iv) that I have not previously held a seaman's Certificate of Nationality and Identity issued under the authority of another Government.

†(v) that I am entitled to hold a British Seaman's Card because I am a *British* *subject by birth and returning to work in a Colonial Territory* (See Note 2.)

*Delete if Discharge Book not required.
†Delete if British Seaman's Card not required.

Left Thumb Print
of Applicant
unable to sign

Signature of Applicant *E.V. Browne*
or of Witness to Thumb Print
of Applicant unable to sign

Date *9th Aug 1961*

PART III. CERTIFICATION

This part of the form need not be completed in every case—see Note 3.
For list of persons eligible to complete this part of the form—see Note 4.

I certify that the applicant has been known *personally* to me for *18 mth* X years and that to the best of my knowledge and belief the facts stated in Parts I and II of this form are correct.   I am a British subject.

Signature ....
Address *64 Brook Lane*
Felixstowe
Profession *Accountant*   Date *9. viii 61*

OFFICE STAMP
(For use by Police
Officers, Bank Officials,
etc.)

Figure 17   *Seamen's papers for Cecil Percival Sealey, born in Barbados in 1901 (BT 372/712/106). A list of ships he served on between 1943 and 1968 is in BT 382/2884*

Maritime Museum holds the remaining 90 per cent of crew lists for 1861, 1862 and all years ending in 5, except 1945. All agreements and crew lists for the period 1939–50 are in BT 380 and BT 381. With the exception of the ten per cent sample at the National Archives and those for 1975 and 1985 at the National Maritime Museum, all other crew lists between 1973 and 1989 have been destroyed.

Records of the deaths of seamen are in BT 153–BT 157 1851–1890, and BT 334 1891–1972, and among the marine deaths held by the General Register Office (see Useful addresses; the indexes are available online from a number of genealogical websites). ADM 80/6–12 are registers of dead men's wages relating to merchant seamen who died on ships travelling to and from the West Indies, 1798–1831. For those who died in the First and Second World Wars you should check the Rolls of Honour in BT 339 and the Commonwealth War Graves Commission (see Useful addresses and www.cwgc.org), and the Caribbean Roll of Honour at http://caribbeanrollofhonour-ww1-ww2.yolasite.com.

BT 351 (online at TNA) contains information on merchant seamen awarded the Mercantile Marine Medal and British War Medal for the First World War. The information includes name, place of birth, date or year of birth, discharge or certificate number and where issued which may be residential address or port. BT 395 (online at TNA) contains a record of Second World War medals claimed and issued to merchant seamen from 1946 to 2002. Medals were not automatically issued but had to be claimed by the veteran. Each entry gives details of the seaman's name and the medals, ribbons and clasps issued, together with a reference to the medal papers file, held at the Registry of Shipping and Seamen. Usually, his discharge book number and date and place of birth are listed too.

6.5.3 Further reading

Bevan, *Tracing Your Ancestors in the National Archives: The Website and Beyond*, Chapter 35

Smith, Watts and Watts, *Records of Merchant Shipping and Seamen*

Watts and Watts, *My Ancestor was a Merchant Seaman: How Can I Find Out More About Him?*

CHAPTER 7
SLAVES AND
SLAVE HOLDERS

Descendants of enslaved Africans comprise the majority of populations on most Caribbean countries. However, if you have African ancestors you cannot assume that they had worked as slave labour in the Caribbean as many Africans freely migrated to the Caribbean from the 1830s, and many Africans freed from illegal slavers from 1808 were also settled in the West Indies.

Capture, transportation and enslavement means that people were separated from their family, heritage, culture, language and customs. Slaves had few rights and were treated as the personal property of their owner. Personal records of slaves are limited: they were not recorded on shipping manifests, they could not possess property, and in some British colonies they were actively discouraged from attending church. Until the introduction of the slave registries from 1812 (see section **7.1**) most records of slaves, their births and deaths, are to be found among the personal papers of their owners and records relating to their owners and estates.

This loss of personal and family identity and lack of official records means that researching enslaved people is more challenging than tracing most other ethnic groups.

Many of the sources for researching slavery and slave ancestry have already been discussed under records of the Colonial Office (Chapter 2), slave trade (section **3.4**), American loyalists (section **3.5**), births, marriages and deaths (section **4.1**), wills (section **4.3**), and plantation records (section **5.3**).

Useful sources for information relating to slaves include:

- mortgage and transfer indentures, property registers and deeds;
- manumission registers and deeds: legal documents freeing slaves, who were often the children of slaves by their owners' and other favoured slaves (section **7.4**);
- wills bequeathing slaves to family and friends (section **4.3**);
- acts legally manumitting slaves by ordinance or by the legislative council (section **7.4**);

- notices in newspapers and gazettes for auctions and runaways (section **2.6.3**);
- records of the slave registry and Slave Compensation Commission (sections **7.1** and **7.2**);
- church records (section **4.1.2**). Although the baptism of slaves was actively discouraged in the Protestant colonies this did occur and from the early-nineteenth century local legislation was relaxed to permit baptism. There are very few references to slave marriages and many slave burials were unrecorded as they occurred on the plantation. It was uncommon for child slaves to be baptised, but when this did occur the mother was usually recorded along with the owner;
- plantation records such as punishment books, stock books, inventories, correspondence, accounts, purchases, loss books and journals or diaries (section **5.3**);
- reports of protectors of slaves, which include punishments, criminal cases, manumissions, baptisms and marriages (section **7.3.1**);
- Colonial Office (Chapter 2) records relating to slaves are numerous and include reports of slave rebellions, reports of protectors of slaves, people in workhouses, slaves granted their freedom, numbers of slaves being imported and registration of slaves.

Most of these records may be found locally in the relevant country's archive or register office but copies of some of these types of documents are found in the National Archives.

The owner or plantation will be found in most of these records, which will help identify family or estate papers for further clues. Often racial information is given, for example, 'black' or 'negro' for predominantly African slaves and 'coloured' or 'mulatto' for slaves of mixed racial ancestry. Some colonies had a grading scale of 'whiteness' denoting the proportion of European to African blood. The term 'creole' is often found which means someone born in the West Indies. Surnames may sometimes be recorded, especially in the slave registers and on runaway notices (see section **1.3** for information on slave surnames). Occasionally, ethnic origin may be recorded but often this is not accurate, having been based on information provided by one of the merchants in the chain from the forts and trading posts (factories) in Africa, or officials on ships, or the merchants selling the slaves on the islands. Often this may be where the slave was transported from rather than his or her true origin, although some records describe tattoos and markings which may give more accurate clues on ethnic origins.

7.1 Slave Registry

The records of the slave registries and the Slave Compensation Commission (section **7.2**) are the most important and comprehensive for slave research in the British West Indies for the period 1812 to 1834. The slave registers provide a census of all slaves and slave holders until the abolition of slavery in the Caribbean colonies on 1 August 1834 and the records of the Slave Compensation Commission complement the registers and give information on compensation paid to slave holders following abolition.

The slave emancipation act was passed in 1833 and registers compiled after this act often give information on apprentices. Although emancipation officially occurred on 1 August 1834 and about 670,000 people were freed, most former slaves were 'apprenticed' to their former masters for up to six years, except for children under the age of six and slaves in Antigua and the Bahamas, where local laws abolishing apprenticeship had been passed. Apprenticeship also ended in the Cayman Islands on 3 May 1835. Following lobbying and unrest apprenticeship ended earlier on 1 August 1838 which is why most Caribbean countries consider that date for emancipation.

The slave trade from Africa to British colonies was made illegal from 1807 but the trade between the islands did not become illegal until 1811. On 26 March 1812 an Order in Council set up a registry of slaves in Trinidad as a means to monitor legally held slaves (PC 2/192; printed in *British and Foreign State Papers*, vol 3, 1815–1816, pp.975–1007). On 24 September 1814 an Order in Council extended the registry to St Lucia and Mauritius (PC 2/196). Between December 1816 and May 1817 most other colonies passed acts to set up their own registries. The acts passed in 1816 and 1817 were submitted to the Privy Council and approved on 9 January 1818 (PC 2/200). However, there were exceptions especially for dependencies, which were usually omitted in the local acts: Bahamas, 1821; Bermuda, 1827, although there was an earlier return in 1821; Cayman Island, April 1834; and British Honduras, 1834. I have not found returns for Barbuda, although owners on Antigua made declarations respecting any slaves held on islands but not living on Antigua.

The Trinidad and St Lucia Orders in Council included detailed instructions on how to complete the registers, to compile indexes and to send copies of the slave registers and indexes to the Colonial Office but these instructions were not repeated in all local laws. A Colonial Office circular of 6 February 1818 (CO 854/1, fos 58–61) was sent to West Indian governors with instructions for the registrars of slaves. The instructions described how a register was to be maintained: each volume was to have an index to owners and plantations at the front, and on completion of each register the registrar was to compile, in a separate book, an index to slaves. I do not know if this later instruction was routinely carried out or even if it was practical in such colonies as Barbados and Jamaica, where few slaves had last names, since the index would contain pages of Williams or Marys; this limitation can be seen in the only index to slaves which did not have registered surnames – St Vincent, 1817 (T 71/464). The National Archives holds indexes to slaves for St Lucia and Trinidad but in these cases most slaves had last names.

The Slave Registration Act 1819 established a central registry of slaves in London, under the Commissioners of the Treasury. Under this act no slaves could be bought, sold or inherited if they had not first been entered in the appropriate island register. A Colonial Office circular of 1 May 1821 (CO 854/1, fo 94) instructed governors to forward duplicates of the slave registers and associated indexes to the London central registry. The records of the central registry are in T 71 (most are online at www.ancestry.co.uk) and the original registers may survive in the relevant country archive or register offices.

The records of the central registry continue until 1834 when slavery was abolished. The registers are arranged by colony, then usually by parish, and many are arranged alphabetically by the name of the owner or estate. Many have separate volumes of indexes which should be looked at first, but most contain internal indexes to owners or estates and a few contain indexes to slaves.

The registers contain much information on the slaves and their owners. For slaves they give at least name, age, colour and country of origin. They record increases and decreases on the last registration period, including births and deaths, purchases, sales, inheritances and manumissions. For the owner they can be used to show deaths, marriages and details of family members. Slaves were bequeathed, inherited and were often given 'in right of marriage' when the wife's slaves became the property of her husband on marriage, and the wife is often named. Slaves of minors were registered by their guardians; many registers give the 'colour' of slave owners.

The information given in the registers differs between colonies. After the first registration most colonies only note increases and decreases in their numbers of slaves, although a few, such as Demerara, St Lucia and Bermuda, list all slaves. Most registers list slaves by sex and age, but some, for example, St Lucia, Honduras and Trinidad, are arranged by family and record other family members such as brothers, sisters and cousins if on the same return. Mothers are occasionally noted in the returns, but fathers are rarely recorded. The Jamaican returns often give baptismal name.

For a detailed analysis of the content of the slave registers and their value for social and family historians see Higman, *Slave Populations of the British Caribbean*.

In 2009 a joint submission on the slave registers was inscribed on the UNESCO Memory of the World register (www.unesco.org). This submission summarises slave registers held by the archives of Bahamas, Belize, Bermuda, Dominica, Jamaica, St Kitts, Trinidad and Tobago and the United Kingdom. The Bermuda National Archives appended their slave registers in 2011.

7.2 Slave Compensation Commission

Slavery was abolished in the Caribbean on 1 August 1834, under the Abolition of Slavery Act 1833, and a sum of £20 million was provided to compensate slave owners. The records of the Slave Compensation Commission are also in T 71 and contain information which was used to compensate slave owners on the abolition of slavery. The Commission was terminated in 1842 but one of the commissioners was appointed to adjudicate on outstanding claims. The National Debt Office dealt with payment of claims, and the records are in NDO 4, West Indies Slave Compensation. Other compensation returns are in AO 14/37–48.

The records of the slave compensation commissioners are arranged by colony and include the following returns:

Valuers' returns – bound volumes of printed forms used for calculating compensation for slaves on 1 August 1834. The categories of slaves used for calculation were praedial (agricultural slaves), non-praedial (domestic slaves), children under the age of six, and the aged, diseased or otherwise non-effective. They may give the name of the estate.

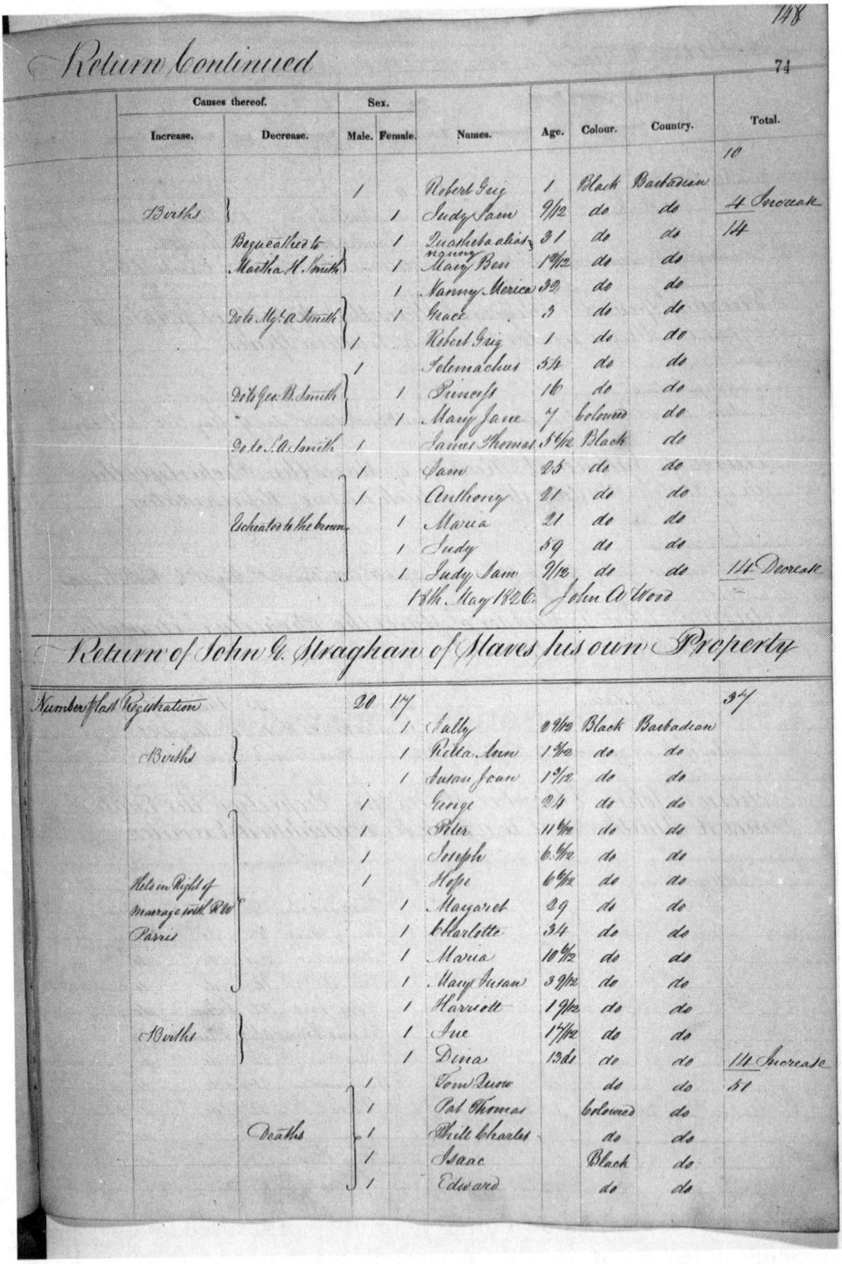

148

Return Continued

74

Causes thereof. Increase.	Decrease.	Sex. Male.	Female.	Names.	Age.	Colour.	Country.	Total.
								10
Births		1		Robert Grig	1	Black	Barbadian	4 Increase
			1	Judy Sam	9/12	do	do	14
	Bequeathed to Martha H. Smith		1	Quasheba alias Nanny	31	do	do	
			1	Mary Ben	1 9/12	do	do	
			1	Nanny Merica	32	do	do	
	Do to Mr A. Smith		1	Grace	3	do	do	
		1		Robert Grig	1	do	do	
		1		Telemachus	5 1/2	do	do	
	Do to Geo B. Smith		1	Princess	16	do	do	
			1	Mary Jane	7	Coloured	do	
	Do to S.A. Smith	1		James Thomas	5 6/12	Black	do	
	Escheated to the Crown	1		Sam	25	do	do	
		1		Anthony	21	do	do	
			1	Maria	21	do	do	
			1	Judy	59	do	do	
			1	Judy Sam	9/12	do	do	14 Decrease

18th May 1826. John A Wood

Return of John G. Straghan of Slaves his own Property

Increase.	Decrease.	Male.	Female.	Names.	Age.	Colour.	Country.	Total.
Number last Registration		20	17					37
Births			1	Sally	2 9/12	Black	Barbadian	
			1	Retta Ann	1 3/12	do	do	
			1	Susan Jean	1 7/12	do	do	
Held in Right of marriage with R.W. Parris		1		George	24	do	do	
		1		Peter	11 6/12	do	do	
		1		Joseph	6 3/12	do	do	
		1		Hope	6 6/12	do	do	
			1	Margaret	29	do	do	
			1	Charlotte	34	do	do	
			1	Maria	10 6/12	do	do	
			1	Mary Susan	3 9/12	do	do	
			1	Harriott	1 9/12	do	do	
Births			1	Sue	1 7/12	do	do	
			1	Dina	13 ds	do	do	14 Increase
	Deaths	1		Tom Drew		do	do	51
		1		Pat Thomas		Coloured	do	
		1		Phill Charles		do	do	
		1		Isaac		Black	do	
		1		Edward		do	do	

Figure 18 *Barbados: slave register, 1826 (T 71/537, p.148). Return of James H Smith, who had died since the previous return in 1823, showing slaves bequeathed. Return of John Grant Straghan who had married since the 1823 return. According to www.familysearch.com he married Rebecca William Parris on 24 April 1826*

Registers of claims – these are in claim number order and show whether there was a claim or counterclaim. A claim was if the slave owners claimed for compensation whereas a counterclaim occurred if there was a dispute on the estate and other parties also claimed for compensation.

Indexes to claims – arranged by the initial letter of the surname, they give the surname, first names, the estate, the parish and claim number.

Original claims and certificates – bound volumes in claim number order, with a copy certificate of claim and the original claim, these are signed and may include further details omitted from the registers, for example, children born to slaves after the final registration.

Counterclaims – loose papers with evidence used in counterclaims. These can contain useful information on the family, the estate, other parties involved such as creditors and slaves, which may pre-date the registers.

Adjudication in contested claims – ledgers in claim number order, with the name of the counterclaim, date of deeds, subject of counterclaim, name of claimant and remarks.

Certificates and awards – copy certificates issued by the compensation commissioners.

Parliamentary returns of awards – these were presented to Parliament and contain the amount paid. The volumes consist of five lists:
- List A: awards made in respect of uncontested claims;
- List B: amount of compensation money forfeited under the 46th Section of the Act 3&4 William IV cap 73;
- List C: awards made in respect of litigated claims;
- List D: awards made for the payment or transfer of the compensation money into court by order of the High Court of Chancery;
- List E: transfers made by the accountant general of the High Court of Chancery in pursuance of orders of the colonial courts.

List A gives the date of award, claim number, the party to whom payment was awarded, number of slaves and the sum payable. The other lists contain the same information as List A but do not include the number of slaves. The returns are in claim number order.

These lists were presented to both Houses of the British Parliament on 16 January 1838 and are printed in the Parliamentary Papers, session 1837–38, volume XLVIII (paper 215). A supplementary list, updating the original return, was compiled in 1840 and is in CO 318/150. These lists are incomplete as a small proportion of contested claims were not resolved until after 1840 and no further returns have been found.

http://compensations.plantations.bb is a database of claims for Barbados and Antigua; you can search by claimant, who was usually the slave holder, or by claim number.

Exhibits: sales of slaves, 1823–30 – were used by the commissioners to assess the values of slaves. They recorded returns of sales of slaves and are filed according to the type of sale, for example, of slaves alone, sales of slaves with land and buildings of estates, and sales through judicial process of the Court of Chancery, or through the marshal's office.

NDO 4, West Indies Slave Compensation, 1835 to 1842, contains payment books which show the sum awarded, the date of the Treasury warrant, and includes the signatures of the claimants' representatives. There are also miscellaneous accounts, correspondence, and some death and marriage certificates.

7.3 Amelioration

To measure the success of the legislation abolishing the slave trade and the slave registers, the Colonial Office requested various returns and reports relating to slaves and slavery. The first circular requesting this information, dated 3 July 1821 (CO 854/1, fos 95–96) asked for the following returns:

- number of slaves imported and exported under licence since 1 January 1808, noting the year, number and sex of slaves imported/ exported, and the place from which they were exported/imported;
- return of manumissions (grants of freedom) since 1 January 1808;
- return of marriages legally solemnised between slaves, as well as free black and coloured people, since 1 January 1808;
- list of people committed to gaols or workhouses as runaways but who had declared themselves free since 1 January 1808, and account of how disposed;
- return of slaves escheated to the Crown (reverted in absence of owners) since 1 January 1808;

- return of population in each year since 1812 with numbers of births and deaths, distinguishing between white, free black or coloured, or slave, by sex and age;
- returns of all slaves taken or sold for debt from 1 January 1818.

There were several further circulars until 1830 to bring the information up to date. Some governors answered these circulars literally and provided nominal returns; others provided statistical information. The returns to the circular of 11 April 1826, including some lists of manumissions for 1821–25, were published in the British Parliamentary Papers, session 1826–27 (128), vol XXII.43 (mfm 29.171–172). Examples of nominal returns mostly for 1821–25 include: Jamaica, CO 137/162; St Vincent, CO 260/42; St Lucia, CO 253/17 (1818–1823) and CO 253/29 (1825–1830); Antigua, CO 7/14; Grenada, CO 101/66; Barbados, CO 28/97; Berbice, CO 111/94 (1818–1820), CO 111/101 (1822–1825), and CO 111/110 (1825–1830); and St Kitts, Nevis and the Virgin Islands, CO 239/22 (1825–1830)

Following prolonged attack from the anti-slavery lobby, Parliament encouraged local governments to improve conditions for slaves, for example, by prohibiting dismemberment as a punishment. This was left to the individual governments to implement but it was considered ineffectual. In 1823 Parliament agreed many measures for the improvement of conditions to better educate and install British social responsibilities on slaves with a view to their eventual emancipation. In addition, colonial governments were required to pass laws to implement these amelioration measures. Between March and July 1823 the Colonial Secretary circulated notes and guidance on amelioration to all Caribbean governors (CO 854/1, fos 114–167 and printed in *British and Foreign State Papers*, 1823–1824, p84–102). The measures included:

- encouragement of church attendance – this was to instil Christian/ Anglican beliefs in slaves and so that they could give evidence in court; this explains the increase in slave baptisms in Church of England registers;
- encouragement of marriage – to instil Christian morals. One inducement was to exempt married mothers from working in the field;
- removal of obstacles to manumission – to make it easier for slaves to be freed and to enable slaves to free themselves;

■ slaves not to be sold alone for debt – this was to stop slaves being sold away from their families, homes and livelihood. This changed the status of slaves from personal estate to real estate;

■ families not to be sold separately – this included lawful and reputed families. There were difficulties if the mother and children were on one estate and the father on another and the protectors of slaves would review cases where families were likely to be moved far apart;

■ maintaining punishment books – to demonstrate that any punishments were justified and that any such punishments were to be carried out in the presence of one free person;

■ setting up savings banks – to encourage saving and long-term use of money. The depositor was to name a beneficiary in case of death and in the absence of any other authority this was declared the equivalent of a will.

This was reinforced by an Order in Council dated 10 May 1824 for improving the conditions of slaves in Trinidad (PC 2/205 and printed in *British and Foreign State Papers*, vol 11, 1823–1824, p124–150); the provisions were later extended to St Lucia, Mauritius and British Guiana.

7.3.1 Reports of protectors of slaves

The protectors of slaves were established under the 1824 Order in Council to look into the welfare of slaves in Trinidad; and extended to St Lucia and British Guiana. Later they became Protectors of Apprentices, during the period of apprenticeship 1834–38, and as Protectors of Immigrants or Protectors of Labourers, to oversee the welfare of East Indian immigrants and other apprenticed labourers. The reports include information on punishments, criminal cases, births, deaths, marriages, free baptisms and manumissions. The National Archives holds reports of protectors of slaves for the following:

1 Berbice, 1826–1834, CO 116/143–153
2 Demerara and Essequibo, 1826–1834, CO 116/156–163
3 St Lucia, 1826–1834, CO 258/5–15
4 Trinidad, 1824–1834, CO 300/19–33

Several of the reports were published in the British Parliamentary Papers: session 1829 (335) vol XXV.255 (mfm 31.153–155) and session 1830–31 (262) vol XV.1 (mfm 33.87–95).

7.4 Manumissions (grants of freedom)

There were three main ways that slaves could be freed.

1 By deed. These were entered into the deeds register or into a separate manumissions register. Rights and fees for grants of manumission were dependent on local legislation.

2 By act of the assembly or court. These were often granted for special services to the colony, such as provision of information leading to the suppression of slave revolts or the capture of rebels. These grants will be found in the appropriate acts or sessional papers; they should also be registered in the deeds registry. Some court records may be found in the National Archives in original correspondence series, but most are to be found locally. Acts of the council or court could also validate or deny freedom and were also used by freedmen and women to confer certain rights. CO 139, Jamaican acts contain many references to slaves being manumitted and petitions from free people for entitlement to the same rights and privileges as English subjects, with certain restrictions. Edward Crawford has summarised Jamaican acts relating to individual slaves and free people between 1760 and 1810 at http://www.rootsweb.ancestry.com/~jamwgw/actass1.htm

3 By will. This did not guarantee freedom as conditions for freedom were often attached such as reaching a certain age or on the death of the owner's widow. Also, since slaves were property, heirs could challenge requests for freedom.

The National Archives does not hold deeds registers or comprehensive lists of those manumitted. The slave registers in T 71 will show those manumitted in the decreases column since these were a reduction to the slave population. Colonial Office circulars between 1821 and 1830 asked for information on manumission: some governors provided returns with names, while others were statistical. These are held in the relevant country's original correspondence series. Manumissions granted by the assembly may be found in the colonial acts (section **2.3**) or sessional papers (section **2.4**). The final series of records in the National Archives which make reference to manumissions are the reports of protectors of slaves. Locally, deeds registers may be in the archive or the register office. See section **4.3** for information on wills.

Figure 19 Antigua: list of slaves manumitted, January to March 1823 (CO 7/14)

Date of such Manumission	Names of Persons Manumitted	Sex	Age	Price in Saving Fund for Slave's Redemption	Lowd Casci – the actions against squaw Effected	Amount of Tax or Levy	Fees paid at the Register Office
1823 January 29	Lucia	Female		" "	Marie Quiona Whitehead		1. 16 "
" 30	Rose Elizabeth	Female		" "	Eliz Xenino		1. 16 "
" "	Catharine	Female		" "	Gabriel Rose		1. 16 "
" 31	Rose James	Female		110 "	James Yaws		1. 16 "
February 7	Nancy	Female		" "	Andrew Marshall		1. 16 "
" 10	Marie Rose	Female	14 Years	" "	Randall Righton		1. 16 "
" "	Josephine	Female	14 Years	" "	Ditto		1. 16 "
" "	Marie Emilia	Female	40 Years	" "	Ditto		1. 16 "
" "	Sabine	Female	5 Years	" "	Ditto		1. 16 "
" "	Selonine	Female	6 Years	" "	Ditto		1. 16 "
" "	Auguste	Female	10 Years	" "	Ditto		1. 16 "
" "	Eloise	Female	95 Years	" "	Ditto		1. 16 "
" "	Jean Joseph	Male	19 Years	" "	Ditto		1. 16 "
" "	Marie Antoinette	Female	21 Years	" "	Ditto		1. 16 "
" "	Mont Rose	Male	15 Years	" "	Ditto		1. 16 "
" "	Marie Roselia	Female	27 Years	" "	Ditto		1. 16 "
" "	Kayta	Female	28 Years	" "	Ditto		1. 16 "
" "	Angela	Female	30 Years	" "	Ditto		1. 16 "
" "	Joseph Rémy	Male	15 Years	" "	Ditto		1. 16 "
" "	Marie Luca	Female	50 Years	" "	Ditto		1. 16 "
" 19	Marie	Female		50 "	Richard Curtis		1. 16 "
" 20	Sally Bartly	Female		100 "	Charles Smith		1. 16 "
" 22	William Southwell	Male		82. 10 "	Geo of Samuel Roots		2. 7 "
" 27	Joania	Female		" "			
" "	Betsey Montbray	Female		" "			
" "	Edward Feb	Male		300 "	Samuel akitt		3. 12 "
" "	Georgiana Feb	Female		" "			
" "	John Edwards	Male		" "			
March 5	Joseph Seal of Alexandrine	Female	39 Years	" "	Randall Righton		1. 16 "
" "	Paul, alias Rosemaine	Male	15 Years	" "	Ditto		1. 16 "
" 7	Selina	Female	4 Years	" "	Jacque Homon		1. 16 "
	23						

7.5 Acts on the status, condition and treatment of slaves

Although these do not name individual slaves they can be used to identify the types of documents created and the officials who had some responsibility for the welfare or conduct of slaves and free people. Laws were also passed to emancipate people, to confirm rights and privileges of freed people, and to enable public departments to sell slaves.

For example, a Jamaican act of 1787 (CO 137/87, fos 86–109) states that justices were to examine mutilated slaves, freed slaves and Indians (Amerindians) without tickets of freedom. Keepers of gaols or workhouses were to advertise names and other details of runaways in their custody in the gazette and chronicles. The clerk of the peace was to attend the trials of slaves and record proceedings. Tickets granted to slaves to work away from their owners or plantations were to be signed by the clerk of the vestry and to be entered into a vestry book for that purpose. Free black and coloured people and Indians were to attend the vestry and give an account of how they had obtained their freedom which was to be entered into a vestry book. Therefore, for Jamaica it may be worth checking parish vestry minutes and records, newspapers and justices of the peace records for further information.

7.6 Further reading

Several genealogical guides for African-Americans research are included in section **1.10**.

Beckles and Shepherd, *Caribbean Slave Society and Economy: A Student Reader*

Burnard, 'Slave naming patterns: Onomastics and the taxonomy of race in eighteenth-century Jamaica'

Craton, *Empire, Enslavement and Freedom in the Caribbean*

Draper, *The Price of Emancipation. Slave-ownership, compensation and British society at the end of slavery*

Draper, '"Possessing slaves": ownership, compensation and metropolitan society in Britain at the time of emancipation 1834–40'

Eltis, 'The traffic in slaves between the British West Indian colonies, 1807–1833'

Gutman, *The Black Family in Slavery and Freedom, 1750–1925*

Handler, 'Slave manumissions and Freedmen in seventeenth-century Barbados'

Handler and Jacoby, 'Slave names and naming in Barbados, 1650–1830'

Higman, *Slave Population and Economy in Jamaica, 1807–1834*

Higman, *Slave Populations of the British Caribbean, 1807–1834*

Legacies of British Slave-ownership – a project by University College, London, recording compensation paid to British-based slave holders (www.ucl.ac.uk/lbs/)

National Archives web pages on slavery and abolition – www.nationalarchives.gov.uk/slavery

Patterson, *The Sociology of Slavery: An Analysis of the Origins, Development and Structure of Negro Slave Society in Jamaica*

CHAPTER 8
THE COLONIAL CIVIL SERVANT

The Personnel Division of the Colonial Office was established on 1 October 1930. Before that the Secretary of State had entire control of the appointments to all but the most subordinate official posts, which were appointed by the governor. Posts were under his 'patronage' and were dealt with in his private office by his private secretaries.

There were three classes of post, based on salary. Class 3 positions were the most subordinate and were appointed entirely by the governor. For class 2 posts the governor would make a provisional appointment which was reported to the Secretary of State for confirmation but seldom refused. The governor could recommend class 1 officers, but on the understanding that the Secretary of State had the final decision. From 1930 there was a gradual unification of the various colonial posts, such as administration, forestry, agriculture, medicine and railways, and the selection of candidates under the control of the Secretary of State was not just by grade, but also by post.

From 1900 there were the rudiments of a centrally managed service. When senior posts in the colonies became vacant, officials of the Colonial Office would review the records and qualifications of officers already in the service and make recommendations to the Secretary of State for filling vacancies by promotion or transfer. Promotion to higher posts was frequently made by transfer from one colony to another. Requests by officers already serving were considered before any posts were filled by outside recruitment, and promotion was based on official qualifications, experience and merit. The Secretary of State recruited and nominated candidates from outside to fill vacancies but could also offer a post in one territory to an officer already serving in another.

The records of the Patronage Department, 1867–1919, are in CO 429. The registers (CO 430) relate to both the department's original correspondence and original correspondence of individual colonies. Letters applying for specific appointments were recorded in the colonial registers. In 1930 the Personnel Division was established, comprising an Appointments Department, dealing with recruitment and training, and a

Colonial Service Department, concerned with promotions and transfers, conditions of employment and pensions. The records of the Personnel Division, 1932–1952, are in CO 850 with the registers in CO 919. Those of the Appointments Department, together with some earlier correspondence from 1920 to 1952, are in CO 877 with the registers in CO 918.

In 1945 the division was renamed the Colonial Service Division, and was changed again to the Overseas Service Division in 1954. The records of the Colonial Services Division and Overseas Service Division, 1948–1966, are in CO 1017. These are continued in OD 16, Department of Technical Co-operation and successors: Personnel Services: Registered Files, 1947–1972, and by FCO 79, Diplomatic Service Administration Office and Foreign and Commonwealth Office: Personnel Departments: Registered Files, 1966–1977, and FCO 77, Diplomatic Service Administration Office and Foreign and Commonwealth Office: Establishment and Organisation Department: Registered Files, 1966–1976.

The starting point for tracing a colonial civil servant's career is the annual *Blue Books* (section **2.6.1**) of each colony, 1820–1940. These list all public employees and provide such information as position, date of appointment, by whom appointed (or under what authority, for example, by letters patent) and annual salary. *Blue Books* also list government pensioners.

The annual *Colonial Office List*, 1862–1966, briefly describes the history and economy of each colony, and lists government employees with their salary. At the back of each volume there are potted biographies of senior colonial officials. The National Archives does not hold applications or personal records for civil servants appointed by colonial government departments; any records that survive will be in the relevant country. However, other useful information may be found in later (or earlier) *Blue Books* (section **2.6.1**) and government gazettes (section **2.5**) which publish notices of appointment, promotion and transfer of officials, retirement, and leave of absence and resumption of duty.

If he or she was appointed by the governor or the Colonial Office it is possible that information will be found in the National Archives. Commissions for the most senior colonial officers, such as governor, chief justice, chief auditor, naval officer, and councillors were recorded in the Privy Council registers (PC 2 and PC 5), letters patent (C 66), and in the Colonial entry books (CO 324). The appointment was also announced in the *London Gazette* (ZJ 1 and online at www.gazettes-online.co.uk) and in colonial gazettes. Colonial appointments by the Secretary of State 1819–1835 are in CO 323.

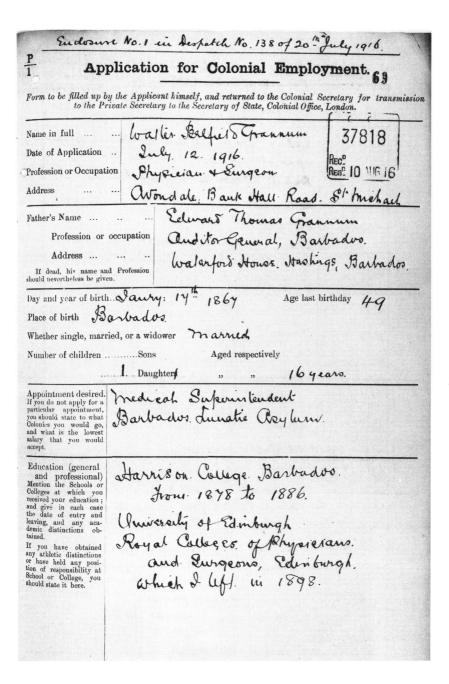

Figure 20 *Application form of Walter Belfield Grannum (1867–1921) for the post of Medical Superintendent, Barbados Lunatic Asylum, 1916 (CO 28/289, fo 69). He is the brother of the author's great-grandfather*

M 64   CIVIL ESTABLISHMENT.

OFFICE.	NAME.	Date of Appointment.	By whom Appointed, and under what Instrument.	Annual Salary.	From what Fund the Salary is paid.
				£ s. d.	
JUDICIAL.					
Chief Justice...	Sir D. P. Chalmers ...	Jan. 22, 1879	By Letters Patent under Mandamus.	2,500 0 0	⎫
Puisne Judge	N. Atkinson ...	June 3, 1885	Royal Warrant.	1,500 0 0	
Puisne Judge	W. A. M. Sheriff ...	May 5, 1887	Ditto ...	1,500 0 0	⎬
Attorney General ...	J. W. Carrington, D.C.L., C.M.G., Q.C.	Dec. 12, 1888	Ditto ...	1,500 0 0	
Clerk to do. ...	C. Chawner ...	Feb. 19, 1886	Governor ...	215 0 0	
Solicitor General ...	Alfred Kingdon, Q.C.	Jan. 29, 1887	Royal Warrant.	400 0 0	⎭
Crown Solicitor ...	Vacant (a)	..	...	400 0 0	
REGISTRAR'S OFFICE.					
Registrar	E. H. G. Dalton ...	May 16, 1876	Governor ...	833 6 8	⎫
Accountant	J. Veecock	April 1, 1888	Secretary of State.	500 0 0	
1st Sworn Clerk and Notary Public.	W. O'Meara (b) ...	Oct. 1, 1882	Governor ...	500 0 0	Fee Fund.
2nd ditto ...	M. P. Olton (c) ..	Oct. 1, 1882	Ditto ...	400 0 0	
3rd ditto ...	E. A. V. Abraham (d)..	Nov. 1, 1882	Ditto ...	400 0 0	
4th ditto ...	J. A. Richardson (d)...	Aug. 23, 1887	Ditto ...	400 0 0	
1st Assistant Sworn Clerk.	J. A. King (e) ...	Aug. 23, 1887	Ditto ...	350 0 0	
2nd ditto ..	J. Walls (f)	Feb. 1, 1890	Ditto ...	300 0 0	⎭

REMARKS.

(a) Mr. F. Abraham acted throughout the year.
(b) Mr. O'Meara acted as Provost Marshal throughout the year.
(c) Mr. Olton acted as 1st Sworn Clerk from 1st Jan. to 16th July, and as Registrar from 17th July to the end of the year.
(d) Mr. Abraham and Mr. Richardson acted respectively as 2nd and 3rd Sworn Clerks from 1st Jan. to 16th July, and as 1st and 3rd from 17th July to the end of the year.
(e) Mr. King acted as 4th Sworn Clerk from 1st Jan. to 16th July and as 3rd from 17th July to 9th December.
(f) Succeeded Mr. Bosch Reitz, who died 9th January.
* Scale £200 to £250.

Figure 21   *Guyana:* Blue Book of Statistics, *1890, staff in the judicial department* (CO 116/259, pp.M64–5)

CIVIL ESTABLISHMENT. M 65

Amount of Fees, Fines, &c., during Year 1890.	Whether a house for his personal Residence; or any Allowance for such be allowed.	Whether the Office is held in connection with any other office. If so, the amount of pay and allowance of such office.	Absent from the Colony during the year 1890.	Whether the Principal enjoy any, and what other Advantage or Profit, not required to be stated in the preceding Columns.	Date of First Appointment under the Colonial Government.
...	...	Judge in Vice-Admiralty Court.	...	...	Aug., 1869
...	...	...	17th July to 29th Octr.	...	Nov. 25, 1874
...	...	...	31st July to end of the year. (a)	...	1872
Patent Fees, £15 12. 6.	...	...	...	...	Decr., 1878
...	...	...	...	...	Feb, 19, 1886
...	...	...	17th July to 12th November. (b)	Private Practice. £200 per annum, as Counsel to Revenue Departments, in Revenue Cases.	Jany., 1881
...	...	...	...	...	...
...	...	Registrar of Vice-Admiralty Court, (Fees). Registrar General of Births and Deaths, £100.	17th July to end of year.	Commissioner of Affidavits, Fees.	Jany., 1860
...	...	...	...	...	Decr., 1860
...	...	...	...	Commissioner of Affidavits, Fees.	Sept. 1868
...	...	...	...	Ditto ..	Jany., 1866
...	...	...	...	...	Jany., 1872
...	...	...	...	Commissioner of Affidavits, Fees.	Decr., 1878
...	...	...	10th to 31st Decr.	...	Jany., 1878
...	...	...	1st to 31st Jany.	...	Feb., 1880

REMARKS.

(a) Mr. H. Kirke acted as Puisne Judge from 29th Oct. to end of year.
(b) Mr. C. S. Davson acted as Solicitor General.

The original correspondence series (section **2.1**) for the relevant country and the several personnel and patronage department series contain appointments by the Secretary of State and governors' recommendations of appointment, promotion and transfer. They can also include individuals' letters to the Secretary of State asking for appointments, promotions and transfers, application forms, medical reports, and applications for leave, half pay, retirement and pension.

Private papers of former colonial civil servants may survive in local and academic archives in the UK and elsewhere, for example, in the countries where they had previously served. Search the National Register of Archives (www.nationalarchives.gov.uk/nra) for surviving papers in the UK. Rhodes House Library (see Useful addresses) holds papers and interviews of former colonial officials collected from the 1960s under the Oxford Colonial Records Project, and the Desk Diaries of the Colonial Office Patronage Department, 1899–1915, which give frank and often colourful descriptions of candidates applying to be colonial civil servants. Concurrent with these Desk Diaries, the London School of Hygiene and Tropical Medicine (see Useful addresses) holds case notes of medical examinations of people seeking appointment in the colonies and protectorates, 1898–1919, 30 volumes (reference: GB 0809 Manson/09).

8.1 Further reading

Bertram, *The Colonial Service*

Colonial Office List (annual publication 1862–1966)

Fiddes, *The Dominions and Colonial Offices*

Jeffries, *The Colonial Empire and its Civil Service*

Jeffries, *Whitehall and the Colonial Service: An Administrative Memoir, 1939–1956*

Kirk-Greene, *A Biographical Dictionary of the British Colonial Service, 1939–1966*

Kirk-Greene, *British Imperial Administrators 1858–1966*

Kirk-Greene, 'Not Quite a Gentleman': The Desk Diaries of the Assistant Private Secretary (Appointments) to the Secretary of State for the Colonies, 1899–1915

Lester and Lambert, *Colonial Lives Across the British Empire: Imperial Careering in the Long Nineteenth Century*

CHAPTER 9
MIGRATION FROM THE WEST INDIES

West Indians are a migratory people. Many early settlers saw the islands as somewhere to make money and then retire to the UK. During the seventeenth and eighteenth centuries newly acquired islands were settled by people from other islands, for example, settlers from St Christopher migrated to Nevis and Barbadians were among the first British settlers in Jamaica. West Indians have also migrated to other British and foreign countries in the West Indies, Central and South America and to the United States and Canada. Much of the migration within the Caribbean and to Latin and South America was seasonal to work on estates, whereas migration to Canada, the US and further afield was often more permanent.

The records of these immigrants are to be found among the usual sources used to find local ancestors such as wills, censuses, church records and civil registration returns. Until the British colonies and dominions such as Canada became independent, British West Indians as British subjects did not need to naturalise, but in foreign countries they may have done so. The Foreign Office looked after British interests in foreign countries and some information regarding British West Indians can be found amongst FO series (see section **9.2.1**).

9.1 Migration to the United Kingdom

Since the settling of the British West Indies, West Indians have returned or emigrated to Britain. Many planters and merchants sent their children to school in England and may themselves have retired to Britain, bringing their servants, including slaves, with them. West Indian merchant seamen, soldiers and sailors were often discharged in the UK and decided to remain and many arrived as businessmen and students. Most settled in the major ports and major towns of London, Cardiff, Hull, South Shields, Liverpool, Edinburgh and Glasgow. However, it was not until this century, and especially after the Second World War, that large numbers of West Indians arrived in Britain.

Until the nineteenth century it is very difficult to know how many West Indians were living in the UK. The decennial censuses can be used to show the growth of Caribbean migration to the UK for the nineteenth and twentieth centuries. A Home Office report of 1963 summarises migration into the UK between 1840 and 1962 and uses figures from the censuses of people born in the Caribbean to show the growth of West Indian immigration (HO 344/76); later figures are provided by the Office of National Statistics:

1851–1881	c7–8,000	(estimates based on analysis of place of birth from online censuses)
1891	8,689	
1901	8,680	
1911	9,189	
1921	9,054	
1931	8,595	(there was no census in 1941)
1951	15,301	
1961	173,773	
1971	306,165	
1981	293,632	
1991	264,591	
2001	253,178	(excludes Guyana and Belize)

Until 1962 there were few restrictions to British West Indian immigration: they were British subjects and did not need to register when they arrived or naturalise when they migrated to Britain to have full rights as a British-born person. To find information on West Indian ancestors in the United Kingdom you need to use the same sources as for the native population. Country of origin is rarely mentioned except in the decennial census returns, though wills may mention family members or property in the West Indies.

Ships' passenger lists, 1878–1960 (BT 26, online at www.ancestry.co.uk; selected lists on Moving Here) contain the names of people arriving in British ports from outside Europe and are arranged by the year and month of arrival, the port of arrival and the name of ship. The information given includes port of departure, name, age, occupation, address in the United Kingdom and country of last residence. British West Indians were also sometimes registered on the certificates and registers of arrivals of aliens, 1810–11 and 1826–69 (CUST 102, FO 83, HO 2 and HO 3, online at www.ancestry.co.uk). These records list aliens (non-British subjects) arriving in the UK giving port of departure, port and date of arrival, name of migrant, occupation and nationality. The master occasionally recorded British colonial subjects as aliens possibly because they were born overseas; these records also list discharged merchant seamen.

Figure 22 1901 census for the family of Walter Belfield Grannum born in Barbados (RG 13/1517, fo 52). He served as Parochial Medical Office for Luton between 1900 and 1902; he returned to Barbados with his family in 1905

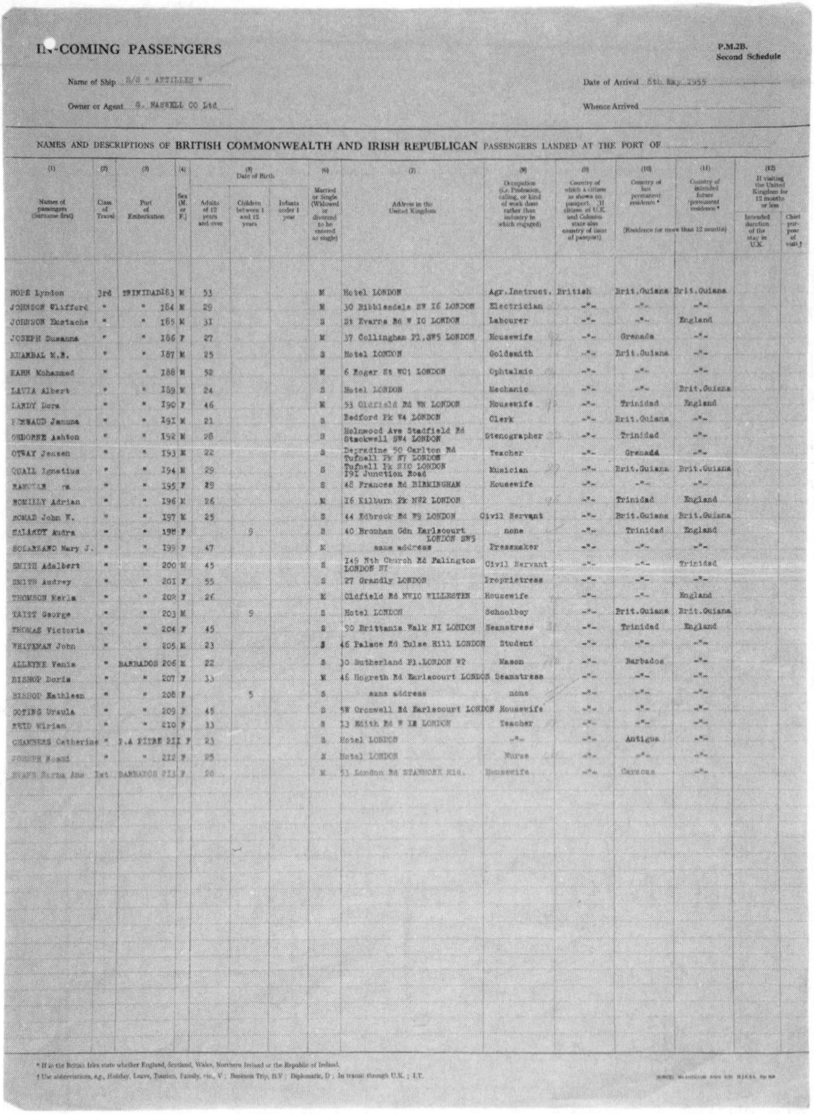

INCOMING PASSENGERS

P.M.2B.
Second Schedule

Name of Ship S/S " ANTILLES "

Date of Arrival 8th May 1955

Owner or Agent S. MASKELL CO Ltd

Whence Arrived

NAMES AND DESCRIPTIONS OF BRITISH COMMONWEALTH AND IRISH REPUBLICAN PASSENGERS LANDED AT THE PORT OF

Figure 23   *Passenger list for SS* Antilles, *arrived Plymouth, 8 May 1955*
(BT 26/1332/56)

Not all people travelled directly from the Caribbean to the UK. Information received by the Ministry of Labour from the Colonial Office relating to West Indians arriving in 1955 (LAB 8/1902 online at Moving Here) shows that many arrived by train at London Victoria, via Calais and Dover, after disembarking from their ships at Continental ports such as Marseilles, Genoa and Vigo. The National Archives does not hold these passenger lists, although they may survive in the country of arrival. There are no records of passengers who travelled by aeroplane.

West Indian communities and individuals can be found in the decennial censuses for Scotland and for England and Wales 1841–1911. Irish returns are less complete: none survive for 1861–91; the returns are incomplete for 1821–51; they are complete for 1901 and 1911. Census returns are arranged by address and provide such information as the names of people at the address, with their relationship to the head of household, age, gender, marital status, occupation and where born; for Caribbean-born people this will usually say 'West Indies, BS' (for British Subject) but may give country or village, parish or town. Most of the censuses for 1841–1911 are online and all allow you to search for people; not all of them, however, allow you to search only by country of birth to help identify communities. The transcription data for the censuses of England and Wales and other population datasets is being made available at the Economic and Social Research Council Data Archive at Essex University (www.data-archives.ac.uk) to enable advance searching.

Other examples include the records of the Committee for the Relief of Poor Blacks 1786–1787, whose aim was to set up a free colony in Africa for freed slaves. In return for relief poor blacks (many of whom were runaway servants and slaves or discharged seamen and soldiers) signed up to be sent to Sierra Leone. The proceedings and other papers of the Committee, including lists of those receiving relief and the intended settlers, are among papers in T 1/631–638 and 641–647.

During the First World War thousands of West Indians joined the British army and worked in munitions factories or as merchant seamen; many remained in Britain. As a result of this settlement, in 1919 there were a number of racial riots in the major seaports, especially Liverpool, Cardiff, Hull, Glasgow and South Shields. Many black and coloured seamen were offered free passage back to West Africa and the West Indies but few took this up. CO 318/351 contains a list of 83 repatriated seamen on SS *Santille* and HO 45/11017/377969 contains the names of 285 coloured West Africans and West Indians in Liverpool, of whom 59 were repatriated.

Other reports and correspondence about the riots can be found in CO 318/349, CO 318/352, CO 323/814 and CO 323/848.

Following the 1919 and other racial riots the government tried to restrict coloured seamen from settling in the UK. The Special Restriction (Coloured Alien Seamen) Order 1925 allowed coloured British seamen discharged in the UK who could not prove their nationality to be treated as aliens who would have to register with the local police force. The National Archives does not hold these aliens' registers but they may survive in local archive services.

Following the outbreak of the Second World War many West Indians were again recruited for war service in the United Kingdom and many stayed after the war. Twelve hundred British Hondurans were recruited to fell timber in Scotland and about 500 remained. Ten thousand West Indians, in particular Jamaicans, were recruited as ground crew in the Royal Air Force, and about 2,000 remained. Many who served in the merchant navy also remained. After the war many of those who served in the RAF used their gratuities to pay for passages back to Britain (see Chapter 6 for records of service personnel and merchant seamen).

However, it was from 1948 with the arrival of the *Empire Windrush* on 21 June 1948 (the passenger list is in BT 26/1237/91, online on www.ancestry.co.uk and Moving Here), and especially after 1952 following the McCarran-Walter Act, which limited the numbers of Caribbean migrants allowed into the United States, that significant numbers of West Indians migrated to the UK. During the 1960s British Rail, London Transport, hospital boards and the British Hotels and Restaurants Association recruited many West Indians. These schemes appear to have been conducted in the West Indies and there are few records in the National Archives.

The 1962 Commonwealth Immigrants Act restricted free migration to the UK from colonies and the Commonwealth except for students, visitors and dependants. People who did not have a passport issued in the UK or were not registered as Citizens of the UK and Colonies had to obtain labour vouchers from the Ministry of Labour in order to be granted entry. There were three categories of vouchers: 'A' for those with a definite offer of a job and 'B' for those who held certain professional qualifications or skills; 'C' was a general category of vouchers issued in order of application, with priority given to those with war service. A selection of vouchers issued to Commonwealth subjects including rejected, returned or unused vouchers are in LAB 42, 1962–1972 and continue, together with foreign applications, in LAB 48, 1973–1975. The 1962 Act also allowed, for the first time, for Commonwealth subjects to be deported, for example HO 372/29, 1962–1963, contains recommendations for deportation, and HO 344/73, 1962–1963, contains cases of deportation.

Some provisions and restrictions of the 1962 Commonwealth Immigrants Act were amended under the 1968 Commonwealth Immigrants Act which gave right of entry to people with a parent or grandparent who had been born in the UK. This act effectively excluded most black and coloured West Indians since they were unlikely to fulfil this condition. This was developed further under the 1971 Nationality Act, which reduced the status of Commonwealth citizens to that of aliens unless at least one parent or grandparent was a citizen of the UK and colonies through birth, naturalisation or registration. Correspondence between governors and the Colonial Office on the subject of citizenship status for newly independent West Indian countries seems to imply that only legitimate children had right of citizenship since this right was through the father. Guidance and information leaflets on nationality acts and immigration can be obtained from the UK Border Agency (www.ukba.homeoffice.gov.uk).

Under the 1948 Nationality Act, people from the self-governing Commonwealth, for example, Canada and India, could register as Citizens of the UK and Colonies. This was extended under the 1962 Commonwealth Immigrants Act to include the colonies. Duplicate certificates of registration as Citizens of the UK and Colonies, 1948–October 1986, are in HO 334. The information includes: name, name at birth if different, address, date and place of birth, marital status, father's name and date and place of birth, and whether he was still alive. Certificates from 1980 are much briefer and include only name, name at birth if different, address and place and date of birth. Certificates of registration are organised by registration number with about 250 certificates in each volume. To use these you need to know the registration number. You can obtain the registration number by writing to the National Archives providing: full name at registration, name at birth if different, date and town and country of birth and date and location of registration. Certificates after October 1986 are held by the UK Border Agency (see Useful addresses).

Many papers reflecting the concerns of Parliament and government departments about immigration in general and coloured immigration in particular are to be found among the records of the Cabinet Office, the Home Office, the Colonial Office, the Commonwealth Relations Office, the Foreign and Commonwealth Office and the Ministry of Labour.

BRITISH NATIONALITY ACT 1948

CONFIRMATION OF REGISTRATION AS A

CITIZEN OF THE UNITED KINGDOM AND COLONIES

174547

Jamaica

This certificate confirms that the person named below, being a British subject or Commonwealth citizen or a citizen of the Republic of Ireland, has been registered as a citizen of the United Kingdom and Colonies under section 6 (1) of the British Nationality Act 1948 as amended by section 12 (2) of the Commonwealth Immigrants Act 1962.

NOTES (1) This certificate is valid only if it bears the embossed stamp of the Home Office.

(2) The personal details are those supplied by the person himself and this document does not certify their accuracy. They are, however, important for the purpose of identification and any unauthorised alterations may render this certificate invalid.

Full name	EVA JULIET BOROUGH
Name at birth if different from above	

Full address	Usual signature of applicant
11, BRAESIDE. PUTNOE, BEDFORD. BEDS.	*E Borough*

Place and country of birth KINGSTON, JAMAICA. W.I.

Date of birth 12th SEPTEMBER, 1908.

Whether single; married; a widower, a widow; divorced (State which) SINGLE.

Details of applicant's father, and of applicant's wife or husband

	Full name	Place of birth	Country of birth	Date of birth	If dead, date of death
Applicant's Father	KENNETH EUGENE BOROUGH.	KINGSTON	JAMAICA W.I.	25th SEPT 1871	12th AUG 1959.
Applicant's Wife or husband					

Issued by K. CULLUM

Date - 2 SEP 1971

by direction of the Secretary of State

HOME OFFICE, LONDON.

Ref. No. B.240177

Figure 24 *Certificate of registration for Eva Juliet Borough, born in Jamaica in 1908, certificate number R1/174547, issued on 2 September 1971 (HO 334/1817)*

Many UK archive and library services are identifying material for the study of minority communities in their localities including black and Caribbean history and some information can be found via the Access to Archives database at www.nationalarchives.gov.uk/a2a. For example, the National Archives hosts two online exhibitions relating to Caribbean immigration: Moving Here, www.movinghere.org.uk and The Black Presence: The History of Black and Asian Peoples in Britain, 1550–1850, www.nationalarchives.gov.uk/pathways/blackhistory/.

9.1.1 Further reading

Bevan, *Tracing Your Ancestors in the National Archives: The Website and Beyond*, Chapter 19

Byron, *Post-war Migration from the Caribbean to Britain: The Unfinished Cycle*

Carberry and Thompson, *A West Indian in England*. Draft copies are in CO 875/59/1

Chater, *Untold Histories: Black People in England and Wales during the Period of the British Slave Trade, c1660–1807*

Chessum, *From Immigrants to Ethnic Minority: Making Black Community in Britain*

Dabydeen, Gilmore, and Jones, *The Oxford Companion to Black British History*

Diamond and Clarke, 'Demographic patterns among Britain's ethnic groups'

File and Power, *Black Settlers in Britain 1555–1958*

Foner, *Jamaica Farewell: Jamaican Migrants in London*

Francis, *With Hope in Their Eyes*

Fryer, *The Politics of Windrush*

Fryer, *Staying Power: The History of Black People in Britain*

Gerzina, *Black London: life before emancipation*

Grannum, 'Caribbean Connections'

Habib, *Black lives in the English archives 1500–1677*

Hoskins, *Black People in Britain 1650–1850*

Kamauesi and Smith, *When will I see you again? Experiences of migration and separation in childhood from the Caribbean to Britain*

Kershaw, *Migration Records: A Guide for Family Historians*

Layton-Henry, *The Politics of Immigration: Immigration, Race and Race Relations in Post-war Britain*

Martin, *Incomparable World*. (Novel of 1790s Black London)

Okokon, *Black Londoners, 1880–1990*

Panayi, *Racial Violence in Britain, 1840–1950*

C. Phillips, *The Final Passage*. (Novel about 1950s migration)

M. Phillips and T. Phillips, *Windrush. The Irresistible Rise of Multi-racial Britain*

Selvon, *The Lonely Londoners*. (Novel of West Indians in 1950s London)

Sewell, *Keep on Moving: The Windrush Legacy*

Shyllon, *Black People in Britain 1555–1833*

David Steel, *No Entry: The Background and Implications of the Commonwealth Migrants Act 1968*

Walvin, *Black and White: The Negro and English Society 1555–1945*

Walvin, *Passage to Britain*

Western, *A Passage to England: Barbadian Londoners Speak of Home*

http://news.bbc.co.uk/1/shared/spl/hi/uk/05/born_abroad/countries/html/caribbean.stm – some statistics about Caribbean migrants in the UK.

9.2 West Indian migration outside the United Kingdom

West Indians have not only migrated to Britain but to other British colonies and Commonwealth countries, as well as to foreign countries, especially in the Caribbean and throughout the Americas. Before the nineteenth century merchants and adventurers moved with their servants and slaves to new British colonies, for example, people from St Christopher moved to Nevis and the other Leeward Islands as they became British during the seventeenth and eighteenth centuries and Barbadians settled in South Carolina and Jamaica in the seventeenth century.

From 1834, with the abolition of slavery, there were much larger movements of people who migrated for land and work to Trinidad and British Guiana, especially from the more populated countries such as Barbados and Jamaica. British West Indians also left their countries to work in non-British countries in the Caribbean and in Central and South America such as Costa Rica, Nicaragua, Cuba, the Netherlands Antilles, the Dominican Republic, and especially Panama. In the 1850s many West Indians, mainly from Barbados and Jamaica, worked on the trans-isthmian railway in Panama; between 1880 and 1914 more than 100,000 left to work on the Panama Canal. However, the United States and Canada saw the greater number of West Indian migrants, who arrived for education, work and to settle.

5. **Ann Lynch** Born at St Almo Hill, Black River District, about 60 years ago. Father was Thomas Lynch and mother, Johanna Chambers, same address; christened at St Mary's Church; came to Panama about forty years ago.
Mental diagnosis: Psychosis associated with arterio sclerosis. Is feeble and requires Hospital treatment.

6. **Catherine Tucker:** Born in Bellfield District St Mary's, christened about 1860 at the Baptist Church, Annotto Bay by Rev. Byron. Married Ebenezer Watts, at the Baptist Church, same place, in 1893. Sisters, Eugenia Campbell, Marcella Palmer, albertha and Beatrice Tucker who were living at Annotto Bay. Came to Panama in April, 1907. Police permit was signed by Inspector Dunham, Sutton St. Station, Kingston.
Diagnosis: Dementia precox - demented, requires Hospital treatment.

7. **Alice Martin:** Born about April, 1895' at Port Antonio (Wayne Road District); father, Samuel Niemeyer Martin, Fellowship P.O., Port Antonio; mother, Eliza Knowland, christened at Baptist Church, Port Antonio; worked for Mrs Millie Abram and Mrs Euginia Scott, Sentry Hill, Port Antonio. Arrived at Bocas del Toro in April 1912. Her husband, Bert. Wright is domiciled at Bocas del Toro.
Diagnosis: constitutional inferiority-may be tried outside the Asylum with proper care.

8. **Henrietta Roden:** (Alias Henrietta O'Neal), born December 1880 at Port Royal Mountain, Dallas Castle, Queen's Hill; father, Robert O'Neal; mother Letitia O'Neal; christened at the Wesleyan Church in Stupport district, St Andrews; married May 10, 1894 to Alexander Roden at the Registrars Office, Kingston; worked for Sargent Kildier at Foster Lane and Barry St.. Arrived in Colon 7th July, 1906. Permit was signed by sar geant Kildier of Sutton St. Station.
Diagnosis: Dementia precox - has lucid intervals. Is pugnacious at times; may be tried outside the Asylum in quiet surroundings.

Figure 25 *Panama: list of British West Indians in the Lunatic Asylum, Canal Zone, Panama, 1918 (CO 318/346, Foreign Office, 25 April 1918)*

Information relating to immigration, recruitment schemes, deportations, welfare, relief, distressed British subjects, West Indian relations, overseas births, marriages and deaths of British subjects, criminal activities, and working conditions is to be found among the records of the Colonial Office, Dominions Office, Commonwealth Relations Office, Commonwealth Office and Foreign Office (before 1967) and the Foreign and Commonwealth Office (from 1967). The International Labour Division and Overseas Department of the Ministry of Labour, 1923–1979 (LAB 13) contains reports from labour attachés on recruitment schemes and employment conditions. The *Labour Gazette* contains advertisements and articles about overseas work, and the National Archives holds copies between 1893 and 1952 in ZPER 45. However, most surviving records relating to individual immigrants will be found in the country of settlement.

The records of the Colonial Office are described in Chapter 2 and information can be found in the original correspondence series for the countries of departure and settlement. Information is also found in the records of the West Indian department (CO 318 and CO 1031), the General department (CO 323 and CO 1032) and the West Indies Development and Welfare Organisation files (CO 1042).

The Dominions Office and Commonwealth Relations Office contain information relating to the self-governing Commonwealth countries such as Canada, Newfoundland, Australia and New Zealand, and West Indian countries which became independent before 1967. The most important series are:

DO 35   Original correspondences 1926–1971

DO 175   General Department and successors: Registered Files, Migration (MIG Series), 1954–1967

DO 200   West Indies Department and Atlantic Department, Registered Files, Commonwealth West Indies (WID Series): 1961–1967

For collections relating to non-Caribbean Commonwealth countries search the Catalogue or see Banton, *Administering the Empire* (see Bibliography).

9.2.1 Records of the Foreign Office

Records relating to West Indian migration and settlement in non-British countries can be found in Foreign Office (FO) series. There are three types of archives: general correspondence, embassy and consular archives, and consular archives.

General correspondence

These papers were created and accumulated in the Foreign Office and are composed of original correspondence and reports from British officials abroad, and drafts of outgoing correspondence. Until 1906 these are arranged by country (FO 1 to FO 84). From 1906 Foreign Office general correspondence is filed in subject series. The most important series is FO 371, Foreign Office political departments. Other series include FO 369, consular departments, which contains references to the protection and welfare of British subjects abroad such as the disposal of estates and wills, and FO 372, treaty departments, which includes papers on naturalisation, extradition and passports.

These records can be accessed by a series of indexes and registers. Before 1906 you need to use FO 605 and FO 566. There is a card index for the period 1906 to 1919 and a printed index (FO 409) for the periods 1920 to 1953, and 1959; later indexes are with the Foreign and Commonwealth Office. Kraus International Publications has published the indexes for the period 1920 to 1951 in 131 volumes (1969–82). With the exception of FO 605, which was compiled by the Foreign Office from the records, these indexes have been compiled from the Foreign Office's registers of incoming correspondence and not all records described in them have survived.

Embassy and consular archives

These papers were created by the British embassies. They contain original correspondence received from the Foreign Office, local correspondence from other embassies and consulates, and with the government of the relevant foreign state. These records include wills, naturalisations, passport registers and papers of the disposal of estates. For example, FO 986 embassy and consular archives for Panama City includes many records on the estates of British West Indians, many of who are named in the catalogue.

Consular archives

These are mainly registers held by the consul, such as registers of births, marriages and deaths of British subjects under the Consular Marriages Act 1848 (see section **9.2.3**) and passport registers.

The Foreign Office and Commonwealth Office merged in October 1967 and the records of the Foreign and Commonwealth Office are in FCO series. These are arranged by broad geographical regions and subject series. For example, most records relating to West Indian migration are in FCO 50, Migration and Visa Department and predecessor: Registered Files, 1967–1971. Before 1782 the records of foreign affairs are in State Papers Foreign (SP) series.

9.2.2 Immigration records

Until the First World War most people did not need passports to emigrate or immigrate, although from the 1880s West Indians needed passports or national identity cards to enter Venezuela. Passport applications or registers may survive in the relevant archive or may still be with the issuing department. However, some registers of passports issued by British embassies and consuls survive in Foreign Office consular archives series.

The National Archives does not hold passenger lists for ships which did not land in the UK. Outward passenger lists may survive in the emigrant's country and inward passenger lists may survive in the country of settlement. For example, passenger lists to the US from 1820 are held by the National Archives and Records Administration (see Useful addresses and online at www.ancestry.com). Between 1892 and 1924 some 22 million passengers and ships' crews came through Ellis Island and the Port of New York; the index to the passenger lists with images of most lists is available online at www.ellisislandrecords.org. Passenger lists to Canada between 1865 and 1935 are held by the National Archives of Canada (see Useful addresses and online at www.ancestry.ca).

9.2.3 Registers of births, marriages and deaths

A Foreign Office circular to embassies and consuls dated 1 May 1816 (FO 83/116, fo 16) instructed them to 'keep an authentic and complete record of marriages celebrated in His Majesties [sic] residences and Foreign Courts'. The returns, which also included births and deaths, were to be sent to the London Registry of the Bishop of London. This registry, known as 'International Memoranda' is at the London Metropolitan Archive (see Useful addresses).

From 1849, under the Consular Marriages Act 1849, consular staff were to register marriages of British subjects in two duplicate registers. One register was sent to the General Register Office (GRO, indexes online). If nationality is recorded the GRO forwards copies to the appropriate register office in Scotland and Northern Ireland; but the GRO has advised me that they do not forward West Indian registrations to the appropriate register officers. The second register was sometimes sent to the Foreign Office and many have been transferred to the National Archives in embassy, legation and consular archive series.

In November 1849 the Foreign Office issued instructions to the consuls to register births and deaths; this instruction was extended to legations in 1859. The legations and consuls were to keep one register for recording births and deaths and to submit annually certified copies of entries to the GRO. When complete, the register was forwarded to the Foreign Office and may have been transferred to the National Archives.

The National Archives also holds miscellaneous non-statutory foreign returns of births, marriages and deaths for 1627 to 1969 in RG 32–RG 35 (online at TheGenealogist); these are indexed in RG 43. These registers were originally held by the GRO and comprise correspondence relating to events, certificates issued by foreign governments and churches, copies of entries in registers kept by British embassies, incumbents of English churches and chaplains, and documents sent by individuals for safe keeping.

Lists of the countries covered by the 'International Memoranda', Foreign Office registers and non-statutory registers are in the Guildhall Library's *The British Overseas* (see Bibliography) and records in the National Archives are covered in section **8.9** of *Tracing Your Ancestors*.

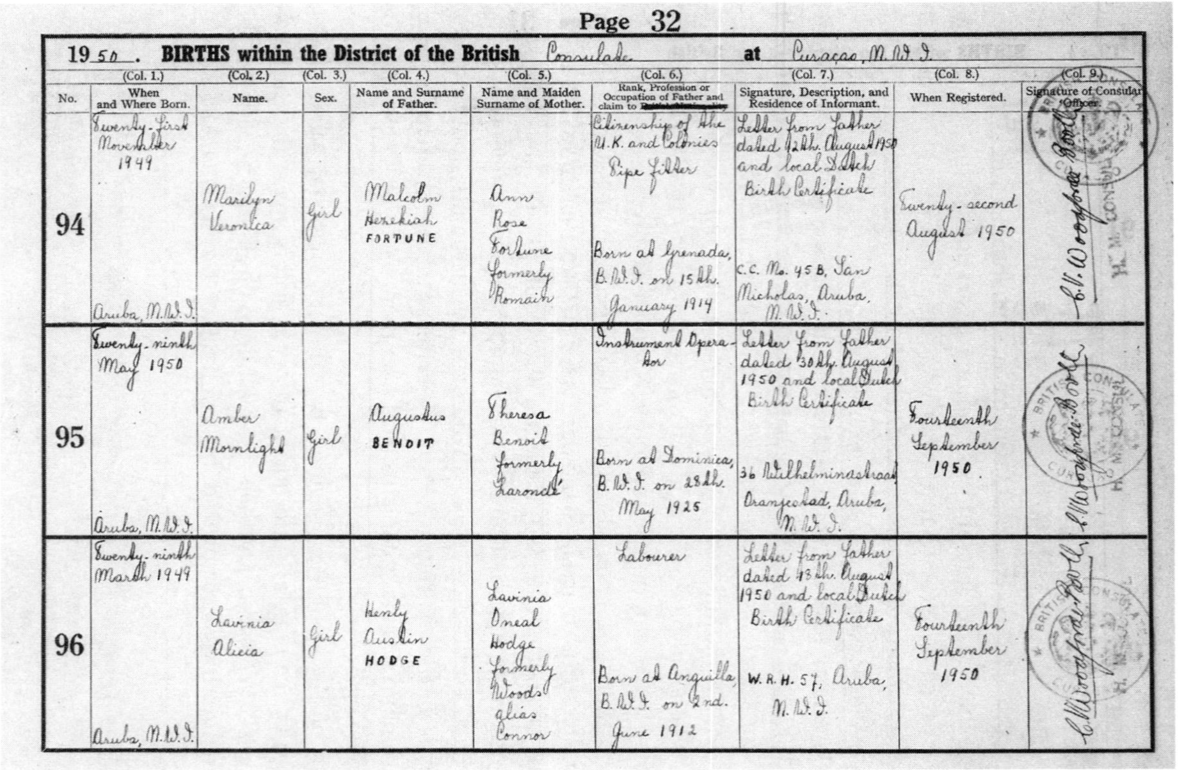

Figure 26 Curaçao: return of births registered at the British Consul, 1950 (FO 907/5, p.32)

9.2.4 Further reading

Anderson, *Caribbean Immigrants: A Socio-demographic Profile*

Atherton, *'Never complain, never explain'. Records of the Foreign Office and State Paper Office, 1500–c1960*

Bevan, *Tracing Your Ancestors in the National Archives: The Website and Beyond*, Chapters 8 and 17

Chamberlain, *Narratives of Exile and Return*

Chamberlain, *Caribbean Migration*

Filby and Meyer, *Passenger and Immigration Lists Index*

Foner, *Islands in the City: West Indian Immigration to New York*

Foner, *New Immigrants in New York*

Gmelch, *Double Passage: The Lives of Caribbean Migrants Abroad and Back Home*

Harney, *Nationalism and Identity: Culture and Imagination in a Caribbean Diaspora*

Kershaw, *Migration Records: A Guide for Family Historians*

Roper, *The Records of the Foreign Office, 1782–1969*

Vickerman, *Crosscurrents: West Indian Immigrants and Race*

Waters, Black Identities: *West Indian Immigrant Dreams and American Realities*

Watkins-Owen, *Blood Relations: Caribbean Immigrants and the Harlem Community*

CHAPTER 10
BRITISH
WEST INDIES
RESOURCES

This chapter describes the primary series at the National Archives for the study of the West Indies and West Indians. Until 1967 most of the records are in the records of the Colonial Office and you will need to refer to Chapter 2 for descriptions of the different series. As countries became independent, diplomatic relations with Britain and matters of British nationality and citizenship were handled by the Commonwealth Office (DO series). After 1967 records are in Foreign and Commonwealth Office series (FCO series, see section **9.2.1**).

Many of the countries were captured and ceded to Britain during the eighteenth and nineteenth centuries and records relating to earlier administrations may survive in the archives of the relevant European power. However, some records, especially those relating to military activities and occupation during the period before the countries became colonies, are in the records of the War Office (WO series). The primary means of reference into these series is through *Public Record Office Lists and Indexes, Volume LIII* (see Bibliography).

Under each country I have included examples of references to baptisms, marriages and burials, nominal censuses (which name at least the head of household), land grants, and other miscellaneous records. These records are not comprehensive but are intended to give an idea of the range and value of records available to researchers in the National Archives. I have also included the more useful records of the London slave registry (see section **7.1**) and the Slave Compensation Commission (see section **7.2**) for family historians. The lists of references are incomplete and other miscellaneous returns and papers, commissioners' hearing notes and assistant commissioners' proceedings, which may contain useful information, are also found in T 71.

I have also provided addresses of country archive and register offices and other useful addresses, published guides to locally held archives and further reading. Unfortunately, there are very few modern published guides to West Indian archives and many of the records described in the guides were not at the time located in the archive or register office. It is possible that many of these records may have since been transferred to these repositories and it is also likely that other genealogical records have come to light. Unfortunately, it is also possible that some no longer survive. Many records have been microfilmed by the Church of Jesus Christ of Latter-day Saints (see section **1.6**) and can be ordered through their Family History Centres. I have included some general books on the history of the West Indies and individual countries. Many other books can be found through online public and university library catalogues, and bookshops.

10.1 British West Indies, general
10.1.1 Colonies general

Colonial papers	1574–1757	CO 1
Original correspondence	1689–1952	CO 323
	1950–1960	CO 1032
Registers of correspondence	1852–1952	CO 378
Registers of out-letters	1871–1925	CO 379
General registers	1623–1849	CO 326
Indexes to correspondence	1795–1874	CO 714

10.1.2 West Indies

Original correspondence	1624–1951	CO 318
	1948–1966	CO 1031
Entry books	1699–1872	CO 319
Registers of out-letters	1872–1926	CO 509
Registers of correspondence	1849–1951	CO 375
Miscellanea	1820–1840	CO 320

There are other series relating to the West Indies.

10.1.3 Colonial Office

West Indies: United States Bases: Original correspondence	1941–1951	CO 971
West Indies: United States Bases: Registers of correspondence	1940–1951	CO 972
West India Royal Commission	1938–1939	CO 950
West Indies Development and Welfare Organisation	1938–1958	CO 1042

10.1.4 Commonwealth Relations Office and Commonwealth Office

Nationality and Consular Department and predecessors: Registered files, Commonwealth nationality (NAT Series)	1952–1967	DO 176
West Indies Department and Atlantic Department: Registered files, Commonwealth West Indies (WID Series)	1961–1967	DO 200

10.1.5 Foreign and Commonwealth Office

American and Latin American Departments: Registered files (A and AL Series)	1967–1979	FCO 7
Atlantic Department: Registered files (G Series)	1966–1968	FCO 23
West Indian Department 'A' and Associated States Department: Registered files, Antigua, Dominica, Grenada, St Kitts-Nevis-Anguilla, St Lucia and St Vincent (WA Series)	1967–1968	FCO 43
West Indian Department 'B' and Foreign and Commonwealth Office, West Indian Department: Registered files, Smaller Commonwealth West Indian Territories (WB and HW Series)	1967–1979	FCO 44
Hong Kong and West Indian Department 'C' and Hong Kong Department: Registered files, Hong Kong, British Honduras, British Indian Ocean Territories and the Seychelles (HW and HK Series)	1967–1979	FCO 40
North American and Caribbean Department and Caribbean Department: Registered files (AN Series)	1968–1977	FCO 63
Foreign and Commonwealth Office: Mexico and Caribbean Department: Registered files (AC file series)	1977–1979	FCO 99

10.1.6 Further reading

Banton, *Administering the Empire, 1801–1968: A Guide to the Records of the Colonial Office in the National Archives of the UK*

Camp, 'Some West Indian sources in England'

Caribbean Historical and Genealogical Journal

Dunn, *Sugar and Slaves: The Rise of the Planter Class in the English West Indies, 1624–1713*

Dyde, *The Caribbean Companion*

Edwards, *The History of the British West Indies*. 5th edn

Greenwood, Hamber and Dyde, *Caribbean Certificate History Book 1*

Greenwood, Hamber and Dyde, *Caribbean Certificate History Book 2*

Greenwood, Hamber and Dyde, *Caribbean Certificate History Book 3*

Gropp, *Guide to Libraries and Archives in Central America and the West Indies, Panama, Bermuda and British Guiana*

Ingram, *Manuscripts Relating to Commonwealth Caribbean Countries in the United States and Canadian Repositories*

Ingram, *Manuscript Sources for the History of the West Indies*

Lawrence-Archer, *Monumental Inscriptions*

Lucas, *Historical Geography of the British Colonies: Volume 2: The West Indies*

Oliver, *Monumental Inscriptions of the British West Indies*

Oliver (ed.), *Caribbeana*

Royal Commission on Public Records, 'Memorandum on official records in the West Indies', pp.115–120

Titford, *My Ancestor Settled in the British West Indies (with Bermuda, British Guiana and British Honduras: A Guide to Sources for Family Historians*

Tyson, *A Guide to Manuscript Sources in United States and West Indian Depositories Relating to the British West Indies During the Era of the American Revolution*

Walne, *A Guide to Manuscript Sources for the History of Latin America and the Caribbean in the British Isles*

www.nationalarchives.gov.uk/caribbeanhistory – The National Archives Caribbean heritage project

www.carbica.org – CARBICA: Caribbean Regional Branch of the International Council on Archives

www.candoo.com/genresources – Jim Lynch's Caribbean genealogical resources

www.cyndislist.com/hispanic.htm – Cyndi Howell's gateway to Caribbean and Hispanic genealogical resources

www.rootsweb.ancestry.com/~caribgw/indexe.html – Caribbean
  Genealogical Web Project
www.worldgenweb.org/index.php/northamgenweb – Web Project,
  includes pages for Central American countries
www.worldgenweb.org/~southamericangenweb – South American
  Genealogical Web Project
www.cavehill.uwi.edu/bnccde/info.htm – University of the West Indies:
  links to Caribbean resources
www.tombstones.bb – database of monumental inscriptions and burials
  in the Caribbean, mostly from Barbados and Antigua

10.2 Anguilla

Anguilla was first settled by the British in 1650 and was attached
administratively to St Christopher. Between 1671 and 1816 Anguilla
formed part of the Leeward Islands federation. When the federation
broke up in 1816 Anguilla formed a separate government with Nevis, St
Christopher and the Virgin Islands. In 1833 they were reunited under
one governor-in-chief and in 1871 the Leeward Islands federation was
reconstituted. In 1882 Anguilla joined with St Christopher and Nevis to
form a single presidency. The Leeward Islands was finally dissolved in
1956 and St Christopher-Nevis-Anguilla became a separate colony with
the capital in St Christopher which, between 1958 and 1962, formed part
of the Federation of the West Indies. In 1971 Britain assumed administrative
responsibility for Anguilla and in 1980 Anguilla was formally separated
from St Christopher and Nevis. Anguilla is a British Overseas Territory.

10.2.1 Colonial Office series

See also under Leeward Islands (section **10.16**) and St Christopher (St
Kitts) (section **10.19**); after 1951 see West Indies (section **10.1**)

Original correspondence	1702–1872	CO 239
Acts	1672–1972	CO 240
Sessional papers	1704–1960	CO 241
Government gazettes	1879–1989	CO 242
Miscellanea	1704–1887	CO 243

10.2.2 Nominal censuses

1716   CO 152/11, no 56 (iii). Printed in *Caribbeana*, vol. 3, p.255
1717   CO 152/12, no 67 (iv)

10.2.3 Slave registers and records of the Slave Compensation Commission

Slave registers, 1827–1834	T 71/261–263
Valuers' returns	T 71/743
Register of claims	T 71/879
Claims and certificates, original	T 71/1033

Other records of the registry and Commission may be found under St Christopher (St Kitts)(section **10.19**).

10.2.4 Archives and other useful addresses

Anguilla was a dependency of St Christopher until 1980 and it is probable that most records relating to Anguilla will be in St Christopher (St Kitts) (section **10.19**). Collections which relate solely to Anguilla may have been transferred to Anguilla.

National Archives, Government Headquarters, Church Street, Box 186, Basseterre, St Kitts, tel: (869) 465-2521, www.nationalarchives.gov.kn

Registrar General, PO Box 236, Basseterre, St Kitts, tel: (869) 465-5251

Anguilla Library Service, The Valley, Anguilla, BWI, tel: (264) 497-2441

Registrar of Births, Deaths and Marriages, Judicial Department, The Valley, Anguilla, BWI, tel: (264) 497-2377

Anguilla National Trust, PO Box 1234, The Valley, Anguilla, BWI, www.axanationaltrust.org

Anguilla Archaeological and Historical Society, PO Box 252, The Valley, Anguilla, http://aahsanguilla.com

10.2.5 Guides to the archives

Baker, *A Guide to Records in the Leeward Islands*

Records for Anguilla are listed under St Christopher. In 1982 a fire destroyed many of the records which were housed in the courthouse, Basseterre, St Christopher; these may be the records described by Baker as being in the Archives' Room, Basseterre.

10.2.6 Further reading

Jones, *Annals of Anguilla*

Titford, *My Ancestor Settled in the British West Indies (with Bermuda, British Guiana and British Honduras): A Guide to Sources for Family Historians)*

Westlake, *Under an English Heaven*

10.3 Antigua and Barbuda

Christopher Columbus named the island after the church, Santa Maria de la Antigua in Seville, in 1493. The Spanish attempted to settle the island in 1520 but found it too dry. In 1629 the French also attempted to settle the island, and also failed. Antigua was eventually colonised by the British from St Christopher under Sir Thomas Warner in 1632. It was captured by the French in 1666 but returned to Britain under the Treaty of Breda in 1667. Between 1671 and 1816 it formed part of the Leeward Islands federation and was its centre of government. The federation broke up in 1816 and Antigua formed a separate government with Montserrat until 1871 when the Leeward Islands federation was reformed. The Leeward Islands federation was finally dissolved in 1956 and Antigua became a separate colony which, between 1958 and 1962, formed part of the Federation of the West Indies. Antigua became independent on 1 November 1981.

10.3.1 Colonial Office series

See also Leeward Islands (section **10.16**); after 1951 see West Indies (section **10.1**)

Original correspondence	1702–1872	CO 7
	1689–1951	CO 152
Registers of correspondence	1850–1951	CO 354
Entry books	1816–1872	CO 393
Acts	1668–1967	CO 8
Sessional papers	1704–1966	CO 9
Government gazettes	1872–1965	CO 156
	1967–1989	CO 1049
Miscellanea	1666–1887	CO 10
	1683–1945	CO 157
Registers of out-letters	1872–1926	CO 507

10.3.2 Colonial Office returns of baptisms etc

1726–1727	CO 152/16	Baptisms and burials: St Peter (fos 213–214)
1733–1734	CO 152/21	Baptisms and burials: St Paul (fos 123–124, 127–128), and St Mary (fos 125–126)
1739–1745	CO 152/25	Burials and marriages: St John, 1745 (fos 100–102); baptisms and burials: St George, 1739–1745 (fos 107–110); St Paul's, Falmouth, 1742–1745 (fos 111–112)

10.3.3 Nominal censuses

1677/8	CO 1/42, fos 229–241	Indicates whether English, Irish, Scottish, French or Dutch. Printed in Oliver, *History of Antigua*, vol. 1, p.lviii
1753	CO 152/27, fos 271–303	Printed in Oliver, *History of Antigua*, vol. 1, p. cix

10.3.4 Miscellaneous

1701–1707	CO 152/6, no 64 (iii)	Sundry account of the Royal Africa Company for slaves imported into Antigua, giving name of purchaser with the numbers of men, women, boy and girl slaves and the cost
1821–1825	CO 7/14	Various slave returns including manumissions

10.3.5 Slave registers and records of the Slave Compensation Commission

Slave registers 1817, 1821, 1824, 1828 and 1832	T 71/244–250 (online at www.ancestry.co.uk)
Valuers' returns	T 71/735–738
Register of claims	T 71/877
Index to claims	T 71/923
Claims and certificates, original	T 71/1027–1029
Counterclaims	T 71/1219–1223
Certificates for compensation and lists of awards	T 71/1333–1334
Amended awards	T 71/1382

Parliamentary returns of awards   T 71/1403, at
http://compensations.plantations.bb/

10.3.6 Archives and other useful addresses

The National Archives, Rappaport Centre, Victoria Park, St John's Antigua,
    West Indies, tel: (268) 462-3946, email: archives@candw.ag
The Registrar General's Office, High Court, High Street, St John's Antigua,
    West Indies, tel: (268) 462-3929
Museum of Antigua and Barbuda, Long Street, 2103, St John's, Antigua
    and Barbuda, West Indies
Antigua and Barbuda Public Library, Market Street, St John's, Antigua and
    Barbuda, West Indies, tel: (268) 462-0229, www.antiguapublib.org
Friends of Antigua Public Library, New York Inc – www.foapl.org
Historical Antigua and Barbuda – www.rootsweb.ancestry.com/~atgwgw/
History of Antigua and Barbuda: a digital archive – http://antiguahistory.net

10.3.7 Guides to the archives

Baker, *Guide to Records in the Leeward Islands*. Note that the records of
    Antigua and Leeward Islands in the care of the Public Record Office
    were returned to Antigua in 1990 and are now held in the National
    Archives of Antigua.

Fires and earthquakes have destroyed many historic records. On 2 April
1841 the Customs House was destroyed by fire; on 19 August 1950 a fire
in the federal building destroyed records relating to Antigua and the
Leeward Islands federation; an earthquake destroyed the public library
in 1974; and in 1999 the records held at the prison were destroyed by fire.

10.3.8 Further reading

Dyde, *Antigua and Barbuda: Heart of the Caribbean*
Dyde, *A History of Antigua: The Unsuspecting Isle*
Kincaid, *A Small Place*
Lannigan, *Antigua and the Antiguans*
Oliver, *History of the Island of Antigua*
Titford, *My Ancestor Settled in the British West Indies (with Bermuda, British
    Guiana and British Honduras): A Guide to Sources for Family Historians*

www.tombstones.bb – database of monumental inscriptions and burials
    in Antigua

10.4 Bahamas

British settlements were established on New Providence from 1629 and on Eleuthera from 1646. The Spaniards attacked New Providence on several occasions between 1680 and 1684 and in 1703 a combined force of French and Spanish destroyed the settlement. After this the Bahamas were popular with pirates of all nations until Captain Woodes Rogers finally removed them in 1718. Between 1670 and 1717 the Bahamas were governed by the lords proprietors of Carolina, who encouraged colonisation, including a large number of German palatines. During the American Revolution the Bahamas were taken by Americans and again by the Spanish in 1781 and were retaken by the British in 1783. After the American Revolution, Loyalists fleeing from Georgia and the Carolinas increased the population. On 10 July 1973 the Bahamas achieved independence.

The Turks and Caicos Islands are part of the Bahamas chain of islands and were annexed to the Bahamas in 1799 but were separated in 1848 to become a dependency of Jamaica.

10.4.1 Colonial Office series

After 1951 see under West Indies (section **10.1**).

Original correspondence	1696–1951	CO 23
	1696–1714	CO 5/1257–1301
Registers of correspondence	1850–1951	CO 333
Entry books	1717–1872	CO 24
Acts	1729–1973	CO 25
Sessional papers	1721–1965	CO 26
Government gazettes	1894–1989	CO 564
Miscellanea	1721–1941	CO 27
Registers of out-letters	1872–1926	CO 508

10.4.2 Nominal censuses

1731	CO 23/3, fos 4–10
1734	CO 23/3, fos 129–132

10.4.3 Land records

1734	CO 23/3, fos 180–181	An account of taxes on plots of land in the Town of Nassau
1847	CO 23/125	Return of land grants, 1841–1846

10.4.4 Miscellaneous

1784	CO 23/25, fo 131	Return of 52 loyalist households who arrived in the Bahamas Islands
1833–1834	CO 23/91, fos 228–236	Returns of people in the workhouse on 29 June 1833 and 29 March 1834. Details include: name, when committed, by whom and for what offence
1763–1783	T 77/19	East Florida claims for people residing in the Bahamas

10.4.5 Slave registers and records of the Slave Compensation Commission

Slave registers, 1822, 1825, 1828, 1831, 1834	T 71/456–460 (online at www.ancestry.co.uk)
Valuers' returns	T 71/772–778
Register of claims	T 71/890
Index to claims	T 71/936
Claims and certificates, original	T 71/1063
Counterclaims	T 71/1262
Certificates for compensation and lists of awards	T 71/1350
Amended awards	T 71/1393
Parliamentary returns of awards	T 71/1414

10.4.6 Archives and other useful addresses

Department of Archives, PO Box SS-6341, Nassau, Bahamas, tel: (242) 393-2175, email: archives@batelnet.bs, www.bahamasnationalarchives.bs

Registrar General's Office, PO Box N532, Nassau, Bahamas, tel: (242) 322-3316

Bahamas Historical Society, PO Box SS-6833, Nassau, Bahamas, http://bahamashistoricalsociety.com

Bahamas Genealogical Web Project – www.rootsweb.ancestry.com/~bhswgw/

10.4.7 Guides to the archives

Public Record Office, *Supplement to the Guide to the Records of the Commonwealth of the Bahamas*

Saunders and Carson, *A Guide to the Records of the Bahamas*

10.4.8 Further reading

British Museum, *List of Documents Relating to the Bahama Islands in the British Museum and Record Office*

Cash, Gordon and Saunders, *Sources for Bahamian History*

Craton, *A History of the Bahamas*

Craton and Saunders, *Islanders in the Stream: A History of the Bahamian People*

Georgia State University bibliography of Bahamian genealogy – www2.gsu.edu/~libpjr/bahgen.htm

Johnson and Hallett (eds), *Early Colonists of the Bahamas: A Selection of Records*

Malcolm, *Historical Documents Relating to the Bahama Islands*

Titford, *My Ancestor Settled in the British West Indies (with Bermuda, British Guiana and British Honduras): A Guide to Sources for Family Historians*

Whittleton, 'Family history in the Bahamas'

10.5 Barbados

Discovered by the Spaniards in 1519 but never settled. The British annexed the island in 1625 and settled in 1627. Many criminals and rebels were transported to Barbados including rebels from Monmouth's Rebellion of 1685 and the Jacobite rebellions of 1715 and 1745. Many people left Barbados to settle other West Indian and American colonies. For example, between 1643 and 1667 12,000 people left Barbados to fight or to settle in Jamaica, Tobago, Trinidad and other islands, Surinam, Carolina, Virginia and New England. Barbados was a member of the Windward Islands group between 1833 and 1885 and the Federation of the West Indies between 1958 and 1962. Barbados became independent on 30 November 1966.

10.5.1 Colonial Office series

Between 1833 and 1885 see also Windward Islands (section **10.25**); after 1951 see West Indies (section **10.1**).

Original correspondence	1689–1951	CO 28
	1874–1885	CO 321
Registers of correspondence	1850–1885	CO 376
	1886–1948	CO 565
Entry books	1627–1872	CO 29
Acts	1643–1966	CO 30

Sessional papers	1660–1965	CO 31
Government gazettes	1867–1975	CO 32
Miscellanea	1678–1947	CO 33
Registers of out-letters	1872–1926	CO 501

10.5.2 Colonial Office returns of baptisms etc

1715–1716 CO 28/15 Baptisms and burials: Christ Church (fos 95–97), St George (fo 102), St John (fo 103), St Andrew (fo 105), St Joseph (fos 107–109), and St Peter (fos 110–114). Printed in Hotten, *Original Lists of People of Quality*

10.5.3 Nominal censuses

1679/80 CO 1/44, no 47 (i–xxii) Printed in Hotten's *Original Lists* and Brandow's *Omitted Chapters from Hotten*

1715 CO 28/16, no 2 Some of the parishes list all white inhabitants with their ages. Printed in Kent's *Barbados and America*; the parishes of St Michael, Christ Church and St George are printed in the *Journal of the Barbados Museum and Historical Society*, vol. IV, p.72

10.5.4 Miscellaneous

1729 CO 28/21, fos 104–109, 165–209 Returns of the Negro Tax, 2/6 levy (some duplication is found in T 1/275, fos 22–44, CO 28/40, fos 37–60, and CO 28/45, fos 107–114)

1832–1835 T 1/4395 (papers 19604/31 and 6198/33) and T 1/4396 (paper 20486/36) Barbados claims following the hurricane of 11 August 1831, money was distributed under the West Indies loans act. Date, name of claimant, parish, return of loss, value and money paid

1821–1825 CO 28/97 Various slave returns including manumissions and a return of paupers and pensioners

1951 CO 32/124 Electoral register

10.5.5 Slave registers and records of the Slave Compensation Commission

Slave registers, 1817, 1820, 1823, 1826, 1829, 1832, 1834	T 71/520–565 (online at www.ancestry.co.uk)
Valuers' returns	T 71/790–803
Register of claims	T 71/895–900
Index to claims	T 71/940
Claims and certificates, original	T 71/1083–1108
Counterclaims	T 71/1280–1287
Certificates for compensation and lists of awards	T 71/1356–1359
Amended awards	T 71/1397
Parliamentary returns of awards	T 71/1418; at http://compensations.plantations.bb/

10.5.6 Archives and other useful addresses

Department of Archives, Lazaretto Building, Black Rock, St Michael, Barbados, tel: (246) 425-1380, email: bda@caribsurf.com

Records Department, Supreme Court of Barbados, Law Courts, Coleridge Street, Bridgetown, Barbados, tel: (246) 426-3461, http://lawcourts.gov.bb/recordbranch.html

Barbados Museum and Historical Society, St Ann's Garrison, St Michael, Barbados, tel: (246) 427-0201, www.barbmuse.org.bb

National Library Service, Public Services Division, Coleridge Street, Bridgetown 2, Barbados, tel: (246) 436-6081, email: natlib@caribsurf.com

Barbados National Trust, Wildey House, Wildey, St Michael, Barbados, http://trust.funbarbados.com/

Bajan Genealogical Web Project – www.rootsweb.ancestry.com/~brbwgw/

10.5.7 Guides to the archives

Chandler, *A Guide to Sources in Barbados*

Handler, *Guide to Source Materials for the Study of Barbados History, 1627–1834*

Handler, *Supplement to a Guide to Source Material for the Study of Barbados History, 1627–1834*

Lane, *Tracing Ancestors in Barbados: A Practical Guide*

Many of the Barbados archives were microfilmed for the University of West Indies.

10.5.8 Further reading

Beckles, *A History of Barbados from Amerindian Settlement to Nation-state*

Brandow, *Genealogies of Barbados Families*

Handler, 'Slave manumissions and freedmen in seventeenth-century Barbados'

Handler, Hughes, Newton, Welch and Wiltshire, *Freedmen of Barbados*

Handler and Jacoby, 'Slave names and naming in Barbados, 1650–1830,' http://jeromehandler.org – digital copies of Handler's articles, many relate to slavery in Barbados

Hoyos, *Barbados: A History from Amerindians to Independence*

Kent, *Barbados and America*

Oliver, *Monumental Inscriptions in Barbados*

Salazar, *Love Child: A Genealogist's Guide to the Social History of Barbados*

Sanders, *Barbados Records* (online at www.ancestry.co.uk)

    Baptisms 1637–1800

    Marriages 1643–1800

    Wills and Administrations 1647–1725

Shilstone, *Monumental Inscriptions in the Burial Ground of the Jewish Synagogue at Bridgetown, Barbados*

Stanford, 'Genealogical sources in Barbados'

Titford, 'Barbados: Some of its parishes, churches and monumental inscriptions'

Titford, *My Ancestor Settled in the British West Indies (with Bermuda, British Guiana and British Honduras): A Guide to Sources for Family Historians)*

www.plantations.bb/manumission/ – database of 377 manumissions granted in Barbados between December 1831 and July 1834

www.plantations.bb/index.php – database of plantation holders and managers in Barbados

www.tombstones.bb – database of monumental inscriptions and burials in Barbados

10.6 Bay Islands

These islands off the coast of Central America were occupied by Britain in 1839 and became a colony under the governorship of Jamaica in 1852. The islands were ceded to the Republic of Honduras in 1859.

10.6.1 Colonial Office series

See also under Jamaica (section **10.15**) and Belize (section **10.7**); after 1859 see under Honduras (section **11.6**).

Original correspondence	1852–1861	CO 34
Registers of correspondence	1852–1854	CO 351
	1854–1861	CO 348
Acts	1852–1859	CO 35
Miscellanea	1855–1859	CO 36

10.7 Belize (formerly British Honduras)

British settlement was first established on the islands off the Mosquito Coast in 1630 and on Honduras in 1638 by adventurers from Jamaica, who logged mahogany and logwood. Although not a British colony at this time, British Honduras was nominally under the superintendence of Jamaica. The Treaty of Paris in 1763 allowed British settlers to continue logging while Spain retained sovereignty. Spain continued to assert sovereignty but did not manage to evict the British settlers and in 1862 British Honduras became a colony under the governorship of Jamaica. In 1884 the colony was separated from Jamaica. Belize became independent on 21 September 1981.

10.7.1 Colonial Office series

See also under Spain (section **11.9**) and Jamaica (section **10.15**) until 1884; after 1951 see West Indies (section **10.1**)

Original correspondence	1744–1951	CO 123
Registers of correspondence	1855–1951	CO 348
Entry books	1630–1872	CO 124
Acts	1855–1977	CO 125
Sessional papers	1848–1965	CO 126
Government gazettes	1861–1975	CO 127
Miscellanea	1807–1943	CO 128
Registers of out-letters	1872–1926	CO 503

10.7.2 Land grants

c1748–1774	WO 55/1815	Names of people who have grants of land in George Town (near Cala Font) Honduras

10.7.3 Slave registers and records of the Slave Compensation Commission

Slave registers, 1834	T 71/251–252 (online at www.ancestry.co.uk)
Valuers' returns	T 71/739
Register of claims	T 71/878
Index to claims	T 71/924
Claims and certificates, original	T 71/1030
Counterclaims	T 71/1223
Certificates for compensation and lists of awards	T 71/1335
Amended awards	T 71/1383
Parliamentary returns of awards	T 71/1404

10.7.4 Archives and other useful addresses

Belize Archives and Records Service, 26/28 Unity Boulevard, Belmopan, Belize, tel: (501) 822-2247, www.belizearchives.gov.bz

Registrar General, Supreme Court, Belize City, Belize, tel: (501) 227-7377

National Library Service, Bliss Institute, PO Box 287, Belize City, Belize

Belize Genealogical Web Project –
    www.worldgenweb.org/index.php/north-america/belize

10.7.5 Guides to the archives

Burdon, *Archives of British Honduras*

Gropp, *Guide to Libraries and Archives in Central America and the West Indies, Panama, Bermuda and British Guiana*

The Spanish attacked British Honduras in 1754 and destroyed every building. In 1918 a fire destroyed the colonial secretary's office and other public buildings and many records were lost following a hurricane and subsequent tidal wave in 1931.

10.7.6 Further reading

Bolland, *The Formation of a Colonial Society: Belize, from Conquest to Crown Colony*

Dobson, *A History of Belize*

Grant, *The Making of Modern Belize: Politics, Society and British Colonialism in Central America*

Humphries, *The Diplomatic History of British Honduras*

Titford, *My Ancestor Settled in the British West Indies (with Bermuda, British Guiana and British Honduras): A Guide to Sources for Family Historians*

10.8 Bermuda

Bermuda, although not in the Caribbean, was considered part of the West Indies by the British government for administrative convenience. It was discovered in 1515 by Juan Bermudes, a Spanish mariner, but the Spanish did not settle on the islands which were uninhabited until 1609 when Admiral Sir George Somers was shipwrecked on one of the reefs. Bermuda also became known as the Somer or Summer Islands. British settlements were established in Bermuda from 1612. Bermuda is a British Overseas Territory.

10.8.1 Colonial Office series

After 1951 see West Indies (section **10.1**)

Original correspondence	1689–1951	CO 37
Registers of correspondence	1850–1951	CO 334
Entry books	1615–1872	CO 38
Acts	1690–1989	CO 39
Sessional papers	1687–1965	CO 40
Government gazettes	1902–1965	CO 647
Miscellanea	1715–1950	CO 41
Registers of out-letters	1872–1925	CO 499

10.8.2 Returns of baptisms and burials

1826–1946	ADM 6/434–436	Baptisms and burials, naval base, Ireland Island; ADM 6/435 includes confirmations, 1849–1900
1903–1918	ADM 6/439	Baptisms, Boaz Garrison
1946–1957	ADM 338/11	Baptisms, Ireland Island

10.8.3 Slave registers and records of the Slave Compensation Commission

Slave registers, 1821, 1827, 1830, 1833–34	T 71/452–455
Valuers' returns	T 71/767–771
Register of claims	T 71/889
Index to claims	T 71/935

Claims and certificates, original	T 71/1059–1062
Counterclaims	T 71/1262
Certificates for compensation and lists of awards	T 71/1349
Amended awards	T 71/1392
Parliamentary returns of awards	T 71/1413

10.8.4 Archives and other useful addresses

Bermuda National Archives, Government Administration Building,
30 Parliament St, Hamilton HM 12, Bermuda, tel: (441) 295-5151

Registry General, Ministry of Labor and Home Affairs, Government
Administration Building, 30 Parliament St, Hamilton, 5–24, Bermuda,
tel: (441) 297-7709, www.registrygeneral.gov.bm

Bermuda Historical Society, c/o Bermuda Library, Par-la-ville Park,
Hamilton, Bermuda

Bermuda National Library, Par-la-Ville, 13 Queen Street, Hamilton HM 11,
Bermuda, www.bnl.bm

The Bermuda National Trust, PO Box HM 61, Hamilton HM AX, Bermuda,
www.bnt.bm

Bermuda Genealogical Web Project –
www.rootsweb.ancestry.com/~bmuwgw/bermuda.htm

Bermuda Online – www.bermuda-online.org

10.8.5 Guides to the archives

Rowe, *A Guide to the Records of Bermuda*

Lefroy, *Memorials of the Discovery and early Settlement of the Bermudas
or Somers Islands 1515–1685*

10.8.6 Further reading

Green, *Monumental Inscriptions of the Royal Naval Cemetery, Ireland
Island, Bermuda*

Hallett, *Bermuda Index, 1784–1914: An Index of Births, Marriages and
Deaths as Recorded in Bermudan Newspapers*

Hallett, *Early Bermuda Wills 1629–1835*

Hallett, *Early Bermudan Records, 1619–1826: A Guide to the Parish and
Clergy Registers with Some Assessment Lists and Petitions*

Mercer, *Bermuda Settlers in the 17th Century: Genealogical Notes from
Bermuda*

Stranack, *The Andrew and the Onions: The Story of the Royal Navy in
Bermuda 1795–1975*

Titford, *My Ancestor Settled in the British West Indies (with Bermuda, British Guiana and British Honduras): A Guide to Sources for Family Historians*

10.9 British Virgin Islands

Tortola was the first of the Virgin Islands to be settled by the Dutch in 1648. The English expelled the Dutch from many of the islands in 1666 and Tortola in 1672, when the islands were included in the Leeward Islands group. When the federation broke up in 1816 the Virgin Islands formed a separate government with Nevis, St Christopher and Anguilla. In 1833 they were reunited under one governor-in-chief and in 1871 the Leeward Islands federation was reconstituted. The islands continued to be administered by the Leeward Islands until 1960 when the Virgin Islands became a separate colony. The British Virgin Islands are a British Overseas Territory.

10.9.1 Colonial Office series

See also Leeward Islands (section **10.16**) and St Christopher (section **10.19**); after 1951 see West Indies (section **10.1**)

Original correspondence	1711–1872	CO 314
	1816–1853	CO 239
	1874–1951	CO 152
Registers of correspondence	1850–1951	CO 354
Acts	1774–1965	CO 315
Sessional papers	1773–1965	CO 316
Miscellanea	1784–1896	CO 317
Registers of out-letters	1872–1926	CO 507

10.9.2 Nominal censuses

1716	CO 152/11, no 6 (vi)	Account of householders for Spanish Town, Beef Island, Tortola and Widdows
1716	CO 152/11, no 45 (iv)	List of households for Spanish Town and Beef Island
1717	CO 152/12/2, no 67 (vi and viii)	List of households for Spanish Town (vi) and Tortola (viii), includes nationality. CO 152/12/2, no 67 (ix) contains a list of men able to bear arms and the number of slaves on Crabb Island

10.9.3 Slave registers and records of the Slave Compensation Commission

Slave registers, 1818, 1822, 1825, 1828, 1831, 1834	T 71/370–375 (online at www.ancestry.co.uk)
Valuers' returns	T 71/753
Register of claims	T 71/883
Index to claims	T 71/929
Claims and certificates, original	T 71/1040
Counterclaims	T 71/1238–1240
Certificates for compensation and lists of awards	T 71/1341
Amended awards	T 71/1388
Parliamentary returns of awards	T 71/1409

10.9.4 Archives and other useful addresses

National Archives and Records Management Unit, Deputy Governor's Office, Government of the Virgin Islands (UK), 33 Admin Drive, Road Town, Tortola, Virgin Islands, tel: (284) 494-3701 www.nationalarchives. gov.vg

Caribbean Studies Unit, Library Services Department, Flemming St, Road Town, Tortola, British Virgin Islands, tel: (284) 494-3428, www.bvilibrary.gov.vg

Civil Registry and Passport Office, Government of the British Virgin Islands, Central Administration Complex, Road Town, Tortola, British Virgin Islands, tel: (284) 494-3701, www.dgo.gov.vg/index.php?mpageid=247

British Virgin Islands Genealogical Project – www.rootsweb.ancestry.com/~bviwgw/

10.9.5 Published guides to the archives

Baker, *A Guide to Records in the Leeward Islands*

10.9.6 Further reading

Dookhan, *A History of the British Virgin Islands*

Jenkins, *Tortola: A Quaker Experiment of Long, Long Ago in the Tropics*

Titford, *My Ancestor Settled in the British West Indies (with Bermuda, British Guiana and British Honduras): A Guide to Sources for Family Historians*

10.10 Cayman Islands

Christopher Columbus first discovered the Cayman Islands in 1503. The Cayman Islands were frequently visited by Spanish, English and French ships for revictualling but it was not until 1670 that they were ceded to Britain by the Treaty of Madrid. In 1734 they were settled by colonists from Jamaica, and justices of the peace were appointed by the Governor of Jamaica to administer the affairs of the islands, which were loosely seen as part of Jamaica. However, it was not until 1863 that the relationship was recognised by an Act of British Parliament and the islands officially became a dependency of Jamaica. In 1957 the Cayman Islands, as a dependency of Jamaica, joined the Federation of the West Indies but this alliance was short-lived. In 1962, when Jamaica became independent, the Cayman Islands decided to remain as a dependent territory of the United Kingdom and this status continues today.

10.10.1 Colonial Office series

See also under Jamaica (section **10.15**) and from 1951 West Indies (section **10.1**).

Acts	1898–1966	CO 650
Sessional papers	1908–1965	CO 857
Government gazettes	1956–1990	CO 1019
Miscellanea	1912–1947	CO 651

10.10.2 Nominal censuses

1802	CO 137/108, fos 265–272	Grand Cayman, 1802, general description of the island, together with list of head of households by location (fos 269–271) broken down into white, free coloureds and free blacks, with numbers in each household and number of slaves

10.10.3 Slave registers and records of the Slave Compensation Commission

Slave registers, 1834	T 71/243 (online at www.ancestry.co.uk, under Jamaica)
Valuers' returns	T 71/734
Register of claims	T 71/875

Claims and certificates, original	T 71/1026
Certificates for compensation and	
lists of awards	T 71/1331

Other records are to be found under Jamaica (section **10.15**).

10.10.4 Archives and other useful addresses

Cayman Islands National Archive, Government Administration Building, Grand Cayman, KY1-9000, Cayman Islands, tel: (345) 949-9809, www.cina.gov.ky

General Registry Cayman Islands, First Floor, Citrus Grove, George Town, Grand Cayman, tel: (345) 946-7922, www.vitals.ky

Cayman Islands Genealogical Web Project – www.iukgenweb.org/index.php/british-overseas-territories/cayman-islands

Many records were destroyed by hurricanes in 1876 and 1932, and by a fire in the Government Administration Building in 1972. Also, many Cayman Island records were lost in transit to Jamaica in the early 1900s.

10.10.5 Further reading

Craton, *Founded Upon the Seas: A History of the Cayman Islands and their People*

Hirst, *Notes on the History of the Cayman Islands*

Titford, *My Ancestor Settled in the British West Indies (with Bermuda, British Guiana and British Honduras): A Guide to Sources for Family Historians*

Williams, *A History of the Cayman Islands*

10.11 Dominica

Dominica was in the possession of Caribs when it was settled by the French in 1632. In 1748 the Treaty of Aix-la-Chapelle made Dominica and the other Windward Islands neutral, to be left in the possession of the Caribs. However, the French still settled on the island. Dominica was captured by Britain in 1761 and ceded to her in 1763. French from Martinique recaptured Dominica in 1778 but it was restored to Britain in 1783. In 1763 Dominica was part of the Windward Islands and became a separate colony in 1771. In 1833 it formed part of the Leeward Islands federation but returned to the Windward Islands in 1940 until 1956, when the Windward Islands federation was dissolved. Between 1958 and 1962

Dominica was a member of the Federation of the West Indies. Dominica became independent on 3 November 1978 under the name of Commonwealth of Dominica.

10.11.1 Colonial Office series

See also under France (section **11.4**), the Leeward Islands (section **10.16**) and the Windward Islands (section **10.25**); after 1951 see West Indies (section **10.1**).

Original correspondence	1730–1872	CO 71
	1872–1940	CO 152
	1940–1951	CO 321
Registers of correspondence	1850–1940	CO 354
	1940–1951	CO 376
Entry books	1770–1872	CO 72
Acts	1768–1965	CO 73
Sessional papers	1767–1965	CO 74
Government gazettes	1865–1975	CO 75
Miscellanea	1763–1940	CO 76
	1888–1939	CO 157
Registers of out-letters	1872–1926	CO 507

10.11.2 Land records

1765–1766	CO 76/9	Dominica and St Vincent: Register of grants of land
1766	CO 101/1, fos 279–281	Docket register of plantation grants in the islands of Dominica, St Vincent and Tobago
1765–1767	CO 101/11, fos 219–222, 413	Docket register of plantation grants
1764–1797	CO 106/9–12	Sale of lands in the Ceded Islands
1766	T 1/453, fos 153–164	An account of lands granted on lease by the Commissioners to the French inhabitants of Dominica
1790–1803	CO 71/2	Includes returns of quit rents

10.11.3 Slave registers and records of the Slave Compensation Commission

Slave registers, 1817, 1820, 1823, 1826, 1829, 1832	T 71/337–363 (registers for 1817–23 online at www.ancestry.co.uk)
Valuers' returns	T 71/748–750
Register of claims	T 71/881
Index to claims	T 71/927
Claims and certificates, original	T 71/1037
Counterclaims	T 71/1233–1235
Certificates for compensation and lists of awards	T 71/1339
Amended awards	T 71/1386
Parliamentary returns of awards	T 71/1407

10.11.4 Archives and other useful addresses

National Documentation Centre, Government Headquarters, Roseau, Commonwealth of Dominica, tel: (767) 448-2401

General Registrar, Bay Front, Roseau, Commonwealth of Dominica, tel: (767) 448-2401

Dominica Genealogical Web Project – www.iukgenweb.org/dominica/

10.11.5 Guides to the archives

Baker, *A Guide to Records in the Windward Islands*

10.11.6 Further reading

Baker, *Centring the Periphery: Chaos, Order and the Ethnohistory of Dominica*

Honychurch, *The Dominica Story: A History of the Island*

Honychurch and Aird, *Dominica: Island of Adventure*

Imperial Department of Agriculture in the West Indies, *Notes on Dominica and Hints to Intending Settlers*. Copy in CO 318/348 (Agriculture, December 1919)

Titford, *My Ancestor Settled in the British West Indies (with Bermuda, British Guiana and British Honduras): A Guide to Sources for Family Historians*

10.12 Federation of the West Indies

The Federation of the West Indies was formed in January 1958 comprising the following territories and their dependencies: Barbados, Jamaica, Antigua, Montserrat, St Christopher-Nevis-Anguilla, Trinidad and Tobago, Grenada, Dominica, St Lucia and St Vincent. The federation was dissolved in 1962 with the loss of Jamaica (with the Cayman Islands and Turks and Caicos Islands) but was reformed in May 1962, although Trinidad and Tobago did not rejoin. The federation was finally abandoned in 1966.

Original correspondence	1958–1966	CO 1031
Government gazettes	1958–1961	DO 136
Acts	1958–1962	DO 139

10.13 Grenada

Grenada was temporarily settled by the British in 1609 but in 1650 the governor of Martinique purchased the island and established a settlement. It was captured by Britain in 1762 and ceded in 1763 under the Windward Islands. Grenada was recaptured by the French in 1779 and restored to the British in 1783. Between 1833 and 1956 Grenada was part of the Windward Islands federation and between 1958 and 1962 a member of the Federation of the West Indies. On 7 February 1974 Grenada became independent.

10.13.1 Colonial Office series

See also under France (section **11.4**) and Windward Islands (section **10.25**); after 1951 see West Indies (section **10.1**).

Original correspondence	1747–1873	CO 101
	1874–1951	CO 321
Registers of correspondence	1850–1951	CO 376
Entry books	1763–1872	CO 102
Acts	1766–1965	CO 103
Sessional papers	1777–1965	CO 104
Government gazettes	1834–1975	CO 105
Miscellanea	1764–1938	CO 106
Registers of out-letters	1872–1882	CO 504
	1883–1926	CO 377

10.13.2 Nominal censuses

| c1767 | CO 101/11, fo 230 | Carriacou: householder, number of English and French overseers, number of slaves, quantity of land, taxes |
| 1772 | CO 101/5, fos 147–151 | List of landholders, the numbers in the household, acreage, negroes, types of crops and mills |

10.13.3 Land grants

| 1762–1764 | CO 101/1, fos 245–246 | A list of sale of town lots in St George |
| 1764–1797 | CO 106/9–12 | Sale of lands in the Ceded Islands |

10.13.4 Miscellaneous lists

| 1763 | CO 101/1, fos 18–31 | Capitation Tax Rolls of people liable to pay tax on slaves |
| 1821–1825 | CO 101/66 | Various slave returns including manumissions |

10.13.5 Slave registers and records of the Slave Compensation Commission

Slave registers, 1817, annual 1819–1834	T71/264–336 (most volumes are online at www.ancestry.co.uk)
Valuers' returns	T 71/744–747
Register of claims	T 71/880
Index to claims	T 71/926
Claims and certificates, original	T 71/1034–1036
Counterclaims	T 71/1228–1232
Certificates for compensation and lists of awards	T 71/1337–1338
Amended awards	T 71/1385
Parliamentary returns of awards	T 71/1406

10.13.6 Archives and other useful addresses

Public Library, 2 Carenage, St George's, Grenada, tel: (473) 440-2506

Registrar General's Office, Ministerial Complex, Botanical Gardens, St George, Grenada, tel: (473) 440-2806

National Museum, Young Street, St George's, Grenada

Grenada Genealogical Web – www.iukgenweb.org/grenada/

10.13.7 Guides to the archives

Baker, *A Guide to Records in the Windward Islands*

No records survive in Grenada before 1764, possibly having been removed by the French or destroyed during their occupations, or in the several conflicts between the French and British. The governor's records were destroyed in a fire at St George's in 1771.

10.13.8 Further reading

Brizan, *Grenada, Island of Conflict: From Amerindians to People's Revolution 1498-1979*

Burgan, *Some West Indian Memorials: Being a Record of the Tablets in St George's Grenada, With Notes*

Devas, *A History of the Island of Grenada, 1498-1796: With Some Notes and Comments on Carriacou and Events of Later Years*

Titford, *My Ancestor Settled in The British West Indies (with Bermuda, British Guiana and British Honduras): A Guide to Sources for Family Historians*

10.14 Guyana (formerly British Guiana)

The Dutch West India Company first settled the territories of Berbice, Essequibo and Demerara in 1580. These Dutch colonies were captured by Britain in 1796 but were restored to the Dutch in 1802. The British recaptured the colonies in 1803 which were formally ceded to Britain in 1814. Gradually, the administration of the three colonies was centralised; the legal and administrative unification of Demerara and Essequibo was effected in 1812. Finally, the colony of British Guiana was created in 1831 when Demerara, Essequibo and Berbice were all combined and their administration conducted from Georgetown. British Guiana became independent on 26 May 1966 under the name Guyana.

10.14.1 Colonial Office series

Before 1803 see the Netherlands (section **11.7**), although part of the records of the Dutch West India Company's administration, 1686-1792, were transferred to Britain in 1819 and are in CO 116; after 1951 see West Indies (section **10.1**).

Original correspondence	before 1814	WO 1
	1781–1951	CO 111
Registers of correspondence	1850–1951	CO 345
Entry books	1797–1872	CO 112
Acts	1837–1965	CO 113
Sessional papers	1805–1965	CO 114
Government gazettes	1838–1975	CO 115
Miscellanea	1681–1943	CO 116
Registers of out-letters	1872–1926	CO 502

10.14.2 Land records

1819	CO 111/28	Lists of Dutch proprietors of plantations in Demerara, Essequibo and Berbice [in Dutch]
1735–1755	CO 116/73, 75, 76	Berbice: grants of land [in Dutch]
1737–1763	CO 116/78	Berbice: mortgages [in Dutch]

10.14.3 Miscellaneous

1811–1818	T 89/1	Records of the Berbice Commission
1764–1793	CO 116/106–117	Berbice: records of the court of policy and criminal justice [in Dutch]
1765–1794	CO 116/128–135	Berbice: taxation returns – poll tax, church tax etc [in Dutch]
1826–1834	CO 116/143–153, 156–163	Reports of protectors of slaves: punishments, criminal cases, births, deaths, marriages, free baptisms and manumissions for:

1. Berbice: CO 116/143–153
2. Demerara and Essequibo: CO 116/156–163

Several of the reports were published in the British Parliamentary Papers: session 1829 (335), vol. XXV.255 (mfm 31.153–155) and session 1830–31 (262) vol. XV.1 (mfm 33.87–95)

10.14.4 Slave registers and records of the Slave Compensation Commission

Slave registers:

Demerara and Essequibo
1817, 1820, 1823, 1826, 1829, 1832   T 71/391–436
Berbice
1818, 1819, 1822, 1825, 1828, 1831, 1834   T 71/437–446 (registers for 1818, 1819 and 1822 online at www.ancestry.co.uk)

Valuers' returns	T 71/757–765
Register of claims	T 71/885–887
Index to claims	T 71/931–933
Claims and certificates, original	T 71/1045–1057
Counterclaims	T 71/1252–1260
Certificates for compensation and lists of awards	T 71/1343–1347
Amended awards	T 71/1390
Parliamentary returns of awards	T 71/1411

10.14.5 Archives and other useful addresses

National Archives of Guyana, Homestretch Avenue, D'Urban Park, Georgetown, Guyana, tel: (592) 226-3852, email: narchivesguyana@yahoo.com, http://mcys.gov.gy/na_about.html

General Register Office, GPO Building, Robb Street, Georgetown, Guyana, tel: (592) 225-7561

National Library, 76/77 Church & Main Streets, Georgetown, Guyana, www.natlib.gov.gy

Guyana Heritage Museum, 17 Kastev, Meten-Meer-Zorg, West Coast, Demerara, Guyana, www.sdnp.org.gy/ghm/

National Trust of Guyana – www.nationaltrust.gov.gy

The Guyana Genealogical Society – www.worldgenweb.org/~guywgw/

Chinese in Guyana project – www.rootsweb.ancestry.com/~guycigtr/

10.14.6 Guides to the archives

Gropp, *Guide to Libraries and Archives in Central America and the West Indies, Panama, Bermuda and British Guiana*

On 23 February 1945 a fire destroyed a substantial part of Georgetown including the library, the natural history museum, the post office and savings bank and a number of other government buildings.

10.14.7 Further reading

Titford, *My Ancestor Settled in the British West Indies (with Bermuda, British Guiana and British Honduras): A Guide to Sources for Family Historians*
Viotti, *Crowns of Glory, Tears of Blood*

10.15 Jamaica

First settled by Spaniards in 1494, Jamaica was captured by Britain in 1655. Among the immigrants Jamaica received were rebels and other criminals from Britain, 1,500 people from Nevis and adjoining islands, Bermudans, New Englanders, Quakers from Barbados and a large number of Jews. Planters were evacuated to Jamaica from Surinam in 1675, and survivors from the ill-fated Scottish colony of Darien settled in 1699. Jamaica became independent on 6 August 1962.

10.15.1 Colonial Office series

Before 1655 see under Spain (section **11.9**); after 1951 see West Indies (section **10.1**).

Original correspondence	1689–1951	CO 137
Registers of correspondence	1850–1951	CO 351
Entry books	1661–1872	CO 138
Acts	1662–1962	CO 139
Sessional papers	1661–1965	CO 140
Government gazettes	1794–1968	CO 141
Miscellanea	1658–1945	CO 142
Registers of out-letters	1872–1926	CO 494

10.15.2 Colonial Office returns of baptisms etc

1821–1825   CO 137/162   March. Returns of slave marriages in Portland, St James, St Catherine, Kingston and Manchester

10.15.3 Nominal censuses

1670   CO 138/1, pp.61–82   Survey of Jamaica, listing under parish owner and then number of acres (printed in Calendar of State Papers, Colonial, America and West Indies, 1669–1674, pp.99–104)

1680   CO 1/45, fos 96–109   Inhabitants of Port Royal and St John's

1753   CO 137/28, fos 171–174   St Andrews' parish. Plantation, landholder, number of acres, types of crops, livestock etc, numbers of slaves

1754   CO 142/31   List of landholders with number of acres, taken from the Quit Rent Books

1831   CO 140/121, pp.353–378   Return of maroons of Moore-town, Charlestown, Scot's Hall and Accompong. The information includes name and age and some entries give colour and comments (such as son of...), and a return of slaves belonging to the maroons

10.15.4 Land grants

1734–1753   CO 137/28,   Return of setters and lands granted
             fos 175–180, 197–223   to new settlers under several acts to encourage emigration of white settlers

1805–1824   CO 137/162, Jan   Return of land grants

10.15.5 Miscellaneous documents

1675	CO 1/35, fos 178–185	A list of His Majesty's subjects and slaves transported in HM hired ship *Hercules* from Surinam to Jamaica
1740–1751	CO 324/55	Foreign Protestants naturalised in American colonies, including Jamaica. Printed in Giuseppi, *Naturalization of Foreign Protestants*
1802	WO 1/352	Return of Nova Scotians and maroons in Sierra Leone. The maroons had been transported from Jamaica to Nova Scotia in 1796 following the Maroon War; in 1800 they migrated to Sierra Leone
c1800–1817	CO 137/144, fos 156–225	Correspondence and returns on the number of slaves baptised into the Church of England, including nominal returns of slave baptisms by Edmund Pope for St Elizabeth, Vere and Claredon parishes, 1815–1817 (fos 166–175) and by Thomas Stewart for St Elizabeth, 1815–1817 (fos 177–179)
1821–1825	CO 137/162, March	Various slave returns including a return of paupers and a return of people committed to the workhouse and manumissions. The return of manumissions has been transcribed by Edward Crawford at www.rootsweb.com/~jamwgw/manum.htm
1831	CO 137/179	Return of people confined to Kingston workhouse (fos 333–338) and list of negroes convicted in the parish of St Anne (fo 341)
1831	CO 137/181	List of people that have been confined in St Andrew's Workhouse claiming their freedom
1825–1831	CO 137/181 (fos 145–148)	A list of convicts in the St James' Workhouse condemned to hard labour for life, 1788–1831 (fo 411)
1917	CO 137/720 (24 Feb 1917)	Petition of 909 signatures for the repeal of Estate Duty Law, 1916, with name, address/village and occupation

10.15.6 Slave registers and records of the Slave Compensation Commission

Slave registers, 1817, 1820, 1823, 1826, 1829 and 1832	T 71/1–242 (online at www.ancestry.co.uk)
Valuers' returns	T 71/685–733
Register of claims	T 71/852–876
Index to claims	T 71/915–922
Claims and certificates, original	T 71/943–1025
Counterclaims	T 71/1174–1218
Certificates for compensation and lists of awards	T 71/1310–1332, 1371–1374
Amended awards	T 71/1381
Parliamentary returns of awards	T 71/1400–1402

10.15.7 Archives and other useful addresses

Jamaica Archives and Records Department, 59-63 Church Street, Kingston, Jamaica, http://jard.gov.jm

The Registrar General, Vital Records Information, Twickenham Park, Spanish Town, Jamaica, www.rgd.gov.jm

National Library of Jamaica, 12 East Street, Kingston, Jamaica, West Indies, www.nlj.gov.jm

Genealogy of Jamaica –
www.rootsweb.ancestry.com/~jamwgw/index.htm

Jamaican family history: genealogical research library –
http://jamaicanfamilysearch.com

Jamaica Gleaner, 1834 onwards, is online at the newspaper archive www.newspaperarchive.com

10.15.8 Guides to the archives

Ingram, *Sources for Jamaican History 1655-1838: A Biographical Survey with Particular Reference to Manuscript Sources*

Ingram, *Sources for West Indian Studies: A Supplementary Listing with Particular Reference to Manuscript Sources*

Port Royal, the old capital, was destroyed by an earthquake on 7 June 1692 and in 1907 an earthquake destroyed most of Kingston including the courthouse.

10.15.9 Further reading

Crooks, *A Tree Without Roots: The Guide to Tracing British, African and Asian Caribbean Ancestry*

Higman, *Jamaica Surveyed: Plantation Maps and Plans of the Eighteenth and Nineteenth Centuries*

Higman, *Slave Population and Economy in Jamaica, 1807–1834*

http://jamaica-gleaner.com/pages/history/ – articles on Jamaican history from the *Jamaica Gleaner*

Livingston, *Sketch Pedigrees of Some of the Early Settlers in Jamaica*

Mitchell, *Jamaican Ancestry: How to Find Out More*

O'Sullivan-Sirjue and Robinson, *Researching Your Jamaican Family*

Patterson, *The Sociology of Slavery: An Analysis of the Origins, Development and Structure of Negro Slave Society in Jamaica*

Porter, *Jamaican Records: A Research Manual: A Two Part Guide to Genealogical and Historical Research Using Repositories in Jamaica and England*

Robertson, 'Jamaican archival resources for seventeenth and eighteenth-century Atlantic slavery'

Soares, 'Jamaican research in Britain'

Titford, *My Ancestor Settled in the British West Indies (with Bermuda, British Guiana and British Honduras): A Guide to Sources for Family Sources*

Wright, 'Materials for family history in Jamaica'

Wright, *Monumental Inscriptions of Jamaica*

10.16 Leeward Islands

A group of islands under one federal government until 1956 comprising Antigua, Barbuda, Montserrat, St Christopher, Nevis, Anguilla, the British Virgin Islands and, between 1833 and 1940, Dominica. The Leeward Islands temporarily broke up in 1816 and formed two authorities: (1) Antigua, Barbuda and Montserrat and (2) St Christopher, Nevis, Anguilla and the British Virgin Islands. In 1833 the Leeward Islands government was re-established and included Dominica. In 1871 the federal legislature was revived with each colony having an administrator or commissioner responsible to the governor whose administrative office was in Antigua. In 1956 the federation was abolished.

10.16.1 Colonial Office series

See also under the individual territories; after 1951 see West Indies (section **10.1**).

Original correspondence	1689–1951	CO 152
Registers of correspondence	1850–1951	CO 354
Entry books	1670–1816	CO 153
Acts	1644–1956	CO 154
Sessional papers	1680–1956	CO 155
Government gazettes	1872–1965	CO 156
Miscellanea	1683–1945	CO 157
Registers of out-letters	1872–1926	CO 507

10.16.2 Further reading

Baker, *A Guide to Records in the Leeward Islands*

10.17 Montserrat

Montserrat was discovered by Christopher Columbus in November 1493 and named after the Abbey of Montserrat near Barcelona. Montserrat could be considered an Irish colony: the island is known as the Emerald Isle of the Caribbean and a green shamrock is its national logo. English and Irish from St Christopher first settled Montserrat in 1632. Further Irish immigrants arrived during the seventeenth century from Virginia, and from Ireland following Cromwell's victory at Drogheda in 1649.

The island was taken by the French in 1664 and 1667 but was restored to England in 1668 by the Treaty of Breda. The French raided Montserrat in 1712 and destroyed much of the island and most of the records. In 1782 Montserrat was again captured by the French but was returned to Britain in 1783 under the Treaty of Versailles.

Between 1671 and 1816 Montserrat formed part of the Leeward Islands federation. When the federation broke up in 1816 Montserrat formed a separate government with Antigua until 1871, when the Leeward Islands federation was reformed. The federation was finally dissolved in 1956 and Montserrat became a separate colony; for a short time between 1958 and 1962 it formed part of the Federation of the West Indies. Montserrat is now a British Overseas Territory.

10.17.1 Colonial Office series

See also Leeward Islands (section **10.16**); after 1951 see West Indies (section **10.1**).

Original correspondence	1702–1872	CO 7
	1726–1872	CO 175
	1872–1951	CO 152
Registers of correspondence	1850–1951	CO 354
Entry books	1816–1872	CO 393
Acts	1668–1960	CO 176
Sessional papers	1704–1965	CO 177
Government gazettes	1967–1989	FCO 6
Miscellanea	1666–1829	CO 10
	1829–1887	CO 178
	1683–1945	CO 157
Registers of out-letters	1872–1926	CO 507

10.17.2 Colonial Office returns of baptisms etc

1721–1729	CO 152/18	Baptisms and burials: St Anthony, 1723–1729 (fos 51–57), St George (fos 57–61) and St Peter (fos 61–63). Marriages: St Patrick (fo 63), St Anthony (fos 64–65), St George (fos 65–66) and St Peter (fos 66–67)
1739–1745	CO 152/25	Baptisms and burials: various parishes (fo 137)

10.17.3 Nominal censuses

1677/8	CO 1/42, fos 218–228	Indicates whether English, Irish, Scottish, French or Dutch. Printed in Oliver's *Caribbeana*, vol. 2, p.318
1729	EXT 1/258 (extracted from CO 152/18)	Printed in Oliver's *Caribbeana*, vol. 4, p.302

10.17.4 Miscellaneous

1727	CO 152/16, fo 148–151	Account of losses sustained by the attack by the French under Cassart in 1712

10.17.5 Slave registers and records of the Slave Compensation Commission

Slave registers, 1817, 1821, 1824, 1828, 1831	T 71/447–451
Valuers' returns	T 71/766
Register of claims	T 71/888
Index to claims	T 71/934
Claims and certificates, original	T 71/1058
Counterclaims	T 71/1261
Certificates for compensation and lists of awards	T 71/1348
Amended awards	T 71/1391
Parliamentary returns of awards	T 71/1412

10.17.6 Archives and other useful addresses

Montserrat Public Library, BBC Building, Brades Main Road, Brades, Montserrat, tel: (664) 491-4706, email: publiclibrary@gov.ms

Registrar General, Government Headquarters, Brades, Montserrat, tel: (664) 491-2129

The Montserrat National Trust, PO Box 393, Olveston, Montserrat www.montserratnationaltrust.ms holds some photographs and documents relating to history of Montserrat

Montserrat Genealogical Web Project www.rootsweb.ancestry.com/~msrwgw/

10.17.7 Guides to the archives

Baker, *A Guide to Records in the Leeward Islands*

In 1712 Governor John Hart reported that all the Montserrat laws and records had been burnt by the French during their invasion that year (*Calendar of State Papers, Colonial, America and West Indies*, 1724–1725, no. 91, p.66, also CSP, Col, 1719–1920, no 173, p.86 and no 241, p.121). The 1928 hurricane and earthquakes between 1933 and 1935 damaged the courthouse including many of the records held there. In 1972 a fire in the new courthouse destroyed most records held there.

10.17.8 Further reading

Titford, *My Ancestor Settled in the British West Indies (with Bermuda, British Guiana and British Honduras): A Guide to Sources for Family Historians*

10.18 Nevis

Nevis was first colonised by British from St Christopher in 1628. Between 1671 and 1816 it formed part of the Leeward Islands federation. When the federation broke up in 1816 Nevis formed a separate government with St Christopher and the Virgin Islands until 1871, when the Leeward Islands federation was reformed. In 1882 Nevis joined with St Christopher and Anguilla to form a single presidency.

The Leeward Islands federation was finally dissolved in 1956 and St Christopher-Nevis-Anguilla became a separate colony with the capital in St Christopher. For a short time between 1958 and 1962 it formed part of the Federation of the West Indies. In 1971 Britain assumed administrative responsibility for Anguilla and in 1980 Anguilla was formally separated from St Christopher and Nevis. St Christopher and Nevis became independent on 19 September 1983.

10.18.1 Colonial Office series

See also under St Christopher (section **10.19**) and Leeward Islands (section **10.16**); after 1951 see West Indies (section **10.1**).

Original correspondence	1689–1951	CO 152
	1703–1872	CO 184
	1816–1853	CO 239
Registers of correspondence	1850–1951	CO 354
Acts	1664–1882	CO 185
	1882–1972	CO 240
Sessional papers	1721–1882	CO 186
	1882–1960	CO 241
Government gazettes	1879–1975	CO 242
Miscellanea	1704–1882	CO 187
	1704–1887	CO 243
Registers of out-letters	1872–1926	CO 507

10.18.2 Colonial Office returns of baptisms etc

1726–1727	CO 152/16	Baptisms and burials: St Paul (fo 341)
1733–1734	CO 152/21	Baptisms and burials: St John (fo 163), St Thomas (fos 163–164), and St George (fo 164)
1740–1745	CO 152/25	Baptisms and burials: St James (fos 114–115)

10.18.3 Nominal censuses

1677/8	CO 1/42, fos 201–217	Indicates whether English, Irish, Scottish, French or Dutch. Printed in Oliver's *Caribbeana*, vol. 3, p.27
1707/8	CO 152/6, no 47 (vi)	
1707	CO 152/7, fo 47	Printed in *Caribbeana*, vol. 3, p.255

10.18.4 Slave registers and records of the Slave Compensation Commission

Slave registers, 1817, 1822, 1825, 1828, 1831, 1834	T 71/364–369 (most registers are online at www.ancestry.co.uk)
Valuers' returns	T 71/751–752
Register of claims	T 71/882
Index to claims	T 71/928
Claims and certificates, original	T 71/1038–1039
Counterclaims	T 71/1236–1237
Certificates for compensation and lists of awards	T 71/1340
Amended awards	T 71/1387
Parliamentary returns of awards	T 71/1408

10.18.5 Archives and other useful addresses

National Archives, Government Headquarters, Church St, Box 186, Basseterre, St Kitts, West Indies, tel: (869) 465-2521, www.nationalarchives.gov.kn

Registrar General, PO Box 236, Basseterre, St Kitts, West Indies, tel: (869) 465-5251

Nevis Historical and Conservation Society, PO Box 563, Charlestown, Nevis, West Indies, www.nevis-nhcs.org

St Christopher and Nevis genealogical project – www.tc.umn.edu/~terre011/genhome.html

10.18.6 Guides to the archives

Baker, *A Guide to Records in the Leeward Islands*

In 1706 many public records were damaged or destroyed by the French (*Calendar of State Papers, Colonial, America and West Indies*, 1721–1722, no 204, XX and XXIV, p.120 and p.122). Nevis joined with St Christopher in 1882 and most Nevis records have since been transferred to St Christopher. In 1982 a fire at the courthouse in St Christopher destroyed many documents. Many Nevis records described in Baker as being in the archives room at Basseterre, St Christopher, may have been destroyed by that fire.

10.18.7 Further reading

Hubbard, *Swords, Ships and Sugar: A History of Nevis to 1900*

Titford, *My Ancestor Settled in the British West Indies (with Bermuda, British Guiana and British Honduras): A Guide to Sources for Family Historians*

Titford, 'Transcripts of 18th century registers for St George Gingerland'

10.19 St Christopher (St Kitts)

Settled by the English in 1623 and by the French in 1625 under d'Esnambuc, the island was divided with the French having the two ends of the island and the English the middle. The English and French used St Christopher as a base to settle the other islands in the Leeward Islands group. In 1702 Britain took the French portions, which were ceded to Britain in 1713. St Christopher was recaptured by the French in 1782 but was restored to Britain in 1783.

Between 1671 and 1816 St Christopher formed part of the Leeward Islands federation. When the federation broke up in 1816 St Christopher formed a separate government with Nevis, Anguilla and the Virgin Islands until 1871, when the Leeward Islands federation was reformed. In 1882 St Christopher joined with Nevis and Anguilla to form a single presidency. The Leeward Islands was finally dissolved in 1956 and St Christopher-Nevis-Anguilla became a separate colony with the capital in St Christopher. For a short time between 1958 and 1962 it formed part of the Federation of the West Indies. In 1971 Britain assumed administrative responsibility for Anguilla and in 1980 it was formally separated from St Christopher and Nevis. St Christopher and Nevis became independent on 19 September 1983.

10.19.1 Colonial Office series

Before 1783 see also under France (section **11.4**); see also under Leeward Islands (section **10.16**) and from 1951 under West Indies (section **10.1**).

Original correspondence	1689–1951	CO 152
	1702–1872	CO 239
Registers of correspondence	1850–1951	CO 354
Entry Books	1816–1872	CO 407
Acts	1672–1972	CO 240
Sessional papers	1704–1960	CO 241
Government gazettes	1879–1975	CO 242
Miscellanea	1704–1887	CO 243
	1683–1945	CO 157
Registers of out-letters	1872–1926	CO 507

10.19.2 Colonial Office returns of baptisms etc

1721–1730	CO 152/18	Baptisms and burials: Christ Church Nichola Town (fos 25–27); St John, Cabosaterre (fo 34); and St Mary Cayon (fos 36–38)
1733–1734	CO 152/18	Baptisms and burials: Christ Church, Nichola Town (fos 132, 134); St Mary Cayon (fos 133, 135); St George, Basseterre (fos 136–143); St Ann, Sandy Point (fos 143–144, 147–148)
1738–1745	CO 152/25	Baptisms, marriages and burials: St Mary Cayon (fos 118–121). Baptisms and burials: St George, Basseterre, 1743–1745 (fos 123–136)

The British Library (see Useful addresses) holds some transcriptions of population and tax records for the French part of St Christopher, 1776–80 and parish registers, 1730–1823. The Society of Genealogists (see Useful addresses) holds transcripts of parish registers, 1730–1823, compiled by V. L. Oliver.

10.19.3 Nominal censuses

1674	CO 1/31, fos 7–21	Various lists of French proprietors living in or possessing land in the English quarters
1677/8	CO 1/42, fos 195–200	Indicates whether English, Irish, Scottish, French or Dutch. Printed in Oliver's *Caribbeana*, vol. 2, p.68

1707	CO 152/7, fo 47	Includes age of head of household. Printed in *Caribbeana*, vol. 3, p.132
1707/8	CO 152/6, no 47 (iv and v)	
1711	CO 152/9, fos 305–315	

10.19.4 Land records

1712–1716	CO 152/11, no 6 (iii)	Account of grants of land in the former French part of St Christopher noting grantee, by whom granted, quality of land, date, for how long, location
1721	CO 152/13, fos 253–256	List of possessors of the French land in Basseterre and Cabesterre divisions
1729	T 1/275, fos 248–249	A list of contracts made by the Commissioners for Sale of Lands in St Christopher that formerly belonged to the French

10.19.5 Miscellaneous

1706	CO 243/2	Account of losses sustained by the proprietors and inhabitants of the island because of the invasion of the French (other returns are in CO 152/9, fos 250–251, and CO 243/3)
1712–1720	CO 243/4–5	Powers of attorney, together with a number of wills
1717–1718	CO 152/12/1–2	Several lists relating to the French and to French plantations
1825–1830	CO 239/22	Various returns relating to slavery such as manumissions, imports and sales for St Kitts, Nevis, Anguilla and Virgin Islands
1821–1822	CO 239/10 (12 Jan 1824)	Parochial relief paid to paupers noting parish, name, gender, age, colour and residence

10.19.6 Slave registers and records of the Slave Compensation Commission

Slave registers, 1817, 1822, 1825, 1827/8, 1831, 1834	T 71/253–260 (online at www.ancestry.co.uk)
Valuers' returns	T 71/740–742
Register of claims	T 71/879
Index to claims	T 71/925
Claims and certificates, original	T 71/1031–1032
Counterclaims	T 71/1224–1227
Certificates for compensation and lists of awards	T 71/1336
Amended awards	T 71/1384
Parliamentary returns of awards	T 71/1405

10.19.7 Archives and other useful addresses

National Archives, Government Headquarters, Church Street, Box 186, Basseterre, St Kitts, tel: (869) 465-2521, www.nationalarchives.gov.kn

Registrar General, PO Box 236, Basseterre, St Kitts, tel: (869) 465-5251

St Christopher National Trust, PO Box 888, Bay Road, Basseterre, St Kitts, http://stkittsheritage.com/

St Kitts-Nevis Genealogical Web Project – www.tc.umn.edu/~terre011/genhome.html

10.19.8 Guides to the archives

Baker, *A Guide to Records in the Leeward Islands*

National Archives of St Kitts and Nevis, *Understanding and using Archives*

Many records were destroyed during the wars with the French; for example, Governor Stapleton reported in 1674 that all records had been burnt or lost in the late war (*Calendar of State Papers, Colonial*, 1669–1674, p.547). In 1867 a fire destroyed much of Basseterre and in 1982 a fire at the courthouse destroyed many historic records. Those records that survived are split between the National Archives and the new courthouse.

10.19.9 Further reading

Dyde, *St Kitts: Cradle of the Caribbean*

Généalogie et historie de la Caraïbe, www.ghcaraibe.org/ – Sources for researching in the French Caribbean, including St Christopher. This site

includes a transcription of a 1671 census of St Christopher at
www.ghcaraibe.org/docu/st-chr/1671ter/p00.html
Oliver, *The Registers of St Thomas, Middle Island, St Kitts 1729–1832*
Titford, *My Ancestor Settled in the British West Indies (with Bermuda,*
  British Guiana and British Honduras): A Guide to Sources for Family
  Historians

10.20 St Lucia

Temporarily settled by the English in 1605, St Lucia was claimed by the
French in 1635. Settlers from St Christopher and the Bermudas settled in
1638 but were driven off by the Caribs in 1641. A treaty of peace was
made between the French and the Caribs in 1660. St Lucia was then
occupied by the British from St Christopher from 1664 to 1667, when it
was restored to France. France and Britain disputed claims over the
island and in 1723 St Lucia was declared neutral. All settlers were to
leave and the island returned to the Caribs. In 1743 France reoccupied St
Lucia which was made neutral again in 1748. France settled the island
again in 1756. Between 1762 and 1803 St Lucia was frequently captured
by Britain and restored to France. St Lucia was finally captured by Britain
in 1803 and ceded to her in 1814. St Lucia was a member of the Windward
Islands federation between 1838 and 1956 and a member of the Federation
of the West Indies between 1958 and 1962. St Lucia became independent
on 22 February 1979.

10.20.1 Colonial Office series

Before 1814 see under France (section **11.4**); see also Windward Islands
(section **10.25**) and after 1951 see West Indies (section **10.1**).

Original correspondence	1709–1873	CO 253
	1874–1951	CO 321
Registers of correspondence	1850–1881	CO 367
	1882–1951	CO 376
Entry books	1794–1872	CO 254
Acts	1818–1965	CO 255
Sessional papers	1820–1965	CO 256
Government gazettes	1857–1975	CO 257
Miscellanea	1722–1940	CO 258
Registers of out-letters	1872–1882	CO 505
	1883–1926	CO 377

10.20.2 Nominal census
1811   CO 253/7 [in French]

10.20.3 Miscellaneous

1787	CO 884/4, no 44	Description of St Lucia including names of landholders with amount of land and crops grown [in French]; relates to the LaTour Map in CO 700/ St Lucia2
1823	CO 253/17	Various slave returns including manumissions granted between 7 Nov 1818 and 25 August 1823
1831	CO 253/30, fos 488–496A	Account of losses following hurricane of 11 August 1831. Quarter, names, name of plantation or property – with references to particulars in appendix. Unfortunately this letter is a duplicate and does not include the appendix
1833	T 1/4396 (paper 6312/36)	Claims following hurricane of 11 August 1831 distributed under West Indies Loans Act. Quarter, name, purpose, value, money paid
1821–1825	CO 253/17	Various slave returns including manumissions
1825–1830	CO 253/29	Various slave returns including manumissions
1826–1834	CO 258/5–15	Reports of protectors of slaves: information includes punishments, births, deaths, marriages, free baptisms and manumissions. Some of these returns are published in the British Parliamentary Papers: session 1829 (335) vol. XXV.255 (mfm 31.153–155) and session 1830–31 (262) vol. XV.1 (mfm 33.87–95)

10.20.4 Slave registers and records of the Slave Compensation Commission

Slave registers, 1815, 1819, 1822, 1825, 1828, 1831, 1834	T 71/376–390 (registers for 1815 and 1819 online at www.ancestry.co.uk)
Valuers' returns	T 71/754–756
Register of claims	T 71/884
Index to claims	T 71/930
Claims and certificates, original	T 71/1041–1044
Counterclaims	T 71/1241–1251
Certificates for compensation and lists of awards	T 71/1342
Amended awards	T 71/1389
Parliamentary returns of awards	T 71/1410

10.20.5 Archives and other useful addresses

St Lucia National Archives, PO Box 3060, Clarke St, Vigie, Castries, St Lucia, tel: (758) 452-1654, email: stlunatarch_mt@candw.lc

Registrar of Civil Status, Peynier Street, Castries, St Lucia, tel: (758) 468-3195, email: civilreg@candw.lc

St Lucia Archaeological and Historical Society, La Clery, Castries, St Lucia

St Lucia National Trust, PO Box 595, Castries, St. Lucia, www.slunatrust.org

Central Library of St Lucia, Castries, St Lucia, www.education.gov.lc

St Lucia Genealogical Web Project – www.iukgenweb.org/stlucia/

10.20.6 Guides to the archives

Baker, *A Guide to Records in the Windward Islands*

Few if any records survive from before 1800 following the bombardment of Castries during the British invasion in 1796. The fires of 1927 and 1948 destroyed much of Castries and St Lucia's records.

10.20.7 Further reading

Breen, *St Lucia: Historical, Statistical and Descriptive*

Jesse, *Outlines of St Lucia's History*

Titford, *My Ancestor Settled in the British West Indies (with Bermuda, British Guiana and British Honduras): A Guide to Sources for Family Historians*

10.21 St Vincent and the Grenadines

In 1660 Britain and France declared St Vincent neutral but between 1672 and 1748 both disputed sovereignty and attempted to settle on the island. In 1748 St Vincent was again declared neutral by the Treaty of Aix-la-Chapelle and left to the Caribs. The island was captured by Britain in 1762, ceded to her in 1763, and settled. France captured St Vincent in 1779 but it was restored to Britain in 1783. From 1763 until 1776 and then from 1833 to 1956, St Vincent was a member of the Windward Islands. Between 1958 and 1962 it was a member of the Federation of the West Indies. On 27 October 1979 St Vincent and the Grenadines became independent.

10.21.1 Colonial Office series

Before 1783 see also under France (section **11.4**), see also under Windward Islands (section **10.25**) and from 1951 see West Indies (section **10.1**).

Original Correspondence	1668–1873	CO 260
	1874–1951	CO 321
Registers of correspondence	1850–1951	CO 376
Entry books	1776–1872	CO 261
Acts	1768–1969	CO 262
Sessional papers	1769–1965	CO 263
Government gazettes	1831–1975	CO 264
Miscellanea	1763–1941	CO 265
Registers of out-letters	1872–1882	CO 506
	1883–1926	CO 377

10.21.2 Land records

1765–1766	CO 76/9	Dominica and St Vincent: Register of grants of land
1766	CO 101/1, fos 279–281	Docket register of plantation grants in the islands of Dominica, St Vincent and Tobago
1765–1767	CO 101/11, fos 212–217, 411–415	Docket register of plantation grants
1764–1797	CO 106/9–12	Sales of lands in the Ceded Islands
1766	T 1/453, fo 164	Account of one-fourth crops reaped from estates of which temporary possession was granted by the Commissioners in 1765

1766	T 1/453, fos 168–170	Account of the French Inhabitants of St Vincent whose claims were allowed by the Commissioners and who paid their fines in May 1766

10.21.3 Miscellaneous

1832–1833	T 1/4396 (paper 12856/33)	Claims following hurricane of 11 August 1831 distributed under West Indies Loans Act, 1832. Date of payment, claimant, purpose, parish, value and money paid
1821–1825	CO 260/42	Various slave returns including manumissions effected by purchase, bequest or otherwise, slave marriages, runaways committed to gaol who claimed to be free, and slaves sold in the Marshal's Office for debt

10.21.4 Slave registers and records of the Slave Compensation Commission

Slave registers, 1817, 1822, 1825, 1828, 1831, 1834	T 71/493–500 (most volumes are online at www.ancestry.co.uk)
Valuers' returns	T 71/780-782
Register of claims	T 71/892
Index to claims	T 71/938
Claims and certificates, original	T 71/1066-1068
Counterclaims	T 71/1265-1269
Certificates for compensation and lists of awards	T 71/1351
Amended awards	T 71/1395
Parliamentary returns of awards	T 71/1416

10.21.5 Archives and other useful addresses

National Archives, Department of Libraries, Archives and Documentation Service, Lower Middle Street, Kingstown, St Vincent and the Grenadines,
tel: (784) 456-1111, email: archives@caribsurf.com

Registry Department, Court House Building, Kingstown, St Vincent and
the Grenadines, tel: (784) 451-2944, email: svgregistry@caribsurf.com

St Vincent and the Grenadines genealogical research –
http://svgancestry.com/

10.21.6 Guides to archives

Baker, *A Guide to Records in the Windward Islands*

10.21.7 Further reading

Anderson and McDonald, *Between Slavery and Freedom: Special
Magistrate John Anderson's Journal of St Vincent During the
Apprenticeship*

Fraser and Joseph, *Our Country: St Vincent and the Grenadines*

Potter, *St Vincent and the Grenadines*

Shephard, *An Historical Account of the Island of St Vincent*

Titford, *My Ancestor Settled in the British West Indies (with Bermuda,
British Guiana and British Honduras): A Guide to Sources for Family
Historians*

Young, *Account of the Black Charaibs in the Island of St Vincent's*

10.22 Tobago

British settlers from Barbados first arrived in Tobago in 1625. The Dutch
and the Courlanders (Courland was a dukedom situated in the present
Republic of Latvia) set up settlements on either end of the island in 1654;
the Courlanders surrendered to the Dutch in 1659. From then on, the
Dutch, French and British occupied Tobago at different times until Tobago
was declared neutral in 1748. However, it was captured by Britain in 1763,
then captured by France in 1781 and ceded to her in 1783. Tobago was
again captured by Britain in 1793 but was restored to France in 1802.
Britain finally captured Tobago in 1803, and Tobago was formally ceded to
her in 1814. Tobago was a member of the Windward Islands between 1763
and 1783 and from 1833 until 1889 when it merged with Trinidad. Between
1958 and 1962 Trinidad and Tobago was a member of the Federation of the
West Indies. On 31 August 1962 Trinidad and Tobago became independent.

10.22.1 Colonial Office series

See also under France (section **11.4**) and Windward Islands (section
10.25), after 1888 see Trinidad (section **10.23**) and from 1951 West Indies
(section **10.1**).

Original correspondence	1700–1873	CO 285
	1874–1888	CO 321
Registers of correspondence	1850–1888	CO 376
Entry books	1793–1872	CO 286
Acts	1768–1898	CO 287
Sessional papers	1768–1898	CO 288
Government gazettes	1872–1898	CO 289
Miscellanea	1766–1892	CO 290
Registers of out-letters	1872–1882	CO 498

10.22.2 Nominal censuses

1770	CO 101/14, fos 126–127	
1751	CO 285/2, fos 77–78	List of French inhabitants of Little Tobago by P. Drummond of HMS *Tavistock*

10.22.3 Land grants

1766	CO 101/1, fos 279–281	Docket register of plantation grants in the islands of Dominica, St Vincent and Tobago
1765–1767	CO 101/11, fos 209, 413	Docket register of plantation grants
1764–1797	CO 106/9–12	Sale of lands in the Ceded Islands

10.22.4 Slave registers and records of the Slave Compensation Commission

Slave registers, annual 1819–1834	T 71/461–492 (online at www.ancestry.co.uk)
Valuers' returns	T 71/779
Register of claims	T 71/891
Index to claims	T 71/937
Claims and certificates, original	T 71/1064–1065
Counterclaims	T 71/1263–1264
Certificates for compensation and lists of awards	T 71/1351
Amended awards	T 71/1394
Parliamentary returns of awards	T 71/1415

See Trinidad for useful addresses and guides to the archives of Trinidad and Tobago.

10.23 Trinidad

Trinidad was gradually settled by Spain during the sixteenth century and retained by Spain until 1797 when she was captured by Britain. Tobago was united with Trinidad in 1889. Trinidad and Tobago was a member of the Federation of the West Indies between 1958 and 1962, and on 31 August 1962 Trinidad and Tobago became independent.

10.23.1 Colonial Office series

Before 1797 see under Spain (section **11.9**) and between 1797 and 1801 see WO 1; after 1951 see under West Indies (section **10.1**).

Original correspondence	1783–1951	CO 295
Registers of correspondence	1850–1951	CO 372
Entry books	1797–1872	CO 296
Acts	1832–1960	CO 297
Sessional papers	1803–1965	CO 298
Government gazettes	1833–1975	CO 299
Miscellanea	1804–1945	CO 300
Registers of out-letters	1872–1926	CO 497
High Commission, registered files	1962–1966	DO 227

10.23.2 Land grants

1814	CO 295/35	Abstract of all grants of land made by the Spanish government and all permissions of occupancy or petitions of grants from the Capitulation, 14 June 1813

10.23.3 Miscellaneous

1814–1815	CO 385/1	List of people allowed to remain in Trinidad
1824	CO 295/63, fos 284–285	List of freeborn men
1824–1834	CO 300/19–33	Reports of protectors of slaves: punishments, criminal cases, births, deaths, marriages, free baptisms and manumissions. Several of the reports were published in the British Parliamentary Papers: session 1829 (335), vol. XXV.255 (mfm 31.153–155) and

		session 1830–31 (262), vol. XV.1 (mfm 33.87–95)
1821–1823	CO 295/59, fos 62–72	Return of American refugees

10.23.4 Slave registers and records of the Slave Compensation Commission

Slave registers, 1813, 1815, 1816, 1819, 1822, 1825, 1828, 1831, 1834	T 71/501–519 (online at www.ancestry.co.uk)
Valuers' returns	T 71/783–789
Register of claims	T 71/893–894
Index to claims	T 71/939
Claims and certificates, original	T 71/1069–1082
Counterclaims	T 71/1270–1279
Certificates for compensation and lists of awards	T 71/1352–1355
Amended awards	T 71/1396
Parliamentary returns of awards	T 71/1417

10.23.5 Archives and other useful addresses

National Archives, PO Box 763, 105 St Vincent St, Port-of-Spain, Trinidad, tel: (868) 625-2689, www.natt.gov.tt

Registrar General's Office, Registration House, South Quay, Port-of-Spain, Trinidad, tel: (868) 624-1660, www.legalaffairs.gov.tt/rgd.aspx

Tobago Warden's Office, TIDCO Mall, Scarborough, Tobago, tel: (868) 639-2410

Tobago Registrar General's Office, Jerningham Street, Scarborough, Tobago, tel: (868) 639-2652

National Library and Information System Authority, 105 Abercromby Street, Port-of-Spain, Trinidad, www2.nalis.gov.tt

Trinidad and Tobago Genealogical pages – www.rootsweb.ancestry.com/~ttowgw/

10.23.6 Guides to the archives

Gropp, *Guide to Libraries of Central America and the West Indies, Panama, Bermuda and British Guiana*

On 23 March 1903 the government building in Port of Spain was destroyed by fire. All court, legislative and survey office files and most administrative records were lost. Many records relating to Tobago had been transferred to the government building and were also destroyed.

10.23.7 Further reading

Brereton, *A History of Modern Trinidad 1783–1962*

Carmichael, *The History of the West Indian Islands of Trinidad and Tobago 1498–1900*

English Protestant Church of Tobago, *Register of Baptisms, Marriages and Deaths from 1781 to 1817*

John, *The Plantation Slaves of Trinidad 1783–1816*

Ottley, *Story of Tobago*

Titford, *My Ancestor Settled in the British West Indies (with Bermuda, British Guiana and British Honduras): A Guide to Sources for Family Historians*

Uddenberg and Vaucrosson, *Lists from the San Fernando Gazette: 1865–1896*

Williams, *History of the People of Trinidad and Tobago*

Woodcock, *History of Tobago*

10.24 Turks and Caicos Islands

The Turks and Caicos Islands were uninhabited until about 1678 when salt-rakers from the Bermudas frequented the Grand Turk. The Spaniards expelled these settlers in 1710, but they soon returned and held the islands. During and after the American Revolution American Loyalists settled the Caicos Islands. Both these island groups were annexed to and administered from the Bahamas in 1799. In 1848 the Turks and Caicos Islands formed their own government under the governor of Jamaica and in 1874 they became a dependency of Jamaica until 1959. Between 1958 and 1962 the islands were a member of the Federation of the West Indies. Between 1965 and 1973 the islands were governed by the Bahamas. The islands are a British Overseas Territory.

10.24.1 Colonial Office series

Before 1848 see under Bahamas (section **10.4**) and after 1873 see under Jamaica (section **10.15**); after 1951 see under West Indies (section **10.1**).

Original correspondence	1799–1848	CO 23
	1848–1882	CO 301
	1874–1951	CO 137
Registers of correspondence	1868–1882	CO 495
Entry books	1849–1872	CO 409
Acts	1849–1965	CO 302
Sessional papers	1849–1965	CO 303
Government gazettes	1907–1965	CO 681
Miscellanea	1852–1947	CO 304
Registers of out-letters	1872–1881	CO 496
	1882–1926	CO 494

Records of the slave registry and Slave Compensation Commission for the Turks and Caicos Islands are with the records for the Bahamas (section **10.4**).

10.24.2 Archives and other useful addresses

Turks and Caicos National Museum, Guinep House, Front Street, PO Box 188, Grand Turk, Turks and Caicos, BWI, tel: (649) 946-2160, www.tcmuseum.org

Registrar's General Office, Front Street, Turks and Caicos Islands, British West Indies, tel: (649) 946-2800

Turks and Caicos Islands Genealogy Project – www.iukgenweb.org/index.php/british-overseas-territories/turks-and-caicos-islands

There is no guide to the archives of the Turks and Caicos Islands although documents relating to the islands, held in the archives and other repositories in the Bahamas, Jamaica and the National Archives, may be described in guides to their archives. Very few original records have survived on the islands but it is possible that material may survive in Jamaica, the Bahamas or in the National Archives (under Jamaica and the Bahamas).

Minor political disturbances in the early 1970s saw the archive attacked and colonial records destroyed or stolen. In 1997 the archives were moved from the Post Office, where they had suffered from regular flooding, to the prison and many were later moved to the museum. About 20 per cent of the surviving records were in such a poor condition that they were destroyed. Microfilm copies of parish registers from the late-1700s and other material relating to the islands, from Jamaica and the National Archives, and some original records are available in the museum.

10.24.3 Further reading

Pusey, *The Handbook of the Turks and Caicos Islands: being a Compendium of History, Statistics and General Information concerning the Islands from their Discovery to the Present Time*

10.25 Windward Islands

Following the Seven Years War, in 1763 the newly ceded islands of Grenada, St Vincent, Dominica and Tobago were united under a single government called the Southern Caribbee Islands. Dominica was separated in 1771 to form part of the Leeward Islands, St Vincent left in 1776 and Tobago in 1783. In 1833 Grenada, St Vincent, Tobago and Barbados formed the Windward Islands with a single governor based initially in Barbados and later in Grenada. St Lucia was added in 1838, Barbados left in 1885, Tobago left on its merger with Trinidad in 1889 and Dominica was added in 1940. The Windward Islands federation was dissolved in 1956.

10.25.1 Colonial Office series

See also under the individual territories; after 1951 see West Indies (section **10.1**).

Original correspondence	1874–1951	CO 321
Registers of correspondence	1850–1951	CO 376
Registers of out-letters	1883–1926	CO 377

10.25.2 Further reading

Baker, *A Guide to Records in the Windward Islands*

CHAPTER 11
RECORDS OF THE NON-BRITISH WEST INDIES

This chapter describes material for the study of the history of British West Indians in other Caribbean countries.

Most of the records of British subjects on non-British West Indian islands are to be found in the records of the Foreign Office (see sections **9.2.1–9.2.3** for more information). These are predominantly official despatches between Britain's representatives abroad and the Foreign Office but may include lists of British subjects, registers of passports issued and registers of births, marriages and deaths. The records are arranged by country or, for the period they were colonies, under the administrative country. For example, records of St Thomas are under Denmark (before 1917) and the United States of America (after 1917), and those for St Eustatius are under the Netherlands.

Many West Indian islands belonging to other European powers were at times occupied and administered by Britain. For example, Surinam (Suriname) was originally a British settlement. In Saint Domingue (Haiti) British forces joined with the French forces during the slave uprising from 1791, until both countries evacuated in 1803. Most islands, however, were invaded and administered by British forces during periods of war. During the Seven Years War, 1756–63, Guadeloupe (1759–63), Martinique (1762–63) and Havana (1762–63) were occupied by Britain. During the French Revolutionary and Napoleonic Wars, 1793–1815, Curaçao (1800–02 and 1807–14), Guadeloupe (1810–13), Martinique (1794–1815), St Croix (1810–15), St Eustatius (1807–15), St Thomas (1807–15) and Surinam (1799–1802 and 1804–16) were occupied.

Records during these periods of occupation are in the records of the War Office, Colonial Office and the Treasury. Information recorded includes censuses, lists of government officials and plantation returns, and identified references are included here. During periods of occupation foreign troops were often taken into British service. The means of reference to the War Office records is through *Public Record Office Lists and Indexes*, vol. LIII (see Bibliography).

11.1 Cuba

Before 1898 see Spain (section **11.9**).

General correspondence before 1906	1901–1905	FO 108
Embassy and consular archives		
Correspondence	1870–1957	FO 277
Registers of correspondence	1842–1939	FO 278
Letter books	1877–1881	FO 279
Miscellanea	1875–1914	FO 280
Havana:		
Correspondence	1762–1763	CO 117
	1931–1948	FO 1001
Registers of correspondence	1931–1936	FO 747
Slave Trade Commission	1819–1869	FO 313
Santiago de Cuba:		
Letter books	1832–1905	FO 453
Registers of correspondence	1913–1935	FO 454
Nuevitas:		
Register of correspondence	1926–1931	FO 455
Camaguey:		
Register of correspondence	1925–1929	FO 456
Antilla:		
Register of correspondence	1925–1932	FO 457

Archivo Nacional (National Archive), Compostela 906, San Isidro, Habana Vieja, 10100 La Habana, Republic of Cuba, www.arnac.cu
Cuban Genealogical Web Project – www.cubagenweb.org
Carr, *Censos, Padrones y Matrículas de la Población de Cuba*
Carr, *Guide to Cuban Genealogical Research*

11.2 Denmark

Includes St Thomas, St John and St Croix. The Danish Virgin Islands were sold to the US in 1917. See also United States of America (section **11.11**).

State papers foreign	1577–1780	SP 75
General correspondence before 1906	1781–1905	FO 22
Embassy and consular archives	1781–1957	FO 211
St Croix:		
Correspondence etc	1808–1815	CO 244, WO 1
St Thomas:		
Correspondence etc	1808–1815	CO 259, WO 1
Danish emigrants going to St Thomas	1796	FO 95/1/4, fo 258

Rigsarkivet (National Archives), Rigsdagsgården 9, 1218 København K, Denmark, www.sa.dk/content/us

Danish National Archives' website on the history of the Danish West Indies, 1671–1917 – www.virgin-islands-history.dk/eng/default.asp

Westergaard, *The Danish West Indies under Company rule 1671–1754*

Danish Consulate on St Thomas – www.dkconsulateusvi.com (includes copy of Westergaard's book)

Bastian, *Owning Memory. How a Caribbean Community Lost its Archives and Found its History*

US Virgin Islands Genealogical Web Project – www.rootsweb.ancestry.com/~usvi/

The St Croix African Roots Project – digitised records on www.ancestry.com

11.3 Dominican Republic (formerly Santo Domingo)

Before 1824 see under Spain (section **11.9**), and between 1795 and 1844 see also under France (section **11.4**) and Haiti (section **11.5**).

General correspondence before 1906	1848–1905	FO 23
Embassy and consular archives	1848–1948	FO 140
Santo Domingo	1811–1932	FO 683

Archivo General de la Nacion, Calle M E Diaz, Santo Domingo, Dominican Republic, www.agn.gov.do

Dominican Republic Genealogical Web Project –
www.rootsweb.ancestry.com/~domwgw/mhhbcgw.htm

11.4 France

Includes Martinique, Guadeloupe, St Martin, St Barthélemy and French
Guiana (Guyane), and St Lucia (section **10.20**), St Vincent (section **10.21**),
Tobago (section **10.22**), Grenada (section **10.13**), a portion of St Christopher
(section **10.19**) and Dominica (section **10.11**) until these were ceded to Britain.

State papers	1577–1780	SP 78
General correspondence before 1906	1781–1905	FO 27
Embassy and consular archives	1814–1957	FO 146
Martinique:		
Correspondence etc	1693–1815	CO 166, WO 1
Administration of vacated properties	1794	WO 1/31, pp.367–397, listing owners by parish
Guadeloupe:		
Correspondence etc	1758–1816	CO 110, WO 1

Le Centre des Archives d'outre-mer, 29 chemin du Moulin-Detesta, 13090
Aix-en-Provence, France, www.archivesnationales.culture.gouv.fr/caom/
fr/index.html

Archives départementales de la Martinique, BP 649, 19 avenue Saint-John
Perse, 97263 Fort-de-France

Archives départementales de la Guadeloupe, BP 74, 97120 Basseterre

Archives départementales de la Guyane, Place Leopold Heder, 97302
Cayenne

Archives Nationales, *Guide des Sources de l'Histoire de l'Amerique Latine
et des Antilles dans les Archives Francaises*

Archives Nationales, *Les Archives Nationales Etat General des Fonds*.
Especially vol. 3 on overseas records

Généalogie et Histoire de la Caraïbe – www.ghcaraibe.org

France Genealogical Web Project – www.francegenweb.org

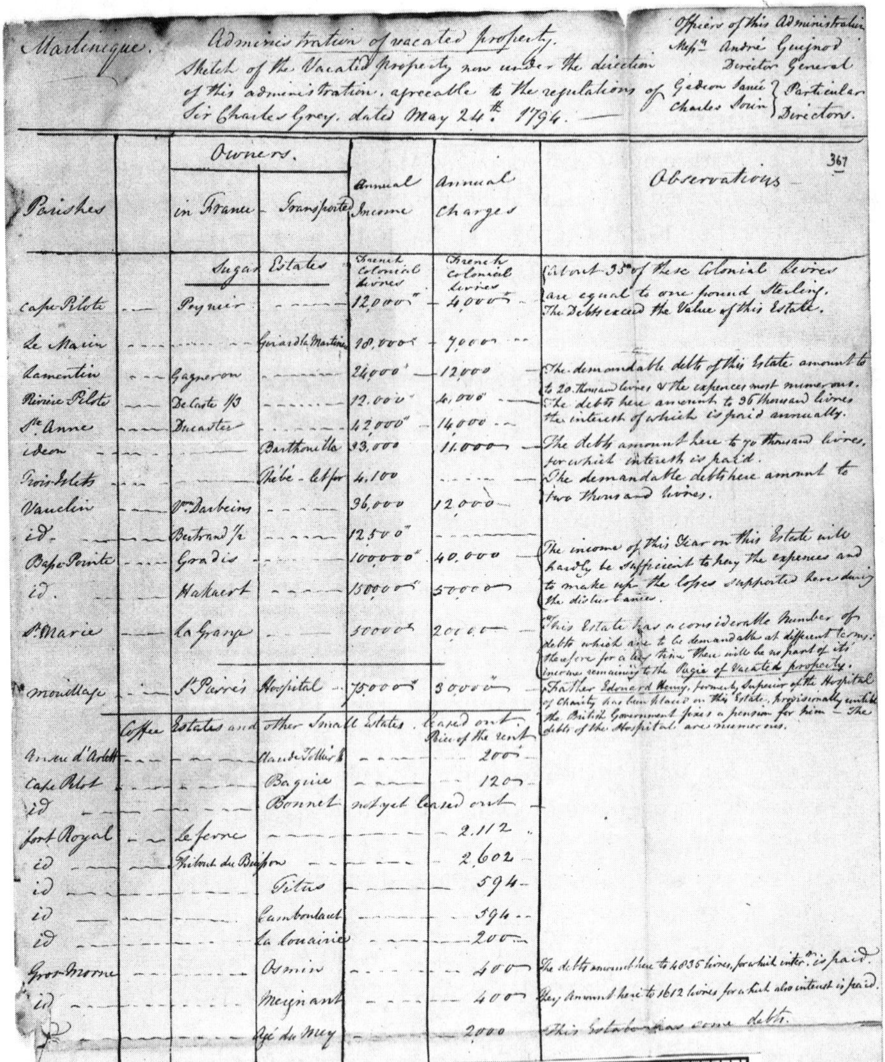

Martinique. Administration of vacated property.
Sketch of the Vacated property now under the direction of this administration, agreeable to the regulations of Sir Charles Grey, dated May 24th. 1794. —

Officers of this Administration
Messrs André Guignod Director General
Gedeon Lamé } Particular
Charles Soin } Directors.

367

Parishes		Owners in France	Owners Transported	Annual Income	Annual Charges	Observations
		Sugar Estates		French Colonial livres	French colonial livres	About 35 of these Colonial livres are equal to one pound Sterling.
Cape Pilote	—	Poyneir	—	12,000	4,000	The Debts exceed the Value of this Estate.
Le Marin	—	—	Girard la Martine	18,000	7,000	
Lamentin	—	Gagneron	—	24,000	12,000	The demandable debts of this Estate amount to 20 thousand livres, & the expences most numerous.
Riviere Pilote	—	De Caste 1/3	—	12,000	4,000	The debts here amount to 36 thousand livres the interest of which is paid annually.
Ste Anne	—	Ducaster	—	42,000	14,000	
idem	—	—	Barthouille	33,000	11,000	The debts amount here to 70 thousand livres, for which interest is paid.
Trois Islets	—	—	Thébé - Colfor	4,100	—	The demandable debts here amount to two thousand livres.
Vauclin	—	Ve Darbeins	—	36,000	12,000	
id.	—	Bertrand 1/2	—	12,500	—	
Basse Pointe	—	Gradis	—	100,000	40,000	The income of this Year on this Estate will hardly be sufficient to pay the expences and to make up the losses supported here during the disturbance.
id.	—	Hakaert	—	150000	50000	
Ste Marie	—	La Grange	—	50000	20000	This Estate has a considerable Number of debts which are to be demandable at different terms; therefore for a long time there will be no part of its income remaining to the Regie of Vacated property.
Moulllage	—	St Pierre's	Hospital	75000	30000	Father Edouard Henry, formerly Superior of the Hospital of Charity has been placed on this Estate, provisionally untill the British Government fixes a pension for him — The debts of the Hospital are numerous.
	Coffee	Estates and	other Small Estates.	Leased out	Price of the rent	
Anse d'Arlett	—	—	Marde Tollier	—	200	
Cape Pilot	—	—	Baguie	—	120	
id	—	—	Bonnet	not yet	leased out	
Fort Royal	—	Le ferne	—	—	2,112	
id	—	Thibault du Buisson	—	—	2,602	
id	—	—	Titus	—	594	
id	—	—	Cambonlaut	—	594	
id	—	—	La Conairie	—	200	
Gros Morne	—	—	Osmin	—	400	The debts amount here to 4835 livres, for which inter^st is paid.
id	—	—	Meignant	—	400	They Amount here to 1612 livres for which also interest is paid.
	—	—	Vve du Mey	—	2000	This Estate has some debts.

Figure 27 *Martinique: list of vacated sugar estates, May 1794 (WO 1/31, p.367)*

11.5 Haiti (formerly Saint-Domingue)

Before 1824 see under France (section **11.4**). Between 1795 and 1803 British troops occupied Saint-Domingue and records in the National Archives often refer to Saint-Domingue as Santo Domingo; it is possible that they refer to the whole island. There is much correspondence relating to Saint-Domingue between 1795–1808 in CO 137 (Jamaica).

General correspondence before 1906	1693–1805	CO 245, WO 1
	1825–1905	FO 35
Embassy and consular archives	1833–1963	FO 866
Aux Cayes consular archives	1870–1907	FO 376
Santo Domingo Claims Committee	1794–1812	T 81
Pay Lists and other documents concerning refugees	1830–1835	T 50/54–56
Accounts of absentee estates	1794–1803	T 64/223–231
Register of marriages in Santo Domingo	1797	ADM 1/3982

Archives Nationales d'Haïti, BP 1299, Angle rues Borgella et Geffrard,
    Port-au-Prince, Haïti, www.anhhaiti.org
Genealogy of Haiti and Saint-Domingue –
    www.rootsweb.ancestry.com/~htiwgw/
Haiti Genealogical Society – www.agh.qc.ca/

11.6 Honduras

Before 1821 see Spain (section **11.9**). Between 1825 and 1838 Honduras was a member of the Federation of Central America, together with Costa Rica, El Salvador, Guatemala and Nicaragua.

General correspondence before 1906	1824–1905	FO 15
	1857–1905	FO 39
Embassy, legation and consulates	1825–1970	FO 252
Consular archives	1861–1948	FO 632

National Archives of Honduras, Avenida Cristóbal Colón, Calle Salvador
    Mendieta, No 1117, Tegucigalpa, M.D.C., Honduras
Honduras Genealogical Web Project –
    www.worldgenweb.org/index.php/north-america/honduras

11.7 Netherlands

Includes the Netherlands Antilles (Aruba, Curaçao, St Eustatius, Saba, Bonaire and St Maarten), Surinam (Suriname) (until 1975) and Berbice, Essequibo and Demerara until captured by Britain in 1803 (section **10.14**). Documents relating to the Dutch West India Company administration of Berbice, Essequibo and Demerara are in CO 116.

State papers	c1560–1780	SP 84
General correspondence before 1906	1781–1905	FO 37
	1967–1974	FCO 33
Embassy and consular archives		
Correspondence	1811–1956	FO 238
Registers of correspondence	1813–1894	FO 240
Miscellanea	1815–1908	FO 241
Netherlands Antilles registers of births, marriages and deaths for Curaçao, Aruba, Paramaribo and Suriname	1889–1966	FO 907
Curaçao:		
Correspondence etc	1800–1816	CO 66, WO 1
St Eustatius:		
Correspondence etc	1779–1783	CO 246
Lists of burghers (Rodney rolls)	1781	CO 318/8, fos 60–86
Surinam:		
Correspondence etc	1667–1832	CO 278, CO 111, WO 1
Surinam absentees Sequestered property Commission	1813–1822	T 75
Census	1811	CO 278/15–27
List of people who have sugar works and plantations in Surinam with the number of slaves	c1674	CO 1/31, fo 293
List of plantation owners	1805	WO 1/149, p.307–357

General State Archives, Postal address PO Box 90520, 2509 LM,
The Hague, www.nationaalarchief.nl
National Archive of Suriname, Doekhieweg-Oost 18A, Paramaribo,
Suriname, http://nationaalarchief.sr
National Archives of the Netherlands Antilles, Scharlooweg 77,
Willemstad, Curaçao, Nederlandse Antillen, www.nationalarchives.an
Netherlands Antilles Genealogical Web Project –
www.rootsweb.ancestry.com/~antwgw/
Sailing letters www.kb.nl/sl/index.html, a project to catalogue
correspondence taken from Dutch ships captured by British ships now
in High Court of Admiralty records at the National Archives; includes
correspondence from Dutch merchants and settlers in the Caribbean

11.8 Panama

Before 1819 see under Spain (section **11.9**). Between 1819 and 1903
Panama was a member of the Republic of Colombia and later the Republic
of New Grenada. From the 1850s many West Indians worked on the
construction of the trans-isthmian railway and later on the construction
of the canal. Between 1906 and 1999 the Panama Canal Zone was under
the jurisdiction of the United States and vital records and census returns
from 1920 are available in the United States (section **11.11**).

General correspondence before 1906	1835–1904	FO 55
	1904–1905	FO 110
Embassy and consular archives		
Colon:		
General correspondence	1890–1948	FO 806
Panama:		
General correspondence	1828–1970	FO 288
Letter books	1827–1904	FO 289
Registers of correspondence	1860–1930	FO 290
Panama City:		
General correspondence	1938–1947	FO 986

Archivo Nacional, Avenida Peru y Calle 31 y 32, Panama 5,
www.archivonacional.gob.pa
Panama Genealogical Web Project –
www.worldgenweb.org/index.php/north-america/panama

11.9 Spain

Includes Cuba (until 1898, section **11.1**), Puerto Rico (until 1898, section **11.11**) and Santo Domingo (until 1844, section **11.3**) and the Caribbean and Central and South America in general until other European powers settled Spanish possessions.

State papers	1577–1780	SP 94
General correspondence before 1906	1781–1905	FO 72
Embassy and consular archives	1783–1962	FO 185

Archivo General de Indias, Edificio de la Lonja, Avenida de la Constitución,
    3, Edificio de La Cilla, C / Santo Tomás, 5, 41071 Sevilla,
    www.mcu.es/archivos/MC/AGI/
Garcia, *Discovering the Americas: The Archive of the Indies*
Tello, Menendez and Herrero, *Documentos Relativos a la Independencia
    de Norteamerica Existentes en Archivos Espanoles*
Spanish Genealogical Web Project – www.genealogia-es.com/

11.10 Sweden

St Bartholomew (St Barths) was Sweden's only Caribbean colony. It was purchased from France in 1784 and was sold back to France in 1878. Before 1784 and after 1878 see under France (section **11.4**).

General correspondence	1784–1878	FO 73

Riksarkivet, Fyrverkarbacken 13, Box 12541, 102 29 Stockholm,
    www.riksarkivet.se
Comité de Liaison et d'Application des Sources Historiques,
    www.memoirestbarth.com

11.11 United States

Includes the US Virgin Islands of St John, St Thomas and St Croix (before 1917 see under Denmark, section **11.2**), Puerto Rico (before 1898 see under Spain, section **11.9**), between 1906 and 1999 the Panama Canal Zone (section **11.8**).

Embassy and consulates archives		
Correspondence	1791–1956	FO 115
Registers of correspondence	1816–1929	FO 117

National Archives and Records Administration, 700 Pennsylvania Avenue,
   NW, Washington, DC 20408, www.archives.gov
St Croix Landmarks Society, 52 Estate Whim, Frederiksted,
   St Croix VI 00840, www.stcroixlandmarks.org
Genealogy of Puerto Rico –
   www.rootsweb.ancestry.com/~prwgw/index.html
US Virgin Islands genealogical web project –
   www.rootsweb.ancestry.com/~usvi/
US Genealogical Web Project – www.usgenweb.org

Many records relating to the US Caribbean dependencies and West Indian migrants to the US have been digitised and are available online at www. archives.gov, www.ancestry.com, and www.fold3.com

USEFUL ADDRESSES

Addresses for Caribbean archives, register offices and other useful addresses can be found under the relevant country in Chapter 10 (for British Caribbean countries) and Chapter 11 (for non-British Caribbean countries).

The National Archives, Kew, Surrey TW9 4DU, tel: 020-8392 5200, www.nationalarchives.co.uk

British Library, 96 Euston Rd, London NW1 2DB, tel: 020-7412 7677, www.bl.uk

Library and Archives Canada, 395 Wellington Street, Ottawa, Ontario K1A 0N3, tel: 613-996-5115, www.collectionscanada.gc.ca

Commonwealth War Graves Commission, 2 Marlow Rd, Maidenhead, Berkshire SL6 7DX, tel: 01628 634221, www.cwgc.org

General Register Office, PO Box 2, Southport, Merseyside PR8 2JD, tel: 0845-603 7788, www.direct.gov.uk/gro

Lambeth Palace Library, London SE1 7JU, tel: 020-7898 1400, www.lambethpalacelibrary.org

London Metropolitan Archives, 40 Northampton Road, London EC1R 0HB, tel: 020-7332 3820, www.cityoflondon.gov.uk/lma

London School of Hygiene and Tropical Medicine, Keppel Street, London WC1E 7HT, tel: 020-7927 2966, www.lshtm.ac.uk/library/archives/index.html

Maritime History Archive, Memorial University of Newfoundland, St John's A1C 5S7, Newfoundland, Canada, tel: (709) 737 8428, www.mun.ca/mha/

Ministry of Defence, www.mod.uk
Enquirers need to complete a subject access request form and a
certificate of kinship form available from
www.veterans-uk.info/service_records/service_records.html.
The Veteran's Agency website contains the contact address for all
armed services.

Ministry of Defence Medal Office: Service Personnel and Veterans
Agency (Joint Personnel Administration Centre), MOD Medal Office,
Building 250, Imjin Barracks, Gloucester GL3 1HW,
www.veterans-uk.info/medals/medals.html

National Archives and Records Administration, National Archives
Building, 700 Pennsylvania Avenue, NW, Washington, DC 20408, US,
www.archives.gov

National Archives of India, Janpeth, New Delhi 110001, India,
http://nationalarchives.nic.in

The National Archives of Scotland, HM General Register House,
2 Princes Street, Edinburgh EH1 3YY, tel: 0131-535 1314, www.nas.gov.uk

Principal Registry of the Family Division, First Avenue House,
42–49 High Holborn, London WC1V 6NP, tel: 020-7947 7000,
www.courtservice.gov.uk. Written enquiries are to be sent to the York
Probate Sub-registry, First Floor, Castle Chambers, Clifford St,
York YO1 7EA

Rhodes House Library, South Parks Rd, Oxford OX1 3RG,
tel: 01865 270909, www.bodleian.ox.ac.uk/rhodes

The Royal Geographical Society, 1 Kensington Gore, London SW7 2AR,
tel: 020-7591 3000, www.rgs.org

Society of Genealogists, 14 Charterhouse Buildings, Goswell Rd, London
EC1M 7BA, tel: 020-7251 8799, www.sog.org.uk

Southampton Archive Service, Civic Centre, Southampton SO14 7LY,
tel: 023 8083 2251,
www.southampton.gov.uk/s-leisure/artsheritage/history/archives

UK Border Agency, Reliance House, 20 Water Street, Liverpool L2 8XU,
email: ukbanationalityenquiries@ukba.gsi.gov.uk,
www.ukba.homeoffice.gov.uk

BIBLIOGRAPHY

Acts of the Privy Council, Colonial Series, 1613–1783, 6 volumes. (Hereford: Anthony Brothers, 1908–12)

Adderley, R. M. *New Negroes from Africa: Free African Immigrants in the Nineteenth-century Caribbean.* (Bloomington, Indiana: Indiana University Press, 2007)

African American Lives (Arlington, Virginia: PBS Paramount, 2006) and *African American Lives 2* (Arlington, Virginia: PBS Paramount, 2008), DVD, hosted by Henry Louis Gates, Junior

Anderson, A. *Caribbean Immigrants: A Socio-demographic Profile.* (Toronto: Canadian Scholars Press, 1993)

Anderson, J. and R. A. McDonald (eds). *Between Slavery and Freedom: Special Magistrate John Anderson's Journal of St Vincent During the Apprenticeship.* (Philadelphia: University of Pennsylvania Press, 2001)

Andrade, J. A. P. M. *A Record of the Jews in Jamaica: From the English Conquest to the Present Time.* (Kingston, Jamaica: *The Jamaica Times,* 1941)

Andrews, C. M. *Guide to Materials for American History to 1783 in the Public Record Office of Great Britain.* (Washington, DC: Carnegie Institution of Washington, 1912 and 1914)

Archives Nationales, *Etat General des Fonds.* (Paris: Archives Nationales, 1978–1980)

Archives Nationales, *Guide des Sources de l'Histoire de l'Amerique Latine et des Antilles dans les Archives Francaises.* (Paris: Archives Nationales, 1984)

Army roll of Honour 1939–45. Soldiers Died in World War Two. (WO304), published on CD-ROM. (Heathfield, England: Naval and Military Press, 2000)

Atherton, L. *'Never complain, never explain'. Records of the Foreign Office and State Paper Office, 1500–c1960.* (London: Public Record Office, 1994)

Atkinson, C. T. 'Foreign regiments in the British army 1793–1802', *Journal of the Society for Army Historical Research,* vol, 22, 1943/4

Baker, E. C. *A Guide to Records in the Leeward Islands.* (Oxford: Basil Blackwell, 1965)

Baker, E. C. *A Guide to Records in the Windward Islands* (Oxford: Basil Blackwell, 1968)

Baker, J. H. *An Introduction to Legal History*, 4th edn. (London: Butterworths Law, 2002)

Baker, P. L. *Centring the Periphery: Chaos, Order and the Ethnohistory of Dominica.* (Montreal: McGill-Queens University Press, 1994)

Ball, E. *The Genetic Strand: Exploring a Family History Through DNA.* (New York: Simon & Schuster, 2007)

Banton, M. *Administering the Empire, 1801–1968: A Guide to the Records of the Colonial Office in The National Archives of the UK.* (London: Institute of Historical Research/The National Archives, 2008)

Barck, O. T. and H. T. Lefler. *Colonial America.* (London: Collier-Macmillan, 1968)

Barrow, C. *Family in the Caribbean: Themes and Perspectives.* (Oxford: James Currey, 1996)

Bastian, J. A. *Owning Memory. How a Caribbean Community lost its Archives and found its History.* (Westport, Connecticut: Libraries Unlimited, 2003)

Beckles, H. *A History of Barbados from Amerindian Settlement to Nation-state.* (Cambridge: Cambridge University Press, 1990)

Beckles, H. and V. Shepherd (eds). *Caribbean Slave Society and Economy: A Student Reader.* (London: James Currey Publishers, 1993)

Bell, H. C. and D. W. Parker. *Guide to British West Indian Archive Materials in London and in the Islands for the History of the United States.* (Washington, DC: Carnegie Institution of Washington, 1926)

Bell H. H. *Notes on Dominica and Hints to Intending Settlers.* (Barbados: Advocate, 1919)

Bertram, A. *The Colonial Service.* (Cambridge: Cambridge University Press, 1930)

Bevan, A. *Tracing Your Ancestors in The National Archives: The Website and Beyond.* (Kew: The National Archives, seventh edition, 2006)

Black, J. *The Atlantic Slave Trade.* (Aldershot, England: Ashgate, 2006)

Bolland, O. N. *The Formation of a Colonial Society: Belize, from Conquest to Crown Colony.* (Baltimore, Maryland: John Hopkins University Press, 1977)

Bousquet, B. and C. Douglas. *West Indian Women at War: British Racism in World War II.* (London: Lawrence and Wishart, 1991)

Braidwood, S. J. *Black Poor and White Philanthropists: London's Blacks and the Foundation of the Sierra Leone Settlement 1786–1791.* (Liverpool: Liverpool University Press, 1994)

Brandow, J. C. *Genealogies of Barbados Families.* (Baltimore, Maryland: Genealogical Publishing Co. Inc., 1983)

Brandow, J. C. *Omitted Chapters from Hotten.* (Baltimore, Maryland: Genealogical Publishing Co. Inc., 1982)

Breen, H. H. *St Lucia: Historical, Statistical and Descriptive.* (London: Frank Cass, 1970)

Brereton, B. *A History of Modern Trinidad 1783–1962.* (Exeter, New Hampshire: Heinemann Educational Books, 1981)

British Library, *Indians Overseas: A guide to source materials in the India Office Records for the study of Indian emigration, 1830–1950.* www.bl.uk/reshelp/pdfs/indiansoverseas.pdf

British Museum, *List of Documents Relating to the Bahama Islands in the British Museum and Record Office. London* (Nassau: 1910)

Brizan, G. *Grenada, Island of Conflict: From Amerindians to People's Revolution 1498–1979.* (London: Zed Books, 1984)

Brooks, R. and M. Little. *Tracing Your Royal Marine Ancestors.* (Barnsley, England: Pen and Sword, 2008)

Brown, W. 'The American Loyalists in Jamaica', *Journal of Caribbean History*, vol. 26, no. 2, 1992, pp.121–46

Buckley, R. N. *Slaves in Red Coats. The British West India Regiments, 1795–1815.* (London: Yale University Press, 1979)

Burdon, J. A. *Archives of British Honduras.* (London: Sifton Praed & Co., 1931–1935)

Burgan W. G. L. *Some West Indian Memorials: Being a Record of the Tablets in St George's Grenada, With Notes.* (Georgetown, Grenada: 1917)

Burnard, T. 'Slave naming patterns: Onomastics and the taxonomy of race in eighteenth-century Jamaica', *Journal of Interdisciplinary History*, vol. XXXI, no. 3, Winter 2001

Burroughs, T. *Black Roots: A Beginner's Guide to Tracing the African American Family Tree.* (New York: Fireside, 2001)

Byron, M. *Post-war Migration from the Caribbean to Britain: The Unfinished Cycle.* (Aldershot, England: Avebury, 1994)

Calendar of State Papers, Colonial, America and West Indies, 1574–1739. (London: HMSO, 1860–1993). Published on CD-ROM, with obsolete references modernised, by Routledge in association with the PRO

(2000) and online, by subscription with digital images of documents from CO 1 by PROQuest http://colonial.chadwyck.com

Calendar of State Papers, Domestic, 1547–1704. (London: HMSO, 1856–1972)

Calendar of Treasury Books, 1660–1718. (London: HMSO, 1904–1962)

Calendar of Treasury Books and Papers, 1729–1745. (London: HMSO, 1898–1903)

Calendar of Treasury papers, 1557–1728. (London: HMSO, 1868–1889)

Camp, A. J. 'Some West Indian sources in England', *Family Tree Magazine*, November 1987, p.11

Carberry, H. D. and D. Thompson. *A West Indian in England.* (Central Office of Information, 1950)

Caribbean Historical and Genealogical Journal, TCI Genealogical Resources, PO Box 15839, San Luis Obispo, California 93406, US

Carmichael, G. *The History of the West Indian Islands of Trinidad and Tobago 1498–1900.* (London: Alvin Redman, 1961)

Carr, P. E. *Censos, Padrones y Matrículas de la Población de Cuba, siglos 16, 17 y 18* (San Luis Obispo, California: TCI Genealogical Resources, 1995)

Carr, P. E. *Guide to Cuban Genealogical Research.* (Baltimore, Maryland: Clearfield Co., 2000)

Cash, P., S. Gordon and G. Saunders. *Sources for Bahamian History.* (London: Macmillan Caribbean Publishing, 1991)

Chamberlain, M. *Narratives of Exile and Return.* (London: Macmillan Caribbean Publishing, 1997)

Chamberlain, M. (ed.). *Caribbean Migration.* (London: Routledge, 1998)

Chandler, M. *A Guide to Sources in Barbados.* (Oxford: Basil Blackwell, 1965)

Chater, K. *Untold Histories: Black People in England and Wales during the Period of the British Slave Trade, c1660–1807.* (Manchester: Manchester University Press, 2009)

Chessum, L. *From Immigrants to Ethnic Minority: Making Black Community in Britain.* (Aldershot, England: Ashgate, 2000)

Clark, P. and D. Souden. *Migration and Society in Early Modern England.* (London: Hutchinson, 1987)

Cock, R. and N. A. M. Rodger (eds). *Guide to the Naval Records in The National Archives of the UK.* (London: Institute of Historical Research, 2006)

Coldham, P. W. *American Loyalist Claims*. (Washington DC: National Genealogical Society, 1992)

Coldham, P. W. *American Wills and Administrations in the Prerogative Court of Canterbury 1610–1857.* (Baltimore, Maryland: Genealogical Publishing Co. Inc., 1989)

Coldham, P. W. *American Wills Proved in London 1611–1775.* (Baltimore, Maryland: Genealogical Publishing Co. Inc., 1992)

Coldham, P. W. *Bonded Passengers to America*. (Baltimore, Maryland: Genealogical Publishing Co. Inc., 1983)

Coldham, P. W. *The Bristol Registers of Servants Sent to Foreign Plantations, 1654–1686.* (Baltimore, Maryland: Genealogical Publishing Co. Inc., 1988)

Coldham, P. W. *The Complete Book of Emigrants, 1607–1776.* (Baltimore, Maryland: Genealogical Publishing Co. Inc., 1987–93)

Coldham, P. W. *The Complete Book of Emigrants in Bondage, 1614–1775.* (Baltimore, Maryland: Genealogical Publishing Co. Inc., 1988)

Coldham, P. W. *More Emigrants in Bondage, 1614–1775.* (Baltimore, Maryland: Genealogical Publishing Co. Inc., 2002)

Coldham, P. W. *Emigrants from England to the American Colonies.* (Baltimore, Maryland: Genealogical Publishing Co. Inc., 1983)

Coldham, P. W. *Emigrants in Chains.* (Baltimore, Maryland: Genealogical Publishing Co. Inc., 1992)

Colonial Office List, annual publication. (London: HMSO, 1862–1966)

Craton, M. *A History of the Bahamas.* (London: Collins, 1962)

Craton, M. *Empire, Enslavement and Freedom in the Caribbean.* (Kingston, Jamaica: Ian Randle Publishers, 1997)

Craton, M. *Founded upon the seas. A History of the Cayman Islands and their People.* (Kingston, Jamaica: Ian Randle Publishers, 2003)

Craton, M. and G. Saunders. *Islanders in the Stream: A History of the Bahamian People.* (Athens, Georgia: University of Georgia Press, 1992 and 1998)

Crewe, D. *Yellow Jack and the Worm: British Naval Administration in the West Indies, 1739–1748.* (Liverpool: Liverpool University Press, 1993)

Crooks, P. *A Tree Without Roots: The Guide to Tracing British, African and Asian Caribbean Ancestry.* (London: BlackAmber Books, 2008)

Cumpston, I. M. *Indians Overseas in British Territories, 1834–1854.* (Oxford: Oxford University Press, 1953)

Cundall, F. *Jamaica's Part in the Great War, 1914–1918.* (London: Institute of Jamaica, 1925)

Dabydeen, D and B. Samaroo (eds). *Across the Dark Waters: Ethnicity and Indian Identity in the Caribbean.* (London: Macmillan, 1996)

Dabydeen, D., J. Gilmore, and C. Jones. *The Oxford Companion to Black British History.* (Oxford: Oxford University Press, 2008)

Devas, R. P. *A History of the Island of Grenada, 1498–1796: With Some Notes and Comments on Carriacou and Events of Later Years.* (St George, Grenada: Carenage Press, 1974)

Diamond, I. and S. Clarke. 'Demographic patterns among Britain's ethnic groups', in *The Changing Population of Britain,* ed. H. Joshi. (Oxford: Basil Blackwell, 1989)

Dobson, D. *Directory of Scots Banished to the American Plantations: 1650–1775.* (Baltimore, Maryland: Genealogical Publishing Co. Inc., 2003)

Dobson, D. *Directory of Scottish Settlers in North America, 1625–1825.* (Baltimore, Maryland: Genealogical Publishing Co. Inc., 1984–86)

Dobson, D. *The Original Scots Colonists of Early America, 1612–1783.* (Baltimore, Maryland: Genealogical Publishing Co. Inc., 1999)

Dobson, N. *A History of Belize.* (Port of Spain, Trinidad and Tobago: Longman Caribbean, 1973)

Donnan, E. *Documents Illustrative of the History of the Slave Trade to America.* (Washington DC: Carnegie Institution, 1930–1935)

Dookhan, I. *A History of the British Virgin Islands.* (Epping, England: Caribbean Universities Press, 1975)

Divall, K. *My Ancestor Was A Royal Marine.* (Society of Genealogists, 2008)

Draper, N. *The Price of Emancipation. Slave-ownership, compensation and British society at the end of slavery.* (Cambridge: Cambridge University Press, 2010)

Draper, N. '"Possessing slaves": ownership, compensation and metropolitan society in Britain at the time of Emancipation 1834–40', *History Workshop Journal,* 64 (Autumn 2007), pp. 74-102

Dunn, R. S. *Sugar and Slaves: The Rise of the Planter Class in the English West Indies, 1624–1713.* (New York: WW Norton & Company, 1973)

Dyde, B. *Antigua and Barbuda: Heart of the Caribbean.* 2nd edn. (London: Macmillan Caribbean, 1993)

Dyde, B. *The Caribbean Companion.* (London: Caribbean Publishing, 1992)

Dyde, B. *The Empty Sleeve: The Story of the West India Regiments of the British Army.* (St John's, Antigua: Hansib Publications, 1998)

Dyde, B. *A History of Antigua: The Unsuspecting Isle.* (London: Macmillan Caribbean, 2000)

Dyde, B. *St Kitts: Cradle of the Caribbean.* (London: Caribbean Publishing, 1999)

Edwards, B. *The History, Civil and Commercial, of the British West Indies: With a Continuation to the Present Time.* 5th edn. (London: G. and W.B. Whittaker, 1819)

Ellis, J. 'George Rose: An exemplary soldier', *Black and Asian Studies Association Newsletter*, no. 31, September 2001

Eltis, D. *The Rise of Atlantic Slavery in the Americas.* (Cambridge: Cambridge University Press, 2000)

Eltis, D. 'The traffic in slaves between the British West Indian colonies, 1807–1833', *Economic History Review*, 2nd series, vol. 25, 1972

English Protestant Church of Tobago, *Register of Baptisms, Marriages and Deaths from 1781 to 1817.* (Port of Spain, Trinidad and Tobago: 1936)

Ferreira, J-A. S. 'Madeiran Portuguese Migration to Guyana, St. Vincent, Antigua and Trinidad: A Comparative Overview', *Portuguese Studies Review*, 14 (2), 2006/7 pp.63–85

Fiddes, G. *The Dominions and Colonial Offices.* (London: G. P. Putnam's Sons, 1926)

Filby, P. W. and M. K. Meyer (eds) *Passenger and Immigration Lists Index.* (Detroit, Michigan: Gale Research Company, 1981–2002)

File, N. and C. Power. *Black Settlers in Britain 1555–1958.* (London: Heinemann Educational Books, 1981)

The First Black Britons [DVD]. (Ramsey, Isle of Man: Beckmann Visual Publishing, 2006)

Foner, N. *Islands in the City: West Indian Immigration to New York.* (Berkeley: University of California Press, 2001)

Foner, N. *Jamaica Farewell: Jamaican Migrants in London.* (London: Routledge, 1979)

Foner, N. (ed.) *New Immigrants in New York.* (New York: Columbia University Press, 2001)

Francis, V. *With Hope in Their Eyes.* (London: X Press, 1998)

Fraser, A. and K. Joseph. *Our Country: St Vincent and the Grenadines.* (London: Macmillan Caribbean, 1998)

Fryer, P. *The Politics of Windrush.* (London: Index Books, 1999)

Fryer, P. *Staying Power: The History of Black People in Britain.* (London: Pluto Press, 2010)

Galenson, D. *White Servitude and Colonial America.* (Cambridge: Cambridge University Press, 1981)

Games, A. *Migration and the Origins of the English Atlantic World.* (Cambridge, Massachusetts: Harvard University Press, 1999)

Garcia, P. G. (ed.) *Discovering the Americas: the Archive of the Indies* (New York: Vendome Press, 1997)

Gates, H. L. (Junior). *In Search of Our Roots: How 19 Extraordinary African Americans Reclaimed Their Past.* (New York: Crown, 2009)

General Register Office, *Abstract of Arrangements Respecting Registration of Birth, Marriages and Deaths in the United Kingdom and the Other Countries of the British Commonwealth of Nations and in the Republic of Ireland.* (London: HMSO, 1952)

Gerzina, G. H. *Black London: Life before Emancipation.* (New Brunswick, New Jersey: Rutgers University Press, 1995)

Giuseppi M. S. *Naturalization of Foreign Protestants in the American Colonies and West Indian Colonies.* (London: Huguenot Society, 1921)

Gmelch, G. *Double Passage: The Lives of Caribbean Migrants Abroad and Back Home.* (Ann Arbor, Michigan: University of Michigan Press, 1993)

Grannum, G. 'Caribbean Connections', *Family History Monthly*, February 2006, pp.26–9

Grannum, K. and N. Taylor. *Wills and Probate Records: A Guide for Family Historians.* 2nd edn. (Kew: The National Archives, 2009)

Grant, C. *A Member of the RAF of Indeterminate Race.* (Bognor Regis, England: Woodfield Publishing, 2006)

Grant, C. H. *The Making of Modern Belize: Politics, Society and British Colonialism in Central America.* (Cambridge: Cambridge University Press, 2008)

Green, T. H. 'Monumental Inscriptions of the Royal Naval Cemetery, Ireland Island, Bermuda' (typescript at the Society of Genealogists, London, 1983)

Greenwood, R., S. Hamber and B. Dyde. *Caribbean Certificate History Book 1: Amerindians to Africans.* (London: Macmillan Education, 2001)

Greenwood, R., S. Hamber and B. Dyde. *Caribbean Certificate History Book 2: Emancipation to Emigration.* (London: Macmillan Education, 2002)

Greenwood, R., S. Hamber and B. Dyde, *Caribbean Certificate History Book 3: Decolonisation and Development.* (London: Macmillan Education, 2001)

Gropp, A. E. *Guide to Libraries and Archives in Central America and the West Indies, Panama, Bermuda and British Guiana.* (New Orleans: Tulane University, 1941)

Guildhall Library, *The British Overseas: A Guide to Records of Their Births, Baptisms, Marriages, Deaths and Burials Available in the United Kingdom*. 3rd edn. (London: Guildhall Library, 1994)

Gutman, H. *The Black Family in Slavery and Freedom, 1750–1925*. (New York: Pantheon, 1976)

Habib, I. *Black Lives in the English Archives 1500–1677: Imprints of the Invisible*. (Aldershot, England: Ashgate, 2008)

Hallett, A. C. H. *Early Bermuda Records, 1619–1826: A Guide to the Parish and Clergy Registers with Some Assessment Lists and Petitions*. (Bermuda: Juniperhill Press, 1991)

Hallett, C. F. E. H. *Early Bermuda Wills 1629–1835*. (Bermuda: Juniperhill Press, 1993)

Hallett, C. F. E. H. *Bermuda Index, 1784–1914: An Index of Births, Marriages, and Deaths as Recorded in Bermudan Newspapers*. (Bermuda: Juniperhill Press, 1989)

Hallett, C. F. E. H. *Forty years of convict labour: Bermuda, 1823–1869*. (Bermuda: Juniper Hill Press, 1999)

Handler, J. S. *Guide to Source Materials for the Study of Barbados History, 1627–1834*. (Carbondale, Illinois: South Illinois University Press, 1971)

Handler, J. S. *Supplement to a Guide to Source Material for the Study of Barbados History, 1627–1834*. (Providence, Rhode Island: The John Carter Brown Library, 1991)

Handler, J. S. 'Slave manumissions and freedmen in Seventeenth century Barbados', *The William and Mary Quarterly*, vol. 41, 1984, pp.390–408

Handler, J. S., R. Hughes, M. Newton, P. L. V. Welch and E. M. Wiltshire. *Freedmen of Barbados. Names and Notes for Genealogical and Family History Research*. (Charlottesville, Virginia: Virginia Foundation for the Humanities, 2007)

Handler, J. S. and J. Jacoby. 'Slave names and naming in Barbados, 1650–1830' *The William and Mary Quarterly*, 3rd series, vol. 53, no. 4, October 1996

Harney, S. *Nationalism and Identity: Culture and Imagination in a Caribbean Diaspora*. (London: Zed Books, 1996)

Hart, A. *How to Interpret Family History and Ancestry DNA Test Results for Beginners: The Geography and History of Your Relatives*. (iUniverse. com, 2004)

Hawkings, D. T. *Criminal Ancestors: A Guide to Historical Criminal Records in England and Wales*. (Stroud, England: Sutton Publishing, 1996)

Healy, M. S. 'Colour, climate, and combat: The Caribbean Regiment in the Second World War', *The International History Review*, vol. XXII, March 2000, pp.65–85

Higman, B. W. *Jamaica Surveyed: Plantation Maps and Plans of the Eighteenth and Nineteenth Centuries*. (Jamaica: Institute of Jamaican Publishers, 1988)

Higman, B. W. *Slave Population and Economy in Jamaica, 1807–1834*. (Jamaica: University of the West Indies, 1995)

Higman, B. W. *Slave Populations of the British Caribbean, 1807–1834*. (Baltimore, Maryland: John Hopkins University Press, 1988)

Higman, B. W. *A Concise History of the Caribbean*. (Cambridge: Cambridge University Press, 2010)

Hirst, G. S. S. *Notes on the History of the Cayman Islands*. (Kingston, Jamaica: P. A. Benjamin Manufacturing Co., 1910)

Holmes, F. *The Bahamas During the Great War*. (Nassau, Bahamas: The Tribune, 1924)

Honychurch, L. *The Dominica Story: A History of the Island*. 3rd edn. (London: Macmillan, 1995)

Honychurch, L. and G. Aird. *Dominica: Island of Adventure*. 3rd edn. (London: Caribbean Publishing, 1998)

Horwitz, H. Chancery Equity Records and Proceedings, 1600–1800, PRO handbook no. 27. (London: Public Record Office, 1998)

Horwitz, H. Exchequer Equity Records and Proceedings, 1649–1841, PRO handbook no. 32. (London: Public Record Office, 2001)

Hoskins, T. *Black People in Britain 1650–1850*. (London: Macmillan Education, 1984)

Hotten, J. C. *The Original Lists of People of Quality...and Others Who Went from Great Britain to the American Plantations 1600–1700*. (Baltimore, Maryland: Genealogical Publishing Co. Inc., 1980)

Howe, G. *Race, War and Nationalism. A Social History of West Indians in the First World War*. (Kingston, Jamaica: Ian Randle Publishers, 2002)

Howell, R. *The Royal Navy and the Slave Trade*. (London: Croom Helm, 1987)

Hoyos, F. A. *Barbados: A History from Amerindians to Independence*. (London: Macmillan Press, 1992)

Hubbard, V. K. *Swords, Ships and Sugar: A History of Nevis to 1900*. (Placentia, California: Premier Editions, 1997)

Humphries, R. A. *The Diplomatic History of British Honduras, 1638–1901*. (Oxford: Oxford University Press, 1961)

Ingham, J. M. *Defence Not Defiance: A History of the Bermuda Volunteer Rifle Corps*. (Bermuda: Ingham, 1992)

Ingram, K. E. N. *Manuscripts Relating to Commonwealth Caribbean Countries in the United States and Canadian Repositories*. (Barbados: Caribbean Universities Press, 1975)

Ingram, K. E. N. *Manuscript Sources for the History of the West Indies*. (Kingston, Jamaica: University of the West Indies, 2000)

Ingram, K. E. N. *Sources for Jamaican History 1655–1838: A Bibliographical Survey with Particular Reference to Manuscript Sources*. (Zug, Switzerland: Inter Documentation Co., 1976)

Ingram, K. E. N. *Sources for West Indian Studies: A Supplementary Listing, with Particular Reference to Manuscript Sources*. (Zug, Switzerland: Inter Documentation Co., 1983)

Jeffries, C. *The Colonial Empire and its Civil Service*. (Cambridge: Cambridge University Press, 1938)

Jeffries, C. *Whitehall and the Colonial Service: An Administrative Memoir, 1939–1956*. (London: The Athlone Press, 1972)

Jenkins, C. F. *Tortola: A Quaker Experiment of Long Ago in the Tropics*. Reprint. (Road Town, Tortola, British Virgin Islands: Caribbean Printing Co. Ltd, 1972)

Jesse, C. *Outlines of St Lucia's History*. (Castries, St Lucia: St Lucia Archaeological and Historical Society, 1964)

John, A. M. *The Plantation Slaves of Trinidad, 1783–1816*. (Cambridge: Cambridge University Press, 1989)

Johnson F. C. and C. F. E. H. Hallett (eds). *Early Colonists of the Bahamas: A Selection of Records*. (Bermuda: Juniperhill Press, 1996)

Jones, S. B. *Annals of Anguilla*. (St Kitts: Progressive Printery, 1937)

Jordan, D. and M. Walsh. *White Cargo: The Forgotten History of Britain's White Slaves in America*. (Edinburgh: Mainstream Publishing, 2007)

Joseph, C. L. 'The British West Indies Regiment 1914–1918', *Journal of Caribbean History*, vol. II, May 1971, pp.94–124

Journals of the Board of Trade and Plantations, 1704–1782. (London: HMSO, 1920–38)

Kamauesi, Z. and N. Smith. *When will I see you again? Experiences of Migration and Separation in Childhood – from the Caribbean to Britain*. (London: Pen Press, 2002)

Kaminkow, J. and M. Kaminkow. *A List of Emigrants from England to America, 1718–1759*. (Baltimore, Maryland: Magna Charta Book Co., 1964)

Kemp, T. J. *International Vital Records Handbook*. 4th edn. (Baltimore, Maryland: Genealogical Publishing Co. Inc., 2000)

Kennett, D. *DNA and Social Networking: A Guide to Genealogy in the Twenty-First Century.* (Stroud, England: The History Press, 2011)

Kent, D. L. *Barbados and America.* (Arlington, Virginia: Carol M. Kent, 1980); reprinted by James Lynch see www.candoo.com/projects/banda.html

Kershaw, R. *Migration Records: A Guide for Family Historians.* (Kew: The National Archives, 2009)

Kieran, B. L. *The Lawless Caymanas: A Story of Slavery, Freedom and the West India Regiment.* (Grand Cayman, Cayman Islands: the author, 1992)

Kincaid, J. *A Small Place.* (New York: Farrar Straus & Giroux, 2000)

Kirk-Greene, A. H. M. *A Biographical Dictionary of the British Colonial Service 1939–1966.* (London: Hans Zell Publishers, 1991)

Kirk-Greene, A. H. M. *British Imperial Administrators 1858–1966.* (Basingstoke, England: Macmillan, 2000)

Kirk-Greene, A. '"Not Quite a Gentleman": The Desk Diaries of the Assistant Private Secretary (Appointments) to the Secretary of State for the Colonies, 1899–1915', *The English Historical Review*, 2002, vol. 117 (472) pp.622–633

Kitzmiller, J. M. *In Search of the 'Forlorn Hope': A Comprehensive Guide to Locating British Regiments and Their Records (1640–WWI).* (Salt Lake City, Utah: Manuscript Publishing Foundation, 1988)

Klein, H. S. *The Atlantic Slave Trade.* (Cambridge: Cambridge University Press, 1999)

Kuczynski, R. R. *Demographic Survey of the British Colonial Empire. Volume 3: West Indian and American Territories.* (London: Oxford University Press, 1953)

Lai, W. L. *Indentured labour, Caribbean sugar: Chinese and Indian migrants to the British West Indies, 1838–1918.* (Baltimore, Maryland: John Hopkins University, 1993)

Lai, W. L. *The Chinese in the West Indies 1806–1995: A Documentary History.* (Kingston, Jamaica: University of the West Indies Press, 1998)

Lane, G. *Tracing Ancestors in Barbados: A Practical Guide.* (Baltimore, Maryland: Genealogical Publishing Co. Inc., 2006)

Lannigan, Mrs. *Antigua and the Antiguans.* Reprint. (London: Macmillan Education, 1991)

Lawrence-Archer, J. H. *Monumental Inscriptions of the British West Indies.* (London: Chatto and Windus, 1875)

Layton-Henry, Z. *The Politics of Immigration: Immigration, Race and Race Relations in Post-war Britain.* (Oxford: Blackwell, 1992)

Lefroy, J. H. *Memorials of the Discovery and Early Settlement of the Bermudas or Somers Islands 1515–1685. Compiled from the Colonial Records and other Original Sources.* (Hamilton, Bermuda: Bermuda Historical Society, 1981)

Lester, A. and D. Lambert (eds). *Colonial Lives Across the British Empire: 'Imperial Careering' in the Long Nineteenth Century.* (Cambridge: Cambridge University Press, 2006)

Livingston, N. B. *Sketch Pedigrees of Some of the Early Settlers in Jamaica.* (Kingston, Jamaica: Educational Supply Company, 1909)

Lloyd, C. C. *The Navy and the Slave Trade: Suppression of the African Slave Trade in the Nineteenth Century.* (London: Longmans, Green and Co., 1949)

Lucas, C. P. *Historical Geography of the British Colonies: Volume 2: The West Indies.* (Oxford: Clarendon Press, 1890)

Malcolm, H. *Historical Documents Relating to the Bahama Islands.* (Nassau, 1910)

Martin, S. I. *Incomparable World.* (London: Quartet Books, 1997)

Mercer, J. E. *Bermuda Settlers of the 17th century: Genealogical Notes from Bermuda.* (Baltimore, Maryland: Genealogical Publishing Co. Inc., 1982)

Metzgen, H. and J. Graham. *Caribbean Wars Untold: A Salute to the British West Indies.* (Kingston, Jamaica: University of the West Indies Press, 2007)

Mitchell, M. E. *Jamaican Ancestry: How to Find Out More.* Revised edition. (Westminster, Maryland: Heritage Books, 2009)

Murray, R. N. *Lest We Forget: The Experiences of World War II Westindian Ex-service Personnel* (Hertford, England: Hansib Publications, 1996)

National Archives of St Kitts and Nevis, *Understanding and using Archives.* (2006)

Noble, E. M. *Jamaica Airman: A Black Man in Britain, 1943 and After* (London: New Beacon Books Ltd, 1984)

Nwokeji, G. U. and Eltis D. 'The Roots of the African Diaspora: Methodological Considerations in the Analysis of Names in the Liberated African Registers of Sierra Leone and Havana', *History in Africa*, 29, 2002

O'Callaghan, S. *To Hell or Barbados: The Ethnic Cleansing of Ireland.* (Dingle, Ireland: Brandon, 2001)

Okokon, S. *Black Londoners, 1880–1990.* (Stroud, England: Alan Sutton, 1998)

Oldham, W. *Britain's Convicts to the Colonies.* (Sydney: Library of Australian History, 1990)

Oliver, V. L. (ed.) *Caribbeana.* (London: Mitchell, Hughes and Clarke, 1910–1919). Reprinted by James Lynch by subscription in 2000 (see www.candoo.com/olivers/caribbeana.html)

Oliver, V. L. *History of the Island of Antigua* (London: Mitchell, Hughes and Clarke, 1894–1899). Reprinted by James Lynch in 1999 (see www.candoo.com/olivers/index.html)

Oliver, V. L. *The Monumental Inscriptions of the British West Indies.* (Dorchester, England: The Friary Press, 1927)

Oliver, V. L. (ed.) *The Monumental Inscriptions in the Churches and Churchyards of the Island of Barbados, British West Indies* (London: 1915)

Oliver, V. L. (ed.) *The Registers of St Thomas, Middle Island, St Kitts 1729–1832.* (London: Huges and Clarke, 1915)

O'Sullivan-Sirjue, J. and P. Robinson. *Researching Your Jamaican Family.* (Kingston, Jamaica: Arawak Publications, 2007)

Ottley, C. R. *The Story of Tobago.* (Port of Spain, Trinidad: Longman, 1973)

Panayi, P. *Racial Violence in Britain, 1840–1950.* (London: Leicester University Press, 1993)

Pappalardo, B. *Tracing Your Naval Ancestors.* (Kew: The National Archives, 2003)

Pariag, F. *East Indians in the Caribbean: An Illustrated History.* (Kingston, Jamaica: Arawak Publications, 2004)

Patterson, O. *The Sociology of Slavery: An Analysis of the Origins, Development, and Structure of Negro Slave Society in Jamaica.* (London: Associated University Press, 1975)

Penfold, P. A. (ed.) *Maps and Plans in the Public Record Office, Volume 2: America and West Indies.* (London: HMSO, 1974)

Phillips, C. *The Final Passage.* (London: Faber and Faber, 1989)

Phillips, M. and T. Phillips. *Windrush: The Irresistible Rise of Multi-racial Britain.* (London: Harper Collins, 1998)

Pomery, C. *DNA and Family History: How Genetic Testing Can Advance Your Genealogical Research.* (Kew: The National Archives, 2004)

Potter, R. B. *St Vincent and the Grenadines* (Santa Barbara, California: ABC Clio Reference Books, 1992)

Porter, S. D. *Jamaican Records: A Research Manual: A Two Part Guide to Genealogical and Historical Research Using Repositories in Jamaica and England*. (London: Stephen D. Porter, 1999)

Public Record Office Lists and Indexes, Volume LIII: *An Alphabetical Guide to Certain War Office and Other Military Records Preserved in the Public Record Office*. (London: HMSO, 1931, reprinted by Kraus Reprint Corporation, 1963)

Public Record Office, *Supplement to the Guide to the Records of the Commonwealth of the Bahamas*. (Nassau, Bahamas: Commonwealth of the Bahamas, 1980)

Pusey, J. H. *The Handbook of the Turks And Caicos Islands: Being a Compendium of History, Statistics, and General Information Concerning the Islands from their Discovery to the Present Time*. (Kingston, Jamaica: M.C. DeSouza, 1897)

Ragatz, L. J. *A Guide to the Official Correspondence of the Governors of the British West India Colonies with the Secretary of State, 1763-1833*. (London: The Bryan Edwards Press, 1923)

Ramdin, R. *Arising from Bondage: A History of the Indo-Caribbean People*. (New York: New York University Press, 2000)

Roberts, A. *The Incredible Human Journey*. (London: Bloomsbury Publishing, 2009)

Robertson, J. 'Jamaican archival resources for seventeenth and eighteenth century Atlantic history', *Slavery and Abolition*, vol. 22, no. 3, December 2001, pp.109-140

Rodger, N. A. M. *Naval Records for Genealogists*. 2nd edn. PRO handbook no. 22 (HMSO, 1998)

Roper, M. *The Records of the Foreign Office, 1782-1969*. (London: Public Record Office, 2002)

Rose, J. M. *Black Genesis: A Resource Book for African-American Genealogy*. (Baltimore, Maryland: Genealogical Publishing Co., 2003)

Rowe, H. *A Guide to the Records of Bermuda*. (Hamilton, Bermuda: The Bermuda Archives, 1980)

Royal Commission on Public Records, vol. II, 1914, 'Memorandum on official records in the West Indies', pp.115-120. (London: HMSO, 1914)

Saha, P. *Emigration of Indian Labour, 1834-1900*. (New Delhi, India: People Publishing House, 1970)

Salazar, L. E. *Love Child: A Genealogist's Guide to the Social History of Barbados.* (St Michael, Barbados: L. E. Salazar, 2001)

Sanders, J. M. *Barbados Records: Baptisms 1637–1800.* (Baltimore, Maryland: Genealogical Publishing Co. Inc., 1984)

Sanders, J. M. *Barbados Records: Marriages 1643–1800.* (Houston, Texas: Sanders Historical Publications, 1982)

Sanders, J. M. *Barbados Records: Wills and Administrations 1647–1725.* (Houston, Texas: Sanders Historical Publications, 1981)

Saunders, D. G. and E. A. Carson. *A Guide to the Records of the Bahamas.* (Nassau, Bahamas: Commonwealth of the Bahamas, 1973)

Saunders, K. (ed.) *Indentured Labour in the British Empire, 1834–1920.* (London: Croom Helm, 1984)

Selvon, S. *The Lonely Londoners.* (London: Penguin, 2006)

Sewell, T. *Keep on Moving: The Windrush Legacy.* (London: The Voice, 1998)

Shephard, C. *An Historical Account of the Island of St Vincent.* Reprinted. (London: Frank Cass, 1997)

Sherwood, M. *Many Struggles: West Indian Workers and Service Personnel in Britain, 1939–45.* (London: Karia Press, 1985)

Sherwood M. and M. Spafford. *Whose Freedom Were Africans, Caribbeans and Indians Defending in World War II?* (London: Savannah Press, 2000)

Shilstone, E. M. *Monumental Inscriptions in the Burial Ground of the Jewish Synagogue at Bridgetown, Barbados.* (London: Jewish Historical Society of England, 1956)

Shyllon, F. *Black People in Britain 1555–1833.* (Oxford: Oxford University Press, 1977)

Smith, K., C. T. Watts and M. J. Watts. *Records of Merchant Shipping and Seamen.* (Kew: Public Record Office, 1998)

Smith, R. *Jamaican Volunteers in the First World War.* (Manchester: Manchester University Press, 2004)

Smolenyak, M. and A. Turner, *Trace Your Roots with DNA.* (Emmaus, Philadelphia: Rodale Press, 2005)

Soares, C. 'Jamaican research in Britain', *Family Tree Magazine*, April 1991, p.35

Soldiers Died in the Great War, first published in 1921, available on CD-ROM (Heathfield, England: Naval and Military Press, 2000)

Spencer, W. *Air Force Records: A Guide for Family Historians.* 2nd edn. (Kew: The National Archives books, 2008)

Spencer, W. *Army Records. A Guide for Family Historians.* (Kew: The National Archives, 2008)

Spencer, W. *Army Service Records of the First World War.* 4th edn. (Kew: The National Archives, 2008)

Stanford, C. J. 'Genealogical sources in Barbados', *The Genealogists' Magazine*, vol. 17, March 1974, pp.489–498

Steel, D. *No Entry: The Background and Implications of the Commonwealth Immigrants Act, 1968.* (London: C. Hurst and Co., 1969)

Stranack, I. *The Andrew and the Onions: The Story of the Royal Navy in Bermuda 1795–1975.* 2nd edn. (Old Royal Navy Dockyard, Bermuda: Bermuda Maritime Museum Press, 1990)

Streets, D. H. *Slave Genealogy: A Research Guide with Case Studies.* (Bowie, Maryland: Heritage Books Inc., 1986)

Syrett, D. and R. L. DiNardo (eds). *The Commissioned Sea Officers of the Royal Navy 1660–1815*: Occasional Publications of the Navy Records Society, Vol. 1. (Aldershot, England: Navy Records Society, 1994)

Tattersfield, N. and J. Fowles. *The Forgotten Trade.* (London: Pimlico, 1998)

Tello, P. L., C. Menendez and C. Herrero. *Documentos Relativos a la Independencia de Norteamerica Existentes en Archivos Espanoles* (Madrid: 1976)

Tepper, M. *Passengers to America.* (Baltimore, Maryland: Genealogical Publishing Co. Inc., 1988)

Thomas, H. *The slave trade: the history of the Atlantic slave trade, 1440–1870.* (London: Phoenix, 2006)

Thomas, T. N. *Indians Overseas: A Guide to Source Materials in the India Office Records for the Study of Indian Emigration, 1830–1950.* (London: British Library, 1985)

Tinker, H. *A New System of Slavery: The Export of Indian Labour Overseas, 1830–1920.* (Oxford: Oxford University Press, 1974)

Titford, J. 'Barbados: Some of its parishes, churches and monumental inscriptions', 2 parts, *Family Tree Magazine,* May and June 1997

Titford, J. *My Ancestor Settled in the British West Indies (with Bermuda, British Guiana and British Honduras): A Guide to Sources for Family Historians.* (London: Society of Genealogists, 2011)

Titford, J. 'Transcripts of 18th century registers for St George Gingerland', *Family Tree Magazine*, January 2000 and March 2000

Tomaselli, P. *Tracing Your Air Force Ancestors.* (Barnsley, England: Pen and Sword, 2007)

Transatlantic Slave Trade database (www.slavevoyages.org)

Tyson, G. F. *A Guide to Manuscript Sources in United States and West Indian Depositories Relating to the British West Indies During the Era of the American Revolution.* (Wilmington, Delaware: Scholarly Resources Inc., 1978)

Uddenberg, T. and K. Vaucrosson. *Lists from the San Fernando Gazette: 1865–1896.* (Uddenberg and Vaucrosson, 2002)

Vickerman, M. *Crosscurrents: West Indian Immigrants and Race.* (Oxford: Oxford University Press, 1999)

Viotti, E. *Crowns of Glory, Tears of Blood.* (Oxford: Oxford University Press, 1997)

Walker, J. W. StG. *The Black Loyalists: The Search for a Promised Land in Nova Scotia and Sierra Leone, 1783–1870.* (Toronto: University of Toronto Press, 1992)

Walne, P. (ed.) *A Guide to Manuscript Sources for the History of Latin America and the Caribbean in the British Isles.* (London: Oxford University Press, 1973)

Walvin, J. *A Short History of Slavery.* (London: Penguin, 2007)

Walvin, J. *Black and White: The Negro and English Society 1555–1945.* (London: Penguin Press, 1973)

Walvin, J. *Passage to Britain.* (Penguin Books, 1984)

Walvin, J. *Making the Black Atlantic: Britain and the African Diaspora.* (London: Cassell, 2000)

Ward, W. E. F. *The Royal Navy and the Slavers: The Suppression of the Atlantic Slave Trade.* (London: Allen and Unwin, 1969)

Wareing, J. 'Preventive and punitive regulation in seventeenth-century social policy: conflicts of interest and the failure to make "stealing and transporting Children, and other Persons" a felony, 1645–73', *Social History*, Volume 27, Issue 3, September 2002, pp. 288–308

Waters, M. C. *Black Identities: West Indian Immigrant Dreams and American Realities* (Cambridge, Massachusetts: Harvard University Press, 1999)

Watkins-Owen, I. *Blood Relations: Caribbean Immigrants and the Harlem Community, 1900–1930.* (Bloomington, Indiana: Indiana University Press, 1996)

Watson, E. *The Carib Regiment of World War II.* (New York: Vantage Press, 1964)

Watts, C. T. and M. J. Watts. *My Ancestor Was in the British Army. Guide to British Army sources for family historians.* (London: Society of Genealogists, 2009)

Watts, C. T. and M. J. Watts. *My Ancestor Was a Merchant Seaman: How Can I Find Out More About Him?* 2nd edn. (London: Society of Genealogists, 2002)

Weiss, J. McNish. *The Merikens: Free Black American Settlers in Trinidad, 1815–1816.* 2nd edn. (London: McNish and Weiss, 2002)

Weiss, J. McNish. 'The corps of Colonial Marines 1814–16: A summary' *Immigrants and Minorities*, vol. 15, no. 1, April 1996

Wells, R. V. *The Population of the British Colonies in America before 1776.* (Princeton, New Jersey: Princeton University Press, 1975

Wells, S. *Deep Ancestry: Inside the Genographic Project.* (Washington, DC: National Geographic Society, 2007)

Westergaard, W. *The Danish West Indies under Company Rule, 1671–1754, with a Supplementary Chapter, 1755–1917.* (New York: Macmillan, 1917)

Western, J. *A Passage to England: Barbadian Londoners Speak of Home.* (Minneapolis, Minnesota: University of Minnesota Press, 1992)

Westlake, D. E. *Under an English Heaven.* (London: Hodder and Stoughton, 1973)

Whittleton, E. H. 'Family history in the Bahamas', *The Genealogists' Magazine*, vol. 18, December 1975, pp.187–191

Williams, E. *History of the People of Trinidad and Tobago.* (London: A Deutsch, 1982)

Williams, N. *A History of the Cayman Islands.* (Grand Cayman, Cayman Islands: Government of the Cayman Islands, 1970)

Willis, J. J. 'Transportation versus imprisonment in eighteenth- and nineteenth-century: Penal power, liberty, and the state', *Law & Society Review*, volume 39, number 1 (2005)

Woodcock, H. I. *History of Tobago.* (London: Frank Cass, 1971)

Woodtor, D. *Finding a Place Called Home: A Guide to African-American Genealogy and Historical Identity.* (New York: Random House, 1999)

Wright, P. *Monumental Inscriptions of Jamaica.* (London: Society of Genealogists, 1966)

Wright, P. 'Materials for family history in Jamaica', *The Genealogists' Magazine*, vol. 15, September 1966, pp.239–250

Young, W. *Account of the Black Charaibs in the Island of St Vincent's.* (London: Frank Cass, 1971)

INDEX